THE LAST HELICOPTER

TWO LIVES IN INDOCHINA

JIM LAURIE

FOCUSASIA PRODUCTIONS LTD.
WASHINGTON, D.C.

© 2020 Jim Laurie All rights reserved.
This publication may not be reproduced, stored in a retrieval system, or transmitted whole or in part, in any form or by any means, electronic, mechanical, photocopying, recording, or otherwise, without prior written permission from the publisher. Brief quotations may be used in literary reviews. Inquiries should be made to focusasia1@gmail.com.

ISBN: 978-1-7351203-0-0
eISBN: 978-1-7351203-1-7
Library of Congress Control Number: 9781735120300

Book Design: Peggy Nehmen
Photos: Jim Laurie

Printed in the United States of America.

Published by: FocusAsia Productions Ltd.
1001 L St NW, Suite 201
Washington, DC 20001
jimlaurie.com/the-last-helicopter

*To Sinan, Christopher, and Xuan Xanh
without whom this book would not have been possible*

Contents

Preface 1
1   A Homecoming 5
2   Events We Could Not Foresee 13
3   Café au Lait 22
4   The Smiles of Bayon 40
5   Scrambled Eggs and Mad Minutes 53
6   War, Love, and Tattered Diaries 68
7   MED Team C 95
8   Dress Rehearsal for the Final Act 101
9   Collapse: Part 1 120
10   Khmer New Year 148
11   Angkar 160
12   Vann, Saorun, and Eric 172
13   New Friends 179
14   Saigon: A Plan 193
15   "No One Should Be Afraid" 203
16   Collapse: Part 2 208
17   "Prison Without Walls" 217
18   Giai Phong 237
19   "Change Will Come Soon" 261
20   Letters of '79 271
21   Reunion 286
22   Food for Thought 300
23   Reflections on Genocide and Survival 312
24   Ashes to Ashes 326
Afterword 333
Acknowledgments 337
Photo Gallery 341
References 356

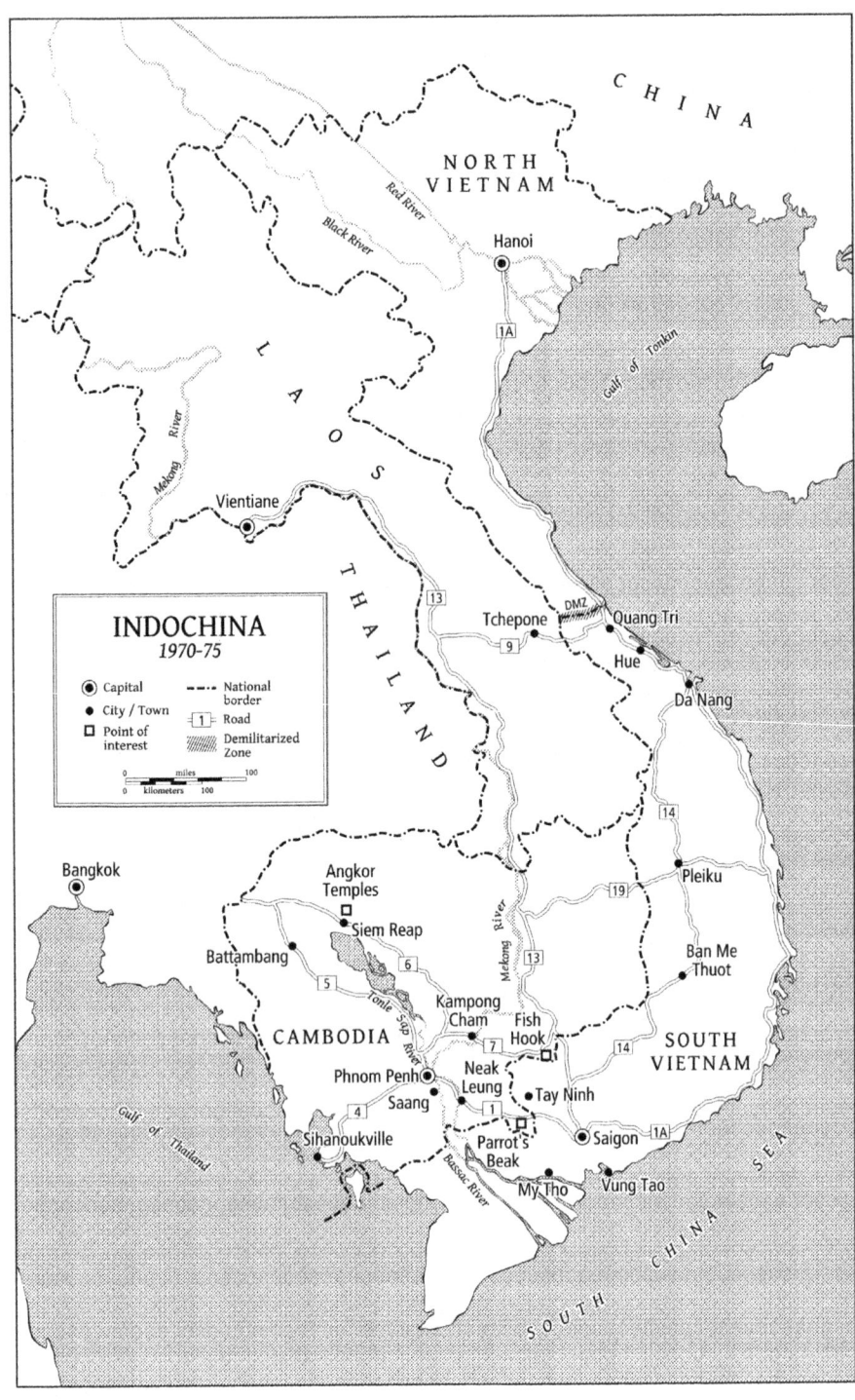

Preface

WHEN YOU ARE YOUNG, you carry out your most daring exploits, experience your most passionate affairs, and create your most unforgettable memories.

This is a story of lives and contrasting cultures that intersect in remarkable and unexpected ways; a story of youth, a thirst for education, travel, romance ... and love—not only for an individual but for an endlessly fascinating place, a region encompassing Vietnam, Cambodia, and Laos—known collectively as Indochina.

The story begins when a curious 22-year-old hitches a ride along Highway Route 1 from Saigon to Phnom Penh in late May 1970. It ends in early 2011 when a still-curious 63-year-old heads bumpily down the same route on a cross-country bus entering Cambodia at the border crossing at Bavet.

The story focuses on a special friend, an extraordinary person at an extraordinary time.

A young woman is engaged in a remarkable struggle for survival amid unimaginable conditions. Along the way she unveils a chronicle of war and recovery, trust and betrayal, lessons learned and lessons forgotten.

A young man is confronted with choices his sheltered life has not prepared him to make. Along the way he witnesses some of Southeast Asia's most cataclysmic events of the late twentieth century.

It is a story of lives interconnected. A story connecting people bound together for a time, by war, pain, and the inability to forget.

■ ■ ■

This book has been a very long time coming.

Soc Sinan and I came together fifty years ago in Cambodia. She was a young professional working for a Khmer French company and I a green but ambitious reporter with a passion for adventure. Over the next five decades we drifted apart and came back together several times. The war that brought us together ultimately drove us apart. Through it all, somehow, we retained a bond, a connection that could not be broken.

Almost from the start, friends and colleagues urged us to tell our stories of survival and rescue. But Sinan was reluctant to tell her story. And I could find little time to tell mine.

Instead, I raced headlong into a twenty-five-year career in American television network news. I bounced from Tokyo to Hong Kong, Saigon to Phnom Penh and Beijing. Over half a century, I spent more time in these places than in my own country.

Whenever NBC or ABC News called me, I was on the next flight out. I immersed myself in breaking news stories from Beirut to Baghdad, Berlin to Belfast, Jerusalem to Johannesburg, Moscow to Mogadishu, and Sarajevo to Srebrenica.

I wrote or produced documentary films on Cambodia, Vietnam, Japan, and China and won awards for reporting from Manila, Beijing, and Saigon of an assassination, a massacre, and a revolution.

Through it all, I put to one side my most personal stories of those who should have mattered more.

Sinan remained through it all consistently kind, yet deeply conflicted. Was she ready to tell the world what she had experienced? She did tell her story but only in bits and pieces over many years.

I recorded her first memories in the spring of 1980 on my old Sony cassette device. The long conversations revealed a quiet reluctance, a tendency to recall parts of her experience while suppressing other, more difficult details. Perhaps it was too traumatic. To recount it all would mean digging deeply into pain, heartache, and the mystery of survival in a place where very many did not survive. I was perhaps too keen to explore. I pushed. She stopped.

As I listen to these recordings now forty years later, her voice with its natural upwardly inflected lilt, common in Cambodian speech, seems somehow too cheery. I suspect she must have been hiding something.

Among the characteristics of this remarkable woman was the ability to maintain a cloak of secrecy over the past and also with great strength to put aside pain and move on.

In June 1981, she began to write her own story, in a simple journal, diary style. She mailed me carefully typed excerpts. She then abandoned the project. Her hundreds of pages, some handwritten, some meticulously typed, remained in a cardboard box in my study for many years.

In 1984, she met a woman, a researcher and a specialist on America's "secret" war in Laos. Comfort lay is confiding not in a man and former lover but in a woman with a sympathetic ear who knew about war and recovery. A partial manuscript emerged. Yet still she could not complete her story.

In her later years, she pulled back the curtain further on more of her secrets.

The account that follows is an assembly of all those bits and pieces merged with the memories of an old war reporter still struggling with early love and his first war.

1
A Homecoming

Saturday, January 29, 2011

I BROUGHT AN OLD FRIEND home again today.

It was not the homecoming I would have wished for her, nor the one she would have wished for herself.

She had departed Cambodia in January 1980. I helped her leave that shattered land after three years, eight months, and twenty-one days of imprisonment under the ultra-radical Khmer Rouge communists, who seized the capital, Phnom Penh, on April 17, 1975, after a bitter war. I flew her out to Singapore under highly unusual and slightly treacherous conditions.

The woman I was returning with had been my first love in a world of war. She provided a passionate introduction to life in a new and, to me, very exotic place.

Her name was Soc Sinan. We used to joke a bit about that. Soc was her family name, not that unusual in Cambodia. But Sinan was rare.

Many Khmer women are given names chosen for just the right meaning. Sophea is the clever one. Sonisay is someone you like at first impression. Sophon means beauty. Sinan or Sonan—as it was sometimes anglicized—embodied all of these qualities, to be sure. Yet Sinan's name in the original Sanskrit-like script seemed absent of meaning.

"You're one of a kind," I told her in 1970. "And besides, in the end your life will provide you meaning."

When we curled up together in the early days of our relationship, she meant to me passion, pleasure, and kindness in a world thrown upside-down by adventure, danger, and fear.

Our return to Cambodia could not have been more different from our departure. For in January 2011, I returned to Cambodia—with only Sinan's remains.

Sinan had died in a Maryland suburb of Washington, DC, in December 2010 at the age of 62.

"Going home" was meant to fulfill one of her last wishes—to return to the place of her birth: a place along the Mekong River.

It was a place where the mango trees grew tall and were said to live more than a hundred years. The place where Sinan said she had been most happy—as a little girl.

Sinan's ashes traveled with me in a small black lacquer box. I wrapped the box in my old 1970s cotton krama (a Khmer scarf) and placed it in a carry-on bag.

She would have laughed at the attention the Homeland Security agents gave her at New York's JFK Airport.

We traveled first to the Chinese city of Hong Kong (my home for more than fifteen years). Sinan had to wait a time while I completed teaching broadcast journalism classes at the university in the Pokfulam area of the island.

With the semester complete, student papers read and graded, my friend and I resumed our journey. We flew two and a half hours south to Ho Chi Minh City—or, as I and millions of others still call it, Saigon.

In Saigon, we paused a day before continuing overland.

We boarded a bus. The Mekong Express Limousine Bus offers one-way service 177 miles to Phnom Penh for $12. We caught the bus at a touristy, backpacker area known as Pham Ngu Lao.

Sinan, I'm sure, would have been pleased that I bought an extra seat on the Mekong Express so I could put the lacquer box by the window next to me. I somehow imagined the window seat would afford her a good view of the much-changed landscape.

If we were lucky, an early departure at 7 would have us in the Cambodian capital in time for a late lunch.

But two obstacles provide a challenge to the traveler. Sometimes the immigration officers are on tea break at the Vietnamese border crossing at Moc Bai or at the Cambodian entry point at Bavet, a short walk away. Once across the border and 103 kilometers or 64 miles later, you enter Neak Leung and face the prospect of delay in the queue for the ferry across the Mekong River.

This day our bus had the right-of-way.

As the ferry chugged on, I disembarked briefly to feel the warm, humid Mekong air hit my face. I spoke to a few local Khmer traders carrying their goods across the river.

"Sok sabai chea tay?" "Aukun." Hello, how are you? Thank you. (I spoke almost no Khmer. I have always been an impossible linguist.)

Business was good.

It had not always been that way.

A misplaced American B-52 bombing raid devastated Neak Leung in 1973. After the American war, the people here suffered, along with all Cambodia, amid the destruction of lives and souls caused by Khmer Rouge rule. Here one trauma replaced another. One atrocity followed the last.

From the Mekong River crossing, our bus now plowed on down Route 1 through heavier traffic.

It is 44 miles to Phnom Penh, the city where Sinan and I first met forty-one years earlier.

We arrived in the capital just after 1 in the afternoon.

I checked in to Le Royal Hotel.

I used to meet Sinan at this hotel from time to time. Not often. In 1970, I was too poor to afford the $19-a-night room charge. A meal by the pool attracted too much attention from curious Khmer and the expat community. We thought it best to avoid local chatter about a scruffy reporter and his far-too-attractive Khmer girlfriend.

The hotel holds a special place in Cambodia's history. Its history mirrored the nation's fate. In French colonial times, it was the place to stay. Charlie Chaplin sipped gin and tonics in the ground-floor bar. After independence, Prince Norodom Sihanouk, the nation's first leader, wined and dined Jacqueline Kennedy there. As war enveloped Cambodia in 1970, it became the favorite haunt of an increasing number of reporters. News agencies rented bungalows at the back, and their reporters debated at poolside the progress or usually lack of progress of the American-backed Khmer military. Later, after the Khmer Rouge were ousted, the hotel reopened for global relief agencies trying to rebuild a shattered land.

Today, totally remodeled by a Singapore hotel chain, Le Royal welcomes businesspeople, well-heeled tourists, and on Sunday, January 30, a small group of friends. Friends with one important thing in common. We were among Sinan's oldest friends.

We gathered at the back of the old hotel adjacent to the pool but sheltered from the sun. Around the small table with me sat Saorun Tchou, San Arun, and Eric Ellul. The atmosphere was reflective and subdued. We sipped glasses of white wine and proposed quiet toasts.

The four of us planned a simple Buddhist ceremony for Sinan the following day at her birthplace in the tiny Mekong River village of Thlok Chhreu. A mutual friend, Chanthou Boua, born in the same village, had old contacts there. With her help all was arranged.

Saorun probably knew Sinan best. They met in the late 1960s. I came to know Saorun in Paris only after the war was over.

"I returned to Cambodia from Paris to live here about ten years ago with Fernand, my second husband," Saorun explained.

They live as comfortable retirees just east of Phnom Penh in a large, airy, palm shrouded house with frontage on the Mekong near Wat Chrouy Ampil.

In the late 1960s and '70s Saorun taught at one of the more prestigious high schools about 7 miles south of Phnom Penh in Takhmau. There 13- to 18-year-old middle-class Khmer children learned French history and world geography from the energetic, always smiling, young teacher.

Young girls also looked to Saorun to learn what was considered most important in those days. The French called the subjects *enseignement ménager et puériculture*—home economics and childcare. Included in the curriculum: sex education.

"I was only a few years older than the students," joked Saorun. "I had little idea how to teach sex."

I saw Saorun as a chatty, quick to laugh, life-of-the-party type, a contrast to the more reserved person I saw in Sinan.

Yet in the small circle of friends closest to Sinan, Saorun emerged as the mother figure, the teacher, the organizer who nonetheless brought an infectious optimism to all around her.

A sense that if everyone stuck together, the future would work out just fine.

"You know, Jim, I didn't see Sinan in more than thirty-five years," recalled Saorun. "We exchanged letters of course, but I never had the chance to visit her and she never came to see me in France. I wish she had."

Saorun paused. Her face suddenly fell into deep sadness. She was no doubt remembering that awful day, April 12, 1975—when after a terrifying night, she and Sinan said goodbye with a long and tearful embrace.

The young man seated to her right put his arm around Saorun. Eric was the second of Saorun's two sons. Eric's father, a noted French scholar, specialized in Khmer anthropology before the war. Professor Ellul and Saorun had divorced not long after the war's end.

This was my first time meeting Eric.

Nearly 40, Eric looked much younger, with his long black hair swept back into a ponytail. He taught at the prestigious Lycée Descartes, a French international school where, since 1951, generations of French students had mingled with the wealthy, privileged French-speaking Khmer.

Barely 3 years old when the war ended, Eric had his head filled with stories of the adoring "Aunt" or "Tante" Sinan. She had showered love and care on Eric in the dark days of 1974–75.

"This gathering gives me a chance to know my mother, the story of Cambodia, and the war better," Eric told me. "There are so many things that were never discussed when I was a child."

San Arun volunteered her time as one of the key organizers of this unusual reunion.

Arun had met Sinan in 1972 before Arun traded war for love and moved to Thailand and then America with her husband-to-be.

I met Arun after the war at her home in Long Beach, California. Over the years, I watched her grow in a career that began in the Cambodian army. She continued in exile as a California real estate agent, and after returning to Phnom Penh, Arun was placed in charge of helping improve the lives of young women as a deputy minister in the Cambodian government's Ministry of Women's Affairs.

Ten years after the war ended, Arun reconnected with Sinan in Long Beach.

"She came to visit me a few years after she arrived in America," Arun recalled. "It was her first time in California. We took in all the sights."

Saorun and Arun represented a small group of women. All had been—in a way—Cambodian "soul sisters." They formed a playful, seemingly carefree group before the ultimate tragedy that was to engulf each of them and their country.

Those absent this day, but on our minds, were Khoeun Rigaud, who now lived in France, and Lisa Vannary or "Vann," who lived in the United States. This group formed a unique social club in the early 1970s.

At that small table in the shade at the rear of Le Royal, Saorun, Arun, Eric, and I sipped another glass and raised it in tribute to Sinan. For several hours more as the sun set over the hotel garden, friends shared memories, told stories, shed tears.

■ ■ ■

On Monday, January 31, the four of us headed out of Phnom Penh.

We drove into a village where life had not changed all that much since the days when I traveled Cambodia's rural roads in the early '70s. As the car picked up speed, I cradled the lacquer box carefully in my lap.

Route 6A leading out of Phnom Penh follows the left bank of the Mekong: first north and then east into Kampong Cham Province. Kicking up dust as we drove bumpily along only partially paved roads, we arrived in the village of Thlok Chhreu in just under two hours.

Soc Sinan was born here in the final years of French colonial rule. Her mother, Sipan, who everyone called "Pan," gave birth to Sinan, villagers said, near a "deep pond to the sounds of the Buddhist drums."

We were to say goodbye to Sinan in the traditional way. Arun arranged for an "achar"—a sort of Buddhist master of ceremonies—to preside over the rituals. Several novice monks helped officiate.

Villagers prepared a substantial meal. The luncheon was not for us but rather for the monks and for much of the village. For the farm families of Thlok Chhreu, our visit would be their highlight of the month, perhaps the year.

With the rituals complete, six people—an oarsman, the boat owner, a young Buddhist monk, the achar, Eric, and I—descended into a rickety sampan. I would spread Sinan's ashes in the middle of the Mekong River a hundred yards or so from the place of her earliest, happiest memories. Arun and Saorun watched and waved from the shore.

We would all say our goodbyes to Soc Sinan—and remember.

2

Events We Could Not Foresee

Saturday, April 12, 1975

THE END, WHEN IT CAME, came with unexpected suddenness. Back in Phnom Penh for only a short time, I had been preoccupied with filing daily news reports on a worsening situation. The war, after five bitter years, closed in. I could see it coming and yet I didn't. The end was near. Yet certainly defeat could be delayed by a few weeks or maybe a few months. The airport remained open. American supplies continued to flow in. Only yesterday, C-130 cargo planes performed another round in their daily airlift from Thailand. I had been out to the front line north of the city. The line was holding. The Cambodians continued to fight, beating back repeated assaults by the Vietnamese-trained, radical Khmer Rouge communists.

I wasn't ready for defeat, and neither were the Cambodian friends I knew—most especially the woman with whom I had developed love, intimacy, and friendship five years before.

Sinan, though she had multiple opportunities, would not leave. She loved Cambodia. She loved her life here.

I promised her that whatever happened, when the time came, I would get her out. Well, the time had come. And Sinan was not with me. I had betrayed her. I had left her behind.

I looked out the tiny window of a US Marine transport helicopter as it flew higher over the city. It banked left, heading south toward the Gulf of Thailand. Phnom Penh's lush, pagoda-dotted terrain disappeared quickly beneath me. I raised my film camera to capture a few final images.

Washington had ordered out American diplomats, military attachés, and journalists. A vote by Congress refusing further economic or military support had ensured the death of a nation. The president had run out of options. For America the war was over. No further assistance for Cambodia would be forthcoming. I was on my way to an aircraft carrier. The Cambodian army would have to go it alone, without the means to succeed. They would certainly, I thought, see it as a final, deadly American betrayal.

I turned away from the window and put my camera down. I couldn't get the thought out of mind. I had left her behind. I tried to get her out. But I had left her behind. For a minute I buried my head in my hands.

I looked around. Other men, a few hardened military officers I recognized from the US Embassy, had done the same, heads bowed as if in prayer or in mourning. One diplomat was sobbing.

"We left a lot of good people, good Cambodian people, behind today," the man next to me shouted over the roar of the aircraft engine. "I don't know what's going to happen to them. It won't be good!"

On the ground, only a block or two from the embassy, it was already not good. Sinan watched as the rescue helicopters pulled away and disappeared over the tree line.

"I stood on the sidewalk, within sight of the embassy building," Sinan wrote nearly ten years later.

"I could hear the extremely loud noises of the helicopters. They were flying northwest to southeast over the city. Everyone wondered what was going on. There was nothing on the radio. All this commotion and yet there were no rockets falling, no enemy attack. Why was this happening?"

"Still, I remembered what Jim had said. 'When the Americans decide to leave, they will do so quickly. You must be ready to go. I will take you out. But you must let me know where you are at all times.'"

But Sinan was not ready. She had not told me where she was going after dinner on the night of April 11. As she recalled the events years later:

On the street, near the embassy, I walked along the Avenue of Liberty. I saw a Cambodian woman I knew standing on the street. "The embassy," she shouted to me, "is leaving. Leaving Cambodia!" A large crowd stood in front of the marine guard house in front of the building. The embassy staff had assembled a small fleet of cars, trucks, and vans to take people to a helicopter landing area at a school a short distance away. Most of the people watching were from the neighborhood nearby.

I saw a few women who used to work at nightclubs in Phnom Penh. They had been dating some of the marine guards. Their marines were clearly leaving without them. The women seemed upset because they sensed their lives would be in danger soon. I talked to one—named Pisey. She was attractive and bright. She told me her marine guard had asked her to leave with him. She could not, she said, because she had two children and couldn't leave her family behind.

As the helicopters flew overhead, most of the crowd across from the embassy remained calm. They were not anxious to leave. They even joked about how panicked the Americans must be.

Those "Yankees" were jumping wildly into their trucks, waving their guns around, in such a hurry to leave.

I looked to the sky. I could see helicopters coming and going. And then they were gone.

After the last helicopter left, I saw the local Khmer police enter the embassy gate. Where the American flag had been, they raised a white flag.

Just after the flag went up, a deadly round of artillery fire crashed into the area on the east side of the Mekong River held by communist forces.

Sinan ran to find shelter.

Two rockets landed on the street nearby. One old man on a bicycle was blown off his bike. I am sure he was killed. I did not have time to stop and look. I just kept running. The streets were now empty. Then I heard the rockets again, this time dropping like drops of rain.

Early Saturday evening, April 12

Sinan slowly made her way back to her apartment on the city's busiest main street—Boulevard Monivong. The boulevard, normally packed with people returning from the Central Market or setting out for a weekend meal in one of the many restaurants, was nearly empty.

Inside her apartment, Sinan positioned herself next to the window. She closed the shutters. She squatted down and peered through the slats.

No one was moving where they would normally be on the corner of Monivong and Keo Chea Street. The quiet was disturbed only by the occasional pass of city police on patrol. The government declared a curfew, which would be enforced when darkness came.

I tried to come to grips with my new situation. Jim was gone. Most of my Khmer friends had gone to stay with their families. I was left very much alone in my apartment. After an hour or so I dried my tears and calmed down.

After a while I walked downstairs to chat with Madame Reine and her family. They were among the three or four friends I had in the building. Mme Reine was married to a captain in the Cambodian army. He sat talking with a few other men. They were eating beef sticks and pickled vegetables.

I wasn't hungry but when Mme Reine offered, I accepted some food.

The men were drinking Larue, the popular beer from South Vietnam. They were upset. As they drank, their faces grew red. The more they drank, the angrier they got: "It was scandalous that the Americans fled Cambodia on their helicopters. They took out their own people. They thought nothing of the Khmer. They created the war here. They spread it from Vietnam. They destroyed our country, and now they're running away, running away, leaving us with nothing."

The men talked about escape. Could we get out of Cambodia? They wanted somehow to get to Vietnam. They realized it was probably too late. Route 1 to Vietnam had been cut off a long time ago by the Khmer Rouge.

At 8:00 I suggested turning on the radio. I always used my small battery radio to hear the VOA, the Voice of America, or sometimes the radio station over in Saigon. The broadcast said that helicopters carrying Americans and some Cambodians had completed their mission and had landed on an aircraft carrier in the Gulf of Thailand. We also heard that Lon Nol, the general who started all this with the American-backed coup d'état back in 1970, was safe and relaxing in Hawaii.

After the broadcast, Mme Reine's husband, still drinking beer, said, "Typical Khmer leaders. Lon Nol and Sihanouk before him. All of them a rotten lot. All claimed to be patriots but at the last minute they didn't give a damn. They just abandoned us. Left us. Took their families with them."

I returned to my apartment. That night I could not sleep. My head was filled with a mixture of sadness, loneliness, and fear.

■ ■ ■

Phnom Penh hung on for four more days after the Americans left. The army fought and then ran out of ammunition. Soldiers deserted to find their families. The defensive perimeter shrank to nothing.

On Thursday morning, April 17, Khmer Rouge soldiers marched into the city. Phnom Penh and soon all of Cambodia came under the control of one of the world's most radical communist movements—the Khmer Rouge.

One of history's greatest episodes of genocide was about to begin.

During five years of fighting, the pre-war city of about 500,000 had swollen to more than two million as refugees fleeing the war flooded into Phnom Penh. I had visited many of them near a sports arena, which the Khmer optimistically called their "Olympic Stadium."

The Khmer Rouge began by ordering the expulsion from the city every man, woman, and child. The frightened procession of people brought meager provisions, only what they could carry. Most left on foot. The wealthy few who tried to drive out of town in their cars soon ran out of gasoline or were ordered to abandon their vehicles at gunpoint.

At Yale University in 1996, scholar Ben Kiernan pored over more than a hundred interviews with evacuee survivors. From these, he estimated about 21,000 people died in the very first days of the communist takeover.

It was just the beginning.

. . .

Sinan refused to obey the commands of the Khmer Rouge on April 17, 1975. Ignoring warnings, ignoring threats, she stalled. She delayed. She tried to prepare.

She carefully observed her surroundings. She began to learn more about the radical communists.

As the Khmer Rouge consolidated their control, she remained, hiding out in her apartment after everyone else had gone.

But as Sinan put it, "On Sunday morning, April 20, there was a sudden change in my situation."

The Khmer Rouge began a door-by-door inspection to see if everyone had obeyed their evacuation orders. One by one they began breaking down people's doors. They used either rifle butts or large pieces of heavy metal. At houses they ran trucks through the front doors.

Khmer people were very good at locking things. But the communists were even better at breaking things.

I remember the speech on the loud hailer: "Trust us! We will take care of your homes and your belongings. Just leave now. It is dangerous to stay. Americans will bomb you here as they have already done all over the countryside."

It was noon. Soldiers searched each apartment, one at a time now. From the ground up, they were going through my building. They got to the top floor. I heard them break into the apartment of my friend Bopha, who had already left, and also that of a hospital nurse down the hall.

My building had forty-six apartments. The building was built in 1965. I had lived here since 1969, when I got my first job.

The Khmer Rouge continued on going door-to-door.

I retreated to the small kitchen at the back of my apartment. I heard them try to open my door. It was locked from the inside. They could not see the lock. They walked away.

It took them 10 minutes to break my neighbors' locked doors. They were laughing.

My heart beat irregularly. I stood in the kitchen and prayed to Buddha and my ancestors to help me. They passed by my door again and went down the hall. Again they came to my door. I heard a soldier say, "Let's try this door, one more time."

I heard a scrape of metal. My door still did not open. Then I heard a gunshot.

They had shot the bolt lock which had kept the steel door shut from the inside. The door finally opened.

I heard one soldier say, "No matter how strong the opposition, the spirit of the revolution will always win."

I remained in the kitchen. I did not know now where to hide. I went behind the curtain which separated the main room from the sleeping area.

After their efforts to break my door, they relaxed for a while on the balcony. They must have been exhausted.

I was shivering in the heat of my apartment. I turned pale.

A few minutes later, they walked boldly in, opened the curtain, and found me—shaking, cowering on the floor, leaning my head against the bed.

Two soldiers pointed rifles at me. I was in that world just between life and death. I put my hands together in a beseeching gesture.

One young soldier shouted, "Enemy, enemy, hiding herself!"

I prayed to them, asking for forgiveness.

They shouted again, "Put your hands down. Don't pray to us. There is no prayer in revolution. We are all equal! Why are you still here? Everyone else has left, evacuated to the countryside. Why are you here?"

I relaxed a little. At least they were not going to shoot me right away.

Sinan's life at that moment was spared. But it was only the start of years of fear and suffering.

Neither Sinan nor I could have foreseen any of the events that would overtake our lives when we met for the first time five years before.

3
Café au Lait

Monday, June 8, 1970

SHE SEEMED SO OUT of place. I first noticed her on Monday morning in the back row of a wartime military briefing. An elegant flower stood out among the weeds.

About fifty reporters assembled for the daily Phnom Penh army briefing at 8. They had come to hear the official view on how the new war in Cambodia was going. The ritual had begun shortly after the installation of the new government in March.

I joined the briefing at the start of my third month as a war reporter.

Running out of money on my first visit to Asia, I accepted a job from a small radio news network where I worked part-time to pay college bills in 1969.

A gig to edit brochures for the opening of the 1970 World's Fair in Osaka, Japan had ended. A week later I failed to find work in Hong Kong writing about China. The China International Travel Service refused me a China visa.

As I checked my bank balance, I was poised to either go home (stashed in my backpack was a round-the-world Pan American Airways ticket) or go to war. I chose war for $250 a week.

I was suddenly thrust into a conflict about which I knew little.

I arrived in Saigon in April, assigned to replace Alan Dawson, a seasoned war reporter who had decided to move on to United Press International (UPI). I was grateful. I now had money in my pocket. Soon, with Alan's help and that of a group of new colleagues, I was shown the ropes. A radio network—Metromedia Radio News (long forgotten today)—got me first to Vietnam and then, when I suggested it, on to Cambodia.

In Phnom Penh, my media colleagues and I introduced American listeners, readers, and viewers to a new list of battlefield locations in a widened war and the names of leaders very few had ever heard of.

Although my stories were leads on many hourly radio news bulletins in 1970, I suspected most Americans were tired of hearing of a distant war that had dragged on for nearly ten years.

Still, Parrot's Beak, Fishhook, Neak Leung, and Pochentong joined Khe Sanh, the DMZ, Hue, and Tan Son Nhut as key wartime place names. And Lon Nol and Sirik Matak, who got rid of a man named Sihanouk, joined Nguyen Van Thieu and Ho Chi Minh as new names to be learned in a wider Indochina war.

■ ■ ■

The daily Cambodia military briefing, where I met Soc Sinan, had its origins in a coup d'état. To this day, the circumstances of the March 17–18, 1970, military coup are debated.

Norodom Sihanouk had dominated Cambodian politics since the early 1950s. He wrested independence from French colonial rule. Too ambitious to be content with his role as playboy prince who would be King, he renounced his royal titles, though in Khmer he was referred to as "Samdech," which loosely translates as "your lordship."

Sihanouk's zenith of power came in the early 1960s. Paying scant attention to domestic realities, running roughshod over any opposition, Sihanouk kept his eyes on two goals.

Borrowing a Louis XIV "L'état, c'est moi" attitude, Sihanouk built a cult of indispensability. He wanted recognition for himself and a place in the world for his tiny nation well above its actual status. Attaching Cambodia to the "neutralist nonaligned movement," he struggled to keep the Khmer people out of war. If he needed compromise and appeasement to achieve that goal—so be it.

While Sihanouk walked a political tightrope from the beginning of his rule, serious challenges emerged in 1967. He was buffeted by the political left and right. He ruthlessly staved off a challenge from the left. He threatened future members of the communist Khmer Rouge with death. They ran. They took refuge in the countryside, the bush, the "maquis" as the French called it, where they slowly built their radical movement.

On his political right, and impossible to expel, Sihanouk faced the urban elite, disaffected students, members of his own royal family, and most importantly an increasingly disgruntled military—individuals he thought he could trust.

The spillover from the escalating war next door had a clear impact.

From 1967 onward, North Vietnam pushed an increasing volume of supplies southward along the Ho Chi Minh Trail crossing into eastern Cambodia. The armies of the North established "sanctuaries" where they could escape the battlefields of South Vietnam. They counted on the United States and its ally in Saigon not to violate Cambodia's "neutrality." The numbers of North Vietnamese troops based in the east rose to 40,000.

The Chinese pressed Sihanouk to allow military supplies to be offloaded at the port of Sihanoukville and funnel them northward to their North Vietnamese allies.

Everybody had their secrets. Sihanouk struck a secret bargain with Beijing. Chinese ships unloaded their cargo. For a "percentage," royal Cambodian troops would help deliver the arms from the Gulf of Thailand port northward.

Sihanouk struck another bargain with Hanoi for food. Again, for a hefty commission, the government diverted Cambodian rice (then in relatively plentiful supply) to North Vietnamese troops.

Sihanouk needed such secret deals. His backers in his army required more money.

In 1965 Sihanouk broke off relations with the United States. He said it was to keep the country out of war. In severing ties, Sihanouk lost American aid money, which included about a third of what he needed to keep his 30,000-man army going.

The Americans had their own secrets. In 1965 President Lyndon Johnson began air attacks on eighty-three strategic North Vietnamese positions in Cambodia.

In February 1969, newly elected President Richard Nixon took one giant step further. He ordered massive B-52 carpet-bombing of eastern Cambodia.

Flying from Guam, over 300 days on more than 4,000 sorties, Boeing B-52 Stratofortresses dropped more than 111,000 tons of explosives.

Nixon hid the carpet-bombing from Congress. US commanders in the know worked hard to maintain the fiction that the bombing struck only "enemy targets in South Vietnam."

The air assaults were no secret, of course, to those under them. Approximately 5,000 Khmer villagers lived in small dwellings in the area. They were the first to feel the impact of the deadly explosives. No accurate accounting was ever made of the total killed. North Vietnamese supply lines were damaged, but Hanoi's commanders moved their base camps deeper into Cambodia.

In Phnom Penh, Sihanouk received reports but did nothing. He had appeased the Chinese and North Vietnamese. Now he appeased the Americans.

By 1969, this "chief of state" was a shadow of his formerly robust self. His nation's image as an "oasis of peace" had been shattered.

Sihanouk retreated into a surreal world in which he became a film director. He made nine feature films between 1966 and 1969. Sihanouk called the hobby a "diversion." Others around him recognized that he had taken his eye off critical issues just as the nation faced great danger.

As my professor of Southeast Asian history, Milton Osborne, wrote later, "farce turned to tragedy." Sihanouk's powers slowly evaporated.

Forces demanding change coalesced. Sihanouk's cousin, Prince Sirik Matak, for years a Sihanouk supporter in diplomatic posts overseas, came home. As 1969 began, he actively if quietly plotted Sihanouk's ouster. Within a year he persuaded Sihanouk's trusted military commander and defense minister, General Lon Nol, to lead a coup d'état. Sihanouk, once considered indispensable to Cambodia's survival, was out. Traveling at the time of his ouster, he began a long residence in China.

■ ■ ■

I met Norodom Sihanouk twice, once in Beijing and then much later in July 1985 in Pyongyang, North Korea.

The Sihanouk I met came across as a smart, highly charismatic man, and always engaging. He also struck me as comical, a character trait that seemed ill-suited to the horrors his country faced. His effusiveness, his high-pitched voice, and his use of language combined to cause in me a suppressed smile. The comic elements of our lengthy meeting in North Korea stick with me.

We met in a forty-room palatial-style building on the outskirts of the capital. North Korea's first leader, Kim Il Sung (grandfather of today's communist "Supreme Leader" Kim Jong Un), installed Sihanouk there.

Kim, the "Great Leader," was an "old friend," Sihanouk told me. Kim offered him the accommodation so that the exiled leader could get a respite from Beijing, his on-again, off-again base since 1970.

Our Korean hosts escorted my television team in two new Mercedes-Benzes from central Pyongyang, down a long tree-lined approach to the hilltop mansion. We were greeted by Sihanouk's elegant wife Monique and their two French poodles.

While Masahiro Ogushi, my camera operator, set up lights for an interview, Sihanouk and I chatted informally. The dogs began to gnaw at the electric cables for the lights. I fantasized for a moment about newspaper headlines proclaiming, "American TV news team kills Cambodian leader's precious poodles." Fortunately, Sihanouk (with what sounded like a high-pitched giggle) called off his dogs. He then offered me some cookies.

"They are American, you know. And Sihanouk has them here in North Korea," he chuckled. He frequently referred to himself in the third person.

The chat before the camera starts rolling often proves the most revealing. I tried to get the measure of a man I had written about often but who remained a mystery to me.

Much had happened in the fifteen years since he was overthrown. Still Sihanouk seemed obsessed with the coup. He blamed the CIA. "Since 1963, Sihanouk has been a target of the CIA. They have always tried to strengthen my opponents and weaken my powers." (I have not been able to find any proof that the CIA directly engineered the coup that ousted him.) By 1985, Sihanouk had tried to reinvent himself several times. He always had a craving to be relevant. Yet each time he tried, he seemed to become less important.

After the coup, with China's help, Sihanouk became the nominal head of the communist Khmer Rouge movement that eventually defeated Lon Nol. When he was of no more use to the Khmer Rouge, they put him under house arrest from 1976 to 1979. Rescued again by the Chinese, he once again became head of a coalition opposed to the Vietnamese who invaded Cambodia in January 1979.

Yet when I met him, he listened intently to my rather positive description of conditions in his Vietnamese-occupied homeland. (I had visited Cambodia five times between 1979 and 1985.)

When I asked, he confirmed that under Khmer Rouge rule five of his children and at least a dozen grandchildren died. He stopped talking for a moment.

Perhaps he might have reflected more on his personal responsibility in supporting a murderous regime. But not quite.

"Sihanouk is not perfect, yes. But I was better than all the others. My only mistake perhaps was the mistake of compromise. But I had no choice."

He paused again. I saw him frown, possibly in sad reflection. But with those TV lights on, he was back in form, back on script.

"You know, these Vietnamese. They lack land and food. So they send more and more Vietnamese into Kampuchea in order to take our land, to take our food, to exploit our natural resources.

This, Sihanouk must resist. We must build peace and a neutral Kampuchea."

As we ended our conversation and prepared to leave the house that Kim built, Sihanouk presented me a gift: an audiocassette tape. Emblazoned on the cover: "The Music of Samdech Norodom Sihanouk as performed by the Pyongyang Symphony Orchestra under the direction of Dear Leader Kim Jong Il" (the son of Kim Il Sung).

He seemed to display great pride in presenting the tape to me. As I accepted the gift, cupping my hands in thanks, I puzzled over his inconsistencies. I wondered whether his better course after 1970 might have been to stick with entertainment.

. . .

In 1970, Cambodia descended into a tragic, all-out war, one that Sihanouk had struggled to avoid. The Lon Nol period was to last five deadly years.

In an initial burst of patriotic enthusiasm for the new "Khmer Republic," 70,000 Cambodian men volunteered for military service. Poorly trained and poorly led, they were no match for the well-trained and disciplined armies sent by Hanoi. Hanoi also began to train an even more fearsome army of Khmer communists, which in a few years would take over the war.

So it was that in 1970 Cambodia began holding its first ever military briefings for the international media.

. . .

I watched the young Khmer woman arrive at the military briefing early. She wore a simple white blouse and a modified Khmer sampot chang kben—a common wraparound skirt popular in the late 1960s. To me the dress seemed not all that different from those worn by the devas in the famous Ramayana myth known as the Reamker.

Soc Sinan was striking in every way. Her broad face reminded me of those on the splendid bas-relief sculptures of the temples of Angkor.

I had not been to Angkor yet. All I knew of Asia, of Cambodia, came from books.

In 1969, I had enrolled in the autumn-semester college course 29.341-C: Introduction to Asian Histories I. There, among the assigned texts by Cœdès and Burling, was a marvelous new illustrated book from Paris. Facing page 110 appeared a captivating close-up. Author Bernard-Philippe Groslier had spent a lifetime studying and restoring temples. Next to his photos he wrote some flowery bits of verse:

Comme la grâce du printemps sur les jardins, it began.

As the grace of spring in the garden, as the day of the full moon— rose a lovely splendid beauty from its fresh youth or find another perfect example of her beauty.

Groslier was describing Sinan! With her wide inviting eyes, full lips, and dark, unblemished beauty, she possessed me totally.

I was 22, she a year younger. Within a week of our meeting, we would quietly celebrate my 23rd birthday together in Phnom Penh.

■ ■ ■

Little in my twenty-two years prepared me for what I was about to do: fall in love in a land that had captured me only in the writings of very old or dead French men.

The first son of a physician and the army nurse he met at the end of World War II, I learned to walk in a house with a broad front porch next to Dad's medical practice in rural Florida. Just when I was getting used to running and playing in hot, muggy air, Dad moved us north. He joined a medical clinic in central Massachusetts to care for war veterans. Those from World War II and Korea kept him steadily busy. As I was flying off to Asia, Dad began to treat veterans of the Vietnam War.

"You sure are fickle," my mother told me more than once. I laughed at that old-fashioned word—fickle. But yes, I constantly moved from one interest to another. As a teenager, I became a global wanderer, at least in my mind.

Mother thought I was cut out, like Dad, to go into science. I learned photomicroscopy in my makeshift basement laboratory. I entered science fairs.

I also toyed with newspapers, starting a neighborhood gossip sheet. I listened to shortwave radio broadcasts alone in my room. As I heard the chimes of "The East Is Red" on Radio Peking or, through the static, the voices of Radio Moscow, I fantasized. I secretly plotted my eventual escape.

My younger brother seemed to have more discipline. "Look how he can memorize everything," boasted Mother. When he was 7, he rattled off in order the names and dates of the thirty-four US presidents. My brother excelled in sports as well: baseball and basketball. I memorized little, dabbled at everything, and excelled at nothing.

Mother argued with Dad. "Can't you push that boy? Teach him some discipline."

"Ah, let him be," replied Dad. "He'll just be a jack of all trades, master of none." Dad always maintained a stash of good old aphorisms, though I'm quite sure he had never read *Greene's Groats-Worth of Wit* of 1592.

My science career came to a screeching halt when I flunked chemistry.

In high school, I landed a weekend announcing job reading the news at a local radio station, which made me a minor celebrity in class.

As I sat in front of a microphone at Worcester's "WNEB—1230 on everybody's dial," I listened to network radio feeds and voices from distant places. The morning CBS *World News Roundup* introduced to me correspondents like David Schoenbrun in Paris, Winston Burdett in Rome, and Peter Kalischer, who roamed Asia. Later in 1965, a young guy named Morley Safer came on the radio from Vietnam.

I took to imagining things—mostly imagining that I was somewhere else.

At university in Washington, DC, I chose to major in history. I experimented with a minor in journalism, taking jobs on the side at a local "all news" radio station, even at one point signing on as theater critic.

I sought something different, anything that might stimulate a poor student.

With too much competition in American and European history, David Brandenberg, the history chair at American University and a French history specialist, suggested I might find Asia of interest. He introduced me to the French colonial past of Indochina. Milton Osborne later deepened my interest.

I may have been one of the few undergrads in those days who focused on Southeast Asia, China, and Japan.

My education failed to include much about the modern era. My college courses were devoid of useful knowledge—social graces, norms of behavior, and language.

Still, George Cœdès laid out for me the "Indianized States of Southeast Asia." Robbins Burling told me of "Hill Farms and Padi Fields." Edwin Reischauer and John King Fairbank introduced me to Japan and China.

I stuffed a few books into my backpack as I departed for Asia. Two of them I thought might be useful if I pitched up in Vietnam or Cambodia.

Bernard Fall's *Hell in a Very Small Place: The Siege of Dien Bien Phu* was one.

I had met the French soldier, writer, and scholar while a freshman in college. Fall taught at Washington's Howard University but in 1966 came to American University to deliver a powerful lecture on how the Americans in Vietnam were repeating the mistakes of the French. I listened intently and believed his every word.

Six months later, the man I met only briefly but who impressed me greatly was dead.

Fall had joined a patrol of US Marines north of Hue, Vietnam. The French dubbed the much-fought-over territory on which Fall walked *La Rue Sans Joie*, "the Street Without Joy." The patrol triggered a land mine. It killed Fall and one American marine instantly.

André Malraux's *La Voie royale* also found its way into the backpack. It was slim. It fit. It gave me a chance to practice my French. I was told my limited, high school French would come in handy in Asia. I was armed with much misinformation.

Writer and later French Minister of Culture, Malraux in his novel told the tale of two adventurers intent on stealing precious statues from the Angkor temples. It drew on Malraux's own experience when at age 22 he was arrested for archeological theft. His description of a 1925 French Cambodge rang true as I watched Cambodia's decline into war.

A blind man chanted the Ramayana as he twanged his ancient guitar. What better personification of Cambodge, of this land of decay, could he have found than that old singer ... a land possessed ... its ancient hymns, like its temples, fallen on evil days; of all dead lands most dead.

Malraux's rather over-the-top description of lust for a Khmer woman also appealed to this 22-year-old's fantasies of new experiences with Sinan.

"Dans la pénombre, elle se couche, nue, son corps lisse et glabre s'affaiblit ..."

"In the darkness, she lies, bare, her body weakens ...", and so on.

In June 1970 Indochina came alive.

■ ■ ■

Sinan said she had never met a person with such ignorance of Cambodia. She set about providing her first American friend an education.

"You must understand much about Cambodge, Jim," Sinan said in a combination of English and French, with a unique Khmer upward inflection in her voice.

First, lessons in social behavior. The intimate side of our relationship must be carefully managed. In romance, Sinan advised, discretion was essential. No holding hands. No public displays of affection. She would conduct herself as a tour guide—guiding me through the sensitivities of Khmer culture and society. Occasionally a younger sister would join us.

In 1970 Cambodia remained—on the surface at least—a highly conservative society. Sinan proved to be an unusual Khmer woman. She was independent. She worked for a respected Khmer French firm. She saw herself as part of an urban middle class, which she hoped would grow if Cambodia could maintain the peace it had enjoyed.

I did not know it then, but Sinan's life was also a troubled one, marred by deep psychological scars born in childhood. The traumas of her early years and her ways of coping, however, would prove beneficial to Sinan's struggle for survival many years later.

■ ■ ■

War can be romantic for everyone except for its victims.

To an impossibly green reporter, the Cambodian military briefing each morning somehow presented a slightly amusing daily habit.

The idea in those days was that reporters would attend the briefing and learn very little of real value but use the military progress reports as clues to where they might go to find a little combat action, and perhaps a real story.

Once the briefing was over, I would join other Phnom Penh–based reporters and stream out of town. A group of enterprising former Angkor tour guides assembled a fleet of somewhat beat-up Mercedes-Benzes. Obligingly, drivers and interpreters filled up coolers with cold drinks. Until the breweries were blown up in

1971, a cooler of Angkor or Bayon beer might come in handy. We'd also stock up on extra cartons of "555" cigarettes to pass out to Cambodian officers and their men.

The roads that exited Phnom Penh were arrayed like spokes of a wheel. I might choose one in search of action. Route 4 headed south through Kampong Speu and on through the dangerous Cardamom Mountains to Sihanoukville (or Kampong Som). Route 5 pointed northwest to Sisophon and Battambang. Route 1 went east to the Vietnamese border.

As a novice radio reporter, I would usually join a more-seasoned correspondent. I wasn't exactly competition for anybody.

The Mercs would at first speed out of town. Slowing down, the Khmer speakers would carefully check military outposts along the way to see how safe the road was ahead.

Often they were not safe at all. About forty reporters lost their lives on the roads of Cambodia. Several more were kidnapped and miraculously lived to tell the tale.

On one return visit to Phnom Penh in 2017, I lit a joss stick and placed it in front of a small memorial to those who did not make it, a marble monument erected on a patch of green near a traffic circle in Phnom Penh at the north end of the French Embassy.

■ ■ ■

In the early days, the Armed Forces of the Khmer Republic issued twice-daily reports from a small walk-up, a former state-run bar just off Post Office Square.

"Salle climatisee—Atmosphere intime," a sign at the entrance proclaimed. In the back of the briefing room another sign read, "Au Salon de Thé du Centre de la Presse Internationale."

A young, fair-skinned Chinese Khmer woman named Phang Ming sat behind a bar. She served café au lait with a smile. She thrust a card into my hand: "Des boisson et des plat francais et cambodgiens, covenant à votre goût et au prix raisonnable. Telephone 2-5800." As the card boasted, the food and drink, French and Cambodian, were pleasant to the taste and offered at a reasonable price.

Two men in uniform stood at the front of the room reading reports from the field. The French-speaking colonel was a man with an unfortunate name for an army information officer—Am Rong. His English translator, a young lieutenant named Chhang Song, assisted the briefing.

It turned out that Lieutenant Chhang Song first invited Sinan to the military briefing a week or so before I met her. Sinan displayed a natural interest in everything. And Chhang Song was known to have an eye for only the most attractive women. The war was new, Sinan's curiosity intense.

■ ■ ■

I did not hesitate. After introducing myself, I thrust my business card at her. I muttered some invention about wanting to chat more about the war and its impact on civilians and the small urban middle class.

Sinan had no card. I quickly pulled out of my pocket a spare card. She wrote on the back:

"Miss Soc Sinan, SONATRAC P.P., 19 Vithei Samdech Pann, Phone 2.3629."

"Merci," I said. "J'espère vous revoir demain ici."

She simply smiled—that broad, inviting, unforgettable smile.

After meeting Soc Sinan that Monday morning in June, I paid scant attention to the military briefing.

A day later came the highlight of my morning, my week, my month. She returned to the next morning's briefing.

I asked Sinan if she might join me at the back of the room for a café au lait. She hesitated but then, after seeing that nearly everyone else in the room had run off—presumably heading for the roads out of town—she agreed.

I peppered her with questions. She answered quietly in short bursts, a mix of halting English and fluent French.

"Where do you work?"

"Une entreprise, ah, une companie, French."

"Why do you come to these boring news conferences?"

"Je suis curieux de cette nouvelle guerre!"

She lobbed questions at me in return. Where was I from? How long had I been in Phnom Penh? Had I visited other Cambodian cities?

She looked at my unkempt appearance, long tangled hair, poorly shaven face. She glanced at my bell-bottomed trousers—too tight at the top, too wide at the bottom, and suddenly asked, "You are how old?"

"As a matter of fact, my birthday is next week," I blurted out. "I'll be 23. Will you celebrate it with me over dinner?"

Again, hesitation. Then acceptance. But only if one of her sisters could join us. I agreed at once. We would go to one of her favorite restaurants—Le Mondiale, near the sports stadium.

"Tu es le premier Américain à qui j'ai parlé!" Sinan observed.

I was the first American she had ever talked to, I confirmed. Ah, she had used the familiar "you"—*Tu*.

I sipped my café au lait with a new friend, a woman I had just met. Covering wars, I thought to myself, could be very pleasant indeed.

■ ■ ■

Sinan maintained her curiosity about military matters. But soon after we met in 1970 she stopped going to the briefings. She sometimes read my dispatches with interest, but we never again had café au lait together at the Salon de Thé du Centre de la Presse Internationale where, as the menu said, the food and drink were pleasant to the taste and offered at a price most "raisonnable."

4

The Smiles of Bayon

THESE WERE INDEED early days.

Anyone who met me discovered a wide-eyed, awkward kid imitating the behavior of those much older and wiser. I was a loner, a young man who kept to himself and was no doubt the greenest war reporter in town.

Unable to afford Le Royal, I lived about a 15-minute walk away at the Hotel de la Poste. I had a spacious ground-floor corner room, shower, large bed, and a sturdy desk on which to plant my durable Olivetti Lettera 32 portable typewriter. On it I pounded out dozens of stories and radio scripts.

The hotel tariff at de la Poste was $5 a night.

The other advantage to my hotel was—as the name suggests—that it stood just opposite the PTT (the Post, Telegraph, and Telephone). In the days long before the internet and instant communications to anywhere, this is where I would file my stories. I would run up the steps to the left of the main post office entrance to the telephone/telex office.

Very early on, the Khmer Republic imposed a system of military censorship. Young English-speaking students read all the copy, whether for radio or newspapers.

I asked one student why he took work as a censor at the post office.

"It's my duty. I support the new Republic," he replied. "The monarchy under Sihanouk was corrupt."

Young and idealistic, he believed supporting the new government would provide a promising future. They were after all in alliance with the Americans.

Censorship was rather a haphazard, laid-back process. If I had a radio voice report to deliver, I would give my script to the young censor to read and "correct." I read my scripts live across shortwave circuits to the United States. The voice-casts were not monitored very carefully, so I could ad-lib back into the stories any changes the young student censor made.

The transmissions were barely intelligible at times. That didn't seem to matter to the editors in Washington or New York. The static added drama to the Phnom Penh dateline.

■ ■ ■

In the early days of our relationship, I tried speaking to Sinan only in French. I soon realized that as my French was extraordinarily poor and my Khmer nonexistent, our conversations would be very limited indeed. Fortunately for me, Sinan, with her disarming smile, let me off the hook and steered me toward English.

Over dinner we talked of her work and her love of Phnom Penh.

Her employer was "SONATRAC," she said, "the "Société Nationale de Tracteurs—the National Tractor Society."

A French firm in the colonial era, now a fully Cambodian-owned company, SONATRAC manufactured and distributed a range of agricultural machinery, trucks, and tractors.

Sinan told me the management was known for its progressive political positions. "Mon entreprise aids à modernizer of the poor farmers du Cambodge," she said with some pride.

SONATRAC also distributed in Cambodia the popular French "Mobylette" or "Moby." This "moped," as it was later called, was the motorized bicycle of the 1960s.

"Only les Khmer in the city with much money could afford one," Sinan quickly added.

Impressed by her organizational skills, her fluency in French, and no doubt her charm, the sales department hired Sinan as a secretary on November 22, 1968. She was barely 20 years old.

"I applied—pour le poste," Sinan told me, "after seeing an advertisement in the newspaper. After some exams, I was chosen from twenty-five other candidates, older than me."

"I didn't tell my father at first," Sinan recalled. "After I got the job, I told him."

Her father, Colonel Soc Sonn, a commander in the 1960s in Sihanouk's army, commanded by General Lon Nol, expressed surprise and doubt at her success.

"How much money did you give them?" he demanded.

"He assumed I had given the managers a bribe. That's how many Khmer got good positions in those days." Cambodia was always impossibly corrupt on every level.

"No, it was pure chance," Sinan told her father.

"I don't think he believed me but he congratulated me all the same."

■ ■ ■

For a few weeks in June and July 1970, when we were not working, Sinan and I were near-constant companions.

I found Phnom Penh an extraordinary city. It had a tranquility and charm that I had not yet found in Asia. It had none of the modernity or sophistication of Tokyo, none of the hustle of Hong Kong, and so far none of the war-weariness of Saigon.

One evening, when Sinan excused herself, explaining that she had an office event to attend, I headed off to one of the floating dance clubs along the Bassac River.

I crossed a slightly wobbly gangway onto a large barge berthed on the river. The lights were turned low, a sprinkling of glittering colored bulbs decorating the edges of the room.

I watched, mesmerized, as a hundred or so Khmer held hands and swayed in a well-choreographed line dance. The display became what the Khmer call the "romvong." Slowly moving in a circle, young men and women stretched out their hands and arms. They seemed to be attempting some of the graceful moves I had seen among dancers of the Royal Ballet.

What struck me was the seeming innocence of the occasion. These were people my age or younger, so far untouched by war, displaying a carefree life that was destined to soon change.

The contrast with what I had seen in Saigon in my first months there could not have been more dramatic. South Vietnamese in their capital partied too. But young Vietnamese adopted the music and dance of the Americans. Energy and tension combined to provide young Vietnamese a mood of watchful waiting: waiting for war to touch their lives.

Young Cambodians had not yet experienced the wrenching experience of terrorist attacks.

In my early months in Saigon, I had witnessed a nightclub bloodbath. I had gone to bed early in the tiny top-floor apartment I rented in the center of the city, just off the main nightclub district, a street known as Tu Do or Liberty Street. At about midnight, I was shaken out of my bed by an explosion. Running the one block to the scene as fast as I could, I was confronted by a screaming phalanx of young girls in miniskirts drenched in blood. The sight of dozens of bodies, lifeless young dancers scattered on the sidewalk, provided a shock that I struggled to erase from my mind. After a time I became hardened to the death and devastation of war.

In both my quiet evenings with Sinan and those graceful moves of the romvong, I witnessed a period of peace and innocence before war would destroy it all. While Phnom Penh's comparative peace remained, I was determined to take it all in. The next few weeks were special.

Sinan got time off from work at SONATRAC to chaperone a naive young foreigner around her city.

We visited the Royal Palace to watch rehearsals of the students of the National Royal Ballet.

We explored the Palace Museum. To the rear of the museum, old men meticulously made copies of ancient Khmer stone heads. I bought several of the replicas. A gray stone image of the most powerful Angkor ruler of all time, King Jayavarman VII (1120–1218), still stares at me from across my study in 2020.

Sinan introduced me to the silver and gold shops in the Chinese part of town. A slightly tarnished silver Khmer goblet Sinan gave me still adorns my bookcase.

We talked about flying to Siem Reap. Was it too late to see Angkor?

I felt nervous. Although it was very early in the war, security had already deteriorated around the temples.

But Sinan wanted to return.

"Let's plan it then. Let's go," I told her.

What could be more romantic? I would take a long weekend and go off among the temples I had only read about. I'd watch the sunset over Angkor Wat and wake up the next morning next to a beautiful Khmer woman.

Malraux, eat your heart out!

I made inquiries of Royal Air Cambodge and asked whether I could afford the finest room either at the Auberge des Temples or at the Grand Hotel D'Angkor. I wanted to make it special, to provide Sinan a different experience at Angkor.

She had been there as a child. Sinan traveled there in April 1959 with her oldest sister Sithan and her brother-in-law. Although she was only 11, Sinan remembered the journey vividly, speaking excitedly of a visit she wanted to repeat.

"We drove nearly six hours north on Route 6 in my brother-in-law's light blue 1956 French Simca." Sinan peered out the Simca's rear window.

"I saw the peasants working in the fields near the temples," she told me. "I thought how difficult it was to work in such a place. The peasant's work dawn to dusk was so hard. How could they do it? I guess they must get used to it, I thought then."

The small city of Siem Reap, on Lake Tonle Sap, provided a gateway to the seat of seventh-century Cambodian civilization. Sinan had a particular fascination with the way people lived there.

"What was Siem Reap like?" I asked.

"What was it like?" She had a habit of repeating my questions before answering. "Well back then, it was a very small town. A variety of people lived there. The Chinese owned the big stone and brick buildings. Or sometimes they took over the homes left behind by the French. Khmer with money lived in sra Lao, which were mahogany or hardwood houses. The poor lived in slaak tnout, houses built with bamboo and dried palm leaves."

It concerned Sinan that the dwellings of the poor far outnumbered those of the rich. Even an 11-year-old realized that tourism had brought little prosperity to the people of Siem Reap.

Sinan's desire for justice, her anger when she saw inequality, impressed me. This was not only a beautiful woman, I thought, but a smart, considerate, and thoughtful one as well.

Talking with Sinan moved me well beyond my world of college texts and those heavy picture books of the Angkor temples compiled by Groslier, the temple's most famous French archeologist.

Sinan described her favorites. Beyond Angkor Wat stood the temple of Ta Prom. As the tourist brochure proclaimed, Ta Prom featured "impossibly intricate stonework seemingly throttled by gnarled, thick trunked Banyan trees."

Sinan's only disappointment, she said, lay in not being able to travel 15 miles further north to the low hills of the Phnom Kulen and the splendid, intricately carved temple of Bantei Srei. That's where *La Voie royale's* Malraux had stolen his statues.

Sinan explained that even in 1959, security in the region north of Angkor could not be guaranteed. Less than six years after independence, rebellion was brewing against the rule of Sihanouk. Small rebel groups formed; many Cambodians believed financed by the Americans.

Sinan repeated that opinion.

"I could not go to Bantei Srei," she said, "because the opponents of Sihanouk were there and funded by the 'SAY, Eee, AH'" (the Khmer pronunciation of "CIA"). "The Americans wanted to drag us into the war in Vietnam, even back then. I'm sure of it."

So it was that suspicions of American interference were planted in the Cambodian mind not long after the French colonials departed the region.

American interference and betrayal, as well as kindness, would influence Sinan for the rest of her life.

. . .

Sinan and I never took our romantic adventure at Angkor. I kept putting things off. I received more telegrams asking me to file more stories. The war grew closer to the temples. It became unsafe. By the end of 1971 access to the temples proved impossible. The last of the French archeologists and restoration experts who had been there for nearly twenty years pulled out. The threat of the growing communist insurgency put a region the size of Manhattan off limits for almost ten years.

In November 1979, I would visit the Angkor complex for the first time. As I traveled then under the protection of units of the Vietnamese army, I thought of Sinan and our plans made a decade before.

In 1970, Sinan and I were left to talk over dinner about the temples that fascinated us most.

"What is your favorite in the books?" she asked.

"Bayon, I think, and all its smiling faces," I replied.

They were remarkable late twelfth-century carvings: smiling faces with their eyes mysteriously closed. Yet somehow they could peer through dense jungle foliage. There must be hundreds of them.

Historians said that King Jayavarman VII wanted to honor the faces of the bodhisattva, the truly enlightened embodiment of Buddha.

Sinan had a simple, optimistic explanation for all the benevolent statuary. "Although they are closed, they are the all-seeing eyes. They are always watching, guarding over and protecting the Khmer people."

In that—as Sinan and I soon discovered—they were not always successful, at least not in this life.

■ ■ ■

In the second week of July, I took a flight back to Saigon. I returned to Phnom Penh twice more in 1970. I could always invent an excuse. I told Metromedia Radio in Washington that I was covering the "wider war." I was really there to visit Sinan. I would remain in Phnom Penh until I was ordered back to Vietnam.

I vacillated in my feelings about Cambodia. I watched as the streets of Phnom Penh slowly become more crowded with war refugees fleeing fresh battles and the fear of American bombing. When I ventured out of town, I became increasingly depressed.

A young colonel I met in Kampong Speu, south of the capital, wore an army beret in the field, its flash positioned fashionably over his left eye. He displayed an impossibly warm, optimistic smile. The brave men he commanded had little training and faced near-certain slaughter. The only defense they seemed to possess against hardened Vietnamese troops and their new Khmer Rouge mentees were the Buddhist pendants that hung from their necks. They would clench the tiny Buddhas in their teeth as they charged into battle. Buddha would protect them.

Yet while I was repelled by war, I was infatuated, obsessed with a woman. My obsession flattered me by displaying insatiable curiosity.

She seemed fascinated by stories of my early explorations of Asia. I described my travels in Japan and the thrill of the Shinkansen: the high-speed "bullet train" which took me from Tokyo to Osaka at speeds up to 140 miles an hour. I told her of Hong Kong and my failed attempts to visit China. I complained about my first months in Saigon and my first wartime experiences. She wanted to visit Hong Kong. To go anywhere—but only for a visit. She seemed so rooted in Phnom Penh.

Sinan guarded her secrets closely, including her previous romantic experience. She did speak of her engagement to a Khmer student when she was 19. He wanted her to go away with him to Paris. This could have been her ticket out. In the end, he went, she declined. She broke off the yearlong engagement and took up her "career" at SONATRAC.

Life in Phnom Penh in 1968–69 was just too good.

While I was struggling with a new culture but entranced by the Khmer woman with whom I spent most evenings, Sinan voiced mixed feeling about Americans. Apart from the young reporter seated opposite her, she hadn't really known any.

"When I was 15, I used to visit the American library at the corner of rue Pasteur and Keo Chea Street," she later wrote. "Our family home was just down rue Pasteur near the library and the embassy residence."

"I tried to learn English. I read books and magazines there in both Khmer and English."

The most impressive American she had ever read about was President John Kennedy. She recalled that Norodom Sihanouk had invited Jacqueline Kennedy to Angkor in 1967. A photo of a fashionably dressed Jackie Kennedy appeared on the cover of *Life* magazine.

"In the early '60s Americans were popular. I loved to read about life in America. We loved President Kennedy. I read everything I could about him, and his wife and children. To us he had a sophisticated, smiling face. Among the Khmer such a character was highly regarded. We thought of him as kind and sincere with a good heart."

Then Sinan recalled, in May 1965, in his radio broadcasts, Sihanouk began to denounce the United States as conspiring against Cambodia. Denunciations fed well-orchestrated demonstrations.

"From my house I could hear people yelling 'Yankee go home.' Red banners streamed down rue Pasteur and swirled in front of the library gate."

Sihanouk saw Vietnamese and Thai conspiracies everywhere. Behind them, he saw Americans. There was a series of disturbances in the northwest of the country.

"'Defeat Yankee racists,' protesters shouted. 'Down with the Yankee dog servants.' Servants referred to Thais and the South Vietnamese. My brother-in-law asked me 'Have you heard the news?'"

"'What's that?' I asked."

"'It was on the radio this morning. Sihanouk is kicking the Americans out! They're closing the embassy now.'"

"But what about the library?"

"Don't be foolish, Sinan. That's going too. And you can forget about those English lessons you were going to take. The teacher must go too."

Sinan and her brother-in-law knew nothing, of course, about the secret deal made at about the same time to allow North Vietnamese forces to "transit" eastern Cambodia. No mention was made of Chinese supplies coming through Sihanoukville or of the money some Cambodians would make selling rice to the communists or assisting Hanoi with transport.

One person who might have known but never spoke of it was Sinan's father—Colonel Soc Sonn.

Sinan spoke guardedly about her father. Only in later years did she open up. Sinan called him "the commander"—the first of two military "commanders" in her life.

For much of Sinan's childhood, Soc Sonn had been posted near the Vietnamese border.

Sihanouk sent Soc Sonn and his troops after elements of the Khmer Serei, a militia group that roamed from Angkor east to the Vietnamese border.

"On Sihanouk's orders, my father pushed forward an army offensive against guerilla groups in Svay Rieng and Prey Veng. We saw little of the commander at home during this time."

What was unclear is whether Soc Sonn was also part of the clandestine trade with North Vietnamese forces in their Cambodian sanctuaries. There was much about Sinan's father that would remain hidden. He wrote a book about his military career. The book disappeared after the communist victory and Soc Sonn's death.

I would learn later that whatever he achieved as a military commander, he failed as a loving father.

She never spoke of it when we were together, but the trauma of her childhood can be found in diaries and writings she left behind.

From the time of her childhood in Thlok Chhreu, Sinan's relations with her father proved distant at best, abusive at worst.

Like many Khmer, the commander sought out soothsayers and mystics for counsel. Famously, General Lon Nol consulted fortune tellers before launching military campaigns against the North Vietnamese and the Khmer Rouge. He made some disastrous decisions.

A Chinese fortune teller advised Soc Sonn that the birth of a girl in April 1948 would be a mistake.

"The child," said the soothsayer, "has very good fortune, much better than the father. Don't keep her, don't raise her," the fortune teller warned. "When she's born, the father will encounter huge destruction."

Sonn told his wife, Pat, she should figure out what to do with the child. The harsh directive explains why Sinan's mother left

Soc Sonn's home in Phnom Penh and went to her native village to give birth. Pat then entrusted the child to her parents to raise for the first seven years of Sinan's life.

Along the Mekong, in Thlok Chhreu, Sinan learned to swim, play, and discover life under the watchful and loving eyes of her grandparents. Not long before her seventh birthday, Sinan's mother died in childbirth, with her seventh child.

Forced to face reality, Soc Sonn sent his lieutenants to Thlok Chhreu to bring his unwanted daughter to Phnom Penh.

Sinan did not want to go. She devised a way to avoid capture—at least for a while.

When Soc Sonn sent his first "agents" to take her to the city, Sinan climbed the tall trees by the riverbank. No one in the village could find her. When the "tormenters" departed, she would leap from a tree into the river and swim home. Recalling those days late in life, she described herself as "happily victorious."

Victory was temporary. The following year Sinan was taken to the commander's house. After a difficult period, Sinan moved in with her sister Sithan and her husband, a much happier situation. The little girl who hid in the trees grew up a city girl.

Colonel Soc Sonn and those early traumatic years may have scarred Sinan psychologically, but they also prepared her. For one thing, given her father's attitude and her mother's death, Sinan could convincingly say later that she was an orphan. For another, she learned a survival skill she would need. Being able to hide in plain sight became essential when living in what Sinan came to call her "prison without walls" under the Khmer Rouge.

5

Scrambled Eggs and Mad Minutes

April–May 1970

IF SINAN PROVIDED ME an education in Cambodian life and society, the two months before we met gave me my first taste of war and an education in what *not* to do when covering combat in Vietnam.

I arrived in Saigon on Cathay Pacific Airways from Hong Kong on April 5, 1970, a date of no particular significance.

I could start on a Monday, transition to my new job, and get to know Saigon. I planned to stay a few months, maybe six, make enough money to restuff my backpack and continue on around the world. Pan American issued that "round-the-world" ticket valid for a year. Vietnam provided a simple diversion.

Looking forward to his new UPI gig, Alan Dawson took the time to meet me at Tan Son Nhut airport and show me the city. Soon after my arrival, I hopped on the back of Dawson's tiny Honda 50 cc motorbike for a tour of the city.

Motorcycles then as now were ubiquitous. Everyone in Saigon seemed to have a Honda. Dubbed the Honda "Super Cub," these motorcycles were cheap and reliable. On the flat roads of Saigon they displayed surprising power, as good as a bigger 125 cc two-stroke. Rumor had it the American civilian assistance program USAID (United States Agency for International Development) subsidized the purchase of Japanese motorbikes, pushing motorized transport instead of bicycles: "It'll give the Vietnamese something to fight the war for," said one wag, not entirely in jest.

For a newcomer, Saigon proved an unrelenting assault on the senses. The wartime capital of the South presented itself as both a sassy and a squalid town.

On the one hand, US Army officers dined on buttered langoustine for a buck twenty-five on the roof of the "Brinks" BOQ (Bachelor Officers Quarters) while poor Vietnamese lived miserably, going hungry in shacks not far away along the narrow waterways flowing with sludge into the Saigon River.

Along lower Tu Do Street and on the side streets heading toward Ham Nghia, bar girls shouted their invitations from gaudily lit doorways: "You buy me Saigon tea?"

A pickpocket positioned himself in front of the USO social club serving cheeseburgers on Nguyen Hue, the street of flowers, as it was once described.

A beggar with shattered legs sat on the sidewalk, an old army hat stretched outward. "You number one!" he shouted in hopes of getting some change. "You—number ten," if you passed by without an offering to the hat.

Burly US military police, along with short, stocky Vietnamese MPs and thin, scrawny local civilian police who the Americans ridiculed as "white mice," broke up fights between soldiers and civilians.

Transvestites and prostitutes of all descriptions mingled with drunken American civilian contractors on the exposed veranda bar of the Hotel Continental Palace, which was helpfully named the "Continental Shelf."

On the other hand, a remarkable gentility coexisted among the upper and middle classes of the city.

The faithful filled the Saigon Notre Dame Cathedral. On early Sunday mornings, I came to find in it a splendid restful escape from war.

The University of Saigon admitted some of the smartest and most enterprising young people in Southeast Asia.

Lunch by the pool or a game of tennis at the Cercle Sportif offered welcome diversions.

An early morning breakfast bowl of pho and a refreshing ca phe sua da (iced coffee) became part of my daily routine. I would sit with friends either on stools in the alleyway off tree-lined Nguyen Du Street or at Givral's Café on Lam Son Square near the National Assembly, housed in the former French opera house. I'd pour a little extra nuoc mam into the pho just to give it an extra kick and down the broth.

And though I never told Sinan about it, I could not resist simply sitting, sipping coffee opposite Lycée Marie Curie Saigon. For a 22-year-old, what could be more enchanting than watching a parade of untouchable, elegant, young Vietnamese women pass through the school gates adorned in their splendid white ao dai—that sleek-fitting silk tunic worn over marvelously tailored trousers?

It took Dawson to find some of the American sites for me. Gunning his two-wheeler, he sped off to Cholon, the Chinese area of the city. He pulled up in front of what apparently was the place every American came to know first—the Cholon Post Exchange.

The PX was the American military's one-stop shop, and the US Army and Airforce Exchange Service had operated Cholon's, the largest PX in the world since early 1965.

They had everything: cigarettes, Johnnie Walker Black Label, beer, wine, clothing, appliances, books, and elephants.

Elephants? For reasons I never understood, rather heavy 15-inch-tall ceramic elephants became popular souvenirs for American servicemen to send home. PX workers shipped the bulky statues through the APO (Army Post Office) to everywhere stateside. The staff thought it a nuisance. They referred to the elephants as BUFEs (pronounced "BUFFYs")—"bloody useless fucking elephants."

■ ■ ■

If Sinan grew impatient with my ramblings about my new life in Vietnam, she never showed it.

I described to her the crash course I received during my first weeks there.

On my first Monday in Saigon, I showed up at the Military Assistance Command Vietnam Joint Public Affairs Office (MACV-JUSPAO) via the ground-floor, corner entrance of the Rex Hotel.

I presented a letter from Metromedia Radio News. WNEW was their well-known flagship station in New York. Within a few minutes, JUSPAO issued me two cards. I suddenly became an accredited radio "correspondent." An officer handed me a second card certifying me as having the equivalent rank of major in the US Army. It would prove useful in boarding planes and helicopters around the country or securing a bunk at military outposts from the Mekong Delta north to the DMZ, the demilitarized zone.

A captain showed me the telephone-booth-sized broadcast facilities and the press room at JUSPAO.

Late in the afternoon each day, 15 minutes would be allotted to "Metromedia News." During that window, I could use the radio booth to file my voice reports on the war. I joined CBS, NBC, ABC, Mutual, Group W, and a few other now long-forgotten radio broadcasters in the queue.

Very soon I met a few colleagues who were generous in educating the novice.

"G'day. 'Ow ya goin', mate?" A Tasmanian named Neil Davis gave the green light for me to rent a simple desk in his office on the second floor of the Passage Eden, an old French office building and residence complex in the heart of the city.

Davis was already a celebrated photojournalist when I met him. He had moved from Australia to Vietnam in 1963 to head the Visnews film agency. Later he would move to Cambodia and work for Reuters and NBC. He turned out to be a true mentor to me.

I was doing Davis a favor at the Passage Eden. He had previously leased part of the news agency office to an Indian money changer, an essential person to know when negotiating Saigon's black market in luxury goods, US dollars, Vietnamese piastres, and American military payment certificates. Visnews management in London and Hong Kong told Davis he really should evict the Indian, who was clearly engaged in "illegal" activities. The young Yank filing reports for an unknown radio network who took the moneychanger's desk would be slightly less notorious.

Into my life during this time also walked two smart, outgoing Vietnamese women. Juliette Suong was the office manager at Visnews Saigon. She knew everyone. Her near-constant companion was Vu Hong Lien, a well-connected journalist with Jiji Press, a Japanese news agency, and the *Asahi Shimbun* newspaper. Hanging out with these two women provided an instant insider's look at Saigon life.

The military briefings in Saigon were a far cry from the one at which I would meet Sinan two months later.

Somebody, I don't know who, dubbed them "the Five O'Clock Follies." The news briefings were actually closer to 4 p.m. when I arrived. The time had been changed to provide broadcast reporters more time to write their stories and file in time for morning radio and TV news shows in the United States.

In those days there was only one morning television news program: *Today* on NBC. More Americans, however, heard their news on car radios during "morning drive time." My daily efforts crackled across the airwaves of WNEW New York during the commutes from Secaucus or Mineola.

■ ■ ■

While a cynical, weary, seasoned approach characterized those in Saigon, extraordinary naivete seemed on display at the military briefing in Phnom Penh, along with a macabre sense of humor. Chhang Song once observed that many Khmer soldiers were transported to battle in commandeered Pepsi-Cola trucks. When the troops were defeated in battle, he was asked what happened. Without missing a beat, Song replied, "It was the trucks. If we had Coca-Cola trucks, we would have won. Why? Because everyone knows that things go better with Coke!" Chhang Song smiled. We laughed.

By contrast, briefings in Saigon seldom displayed good humor. They were raucous, rude, unruly. The first thing that struck me was how jaded all the reporters who attended were.

They featured daily shouting matches between the US military briefer and a few in the press corps. One crusty old reporter who had been there since 1963 seemed noisiest. Joe Fried, the correspondent of the New York *Daily News*, spat out questions and scoffed in disbelief at the answers.

It was said that Fried never left Saigon unless he secured a seat on the helicopter of an American general. He relied on young novices to act as his eyes and ears. After my forays to combat zones "up country," Fried would grill me and a few others on what we saw and heard. Our words would appear as firsthand accounts from sources in the *Daily News* or in the radio stories. Fried also filed for Mutual (another long-extinct radio network).

■ ■ ■

With less than three weeks on the ground in Vietnam, on April 29, 1970, I was thrust into my first big story and a rather dramatic introduction to Cambodia.

Word came that something was afoot from the South Vietnamese military. With American support, the Army of the Republic of Vietnam (ARVN) was preparing to launch a massive ground assault across the border on North Vietnamese installations in an area we came to call the Parrot's Beak.

As seen on a map, the Parrot's Beak provided a salient, a finger of Svay Rieng Province, Cambodia, pointed directly at the South Vietnamese capital. Through its center ran the old French Route 1. From this region, North Vietnamese troops staged attacks on targets in Tay Ninh Province, Vietnam. American planes had bombed the region for years.

Two days later President Nixon provided details of an even larger mission:

"Tonight, American and South Vietnamese units will attack the headquarters for the entire communist military operation in South Vietnam. This key control center has been occupied by the North Vietnamese and Vietcong for five years in blatant violation of Cambodia's neutrality.

This is not an invasion of Cambodia. The areas in which these attacks will be launched are completely occupied and controlled by North Vietnamese forces. Our purpose is not to occupy the areas. Once enemy forces are driven out of these sanctuaries, and once their military supplies are destroyed, we will withdraw."

Appearing to the left of a large red and yellow map of Indochina, Nixon delivered his Cambodia "incursion" address live on the three big American networks at 9 p.m. in Washington on April 30 (8 a.m. May 1 in Vietnam and Cambodia).

In those days there were no live international satellite channels. I heard bits of Nixon's speech on the Saigon Armed Forces Radio station (AFRTS).

For many people, news of the speech came across scratchy shortwave radio transmissions from the Voice of America or the BBC World Service.

By the time of the broadcast, two campaigns were well underway.

With Sihanouk out of the picture and "neutralist" Cambodia a thing of the past, South Vietnamese and American forces launched a major, multi-location, multi-stage invasion. The new government of General Lon Nol and Prince Sirik Matak was not consulted on the operation. US planners assumed the new regime would not object. While Americans may not have triggered the coup, they now had a friendly government in Phnom Penh. They would take full advantage of it.

The American First Air Cavalry division mounted 435 helicopters. Many of them flew west across another salient to the north of Parrot's Beak called the Fishhook. The helicopters supported elements of the 11th Armored Cavalry moving northwest inside Cambodia. The center of North Vietnamese operations hampering American efforts had been located here.

In the first days of May, high-flying B-52s unloaded 15,000-pound "Daisy Cutter" bombs to create instant clearings for helicopter LZs (landing zones) in eastern Cambodia.

In both the Fishhook and Parrot's Beak, Apache "Cobra" helicopters and AC-47 Spooky gunships filled the skies. Small OH-6 "Loach" choppers provided surveillance from the air while on the ground the assault moved against both North Vietnamese troops and their supply lines. The Americans called their offensive Operation Rockcrusher.

The South Vietnamese called their campaign Toan Thang (Total Victory). It was commanded by the flamboyant General Do Cao Tri.

I drove out to meet Tri. After reviewing his forces' positions, he helicoptered in to see a group of us on the Cambodian border. The General Tri I met came across as a rather overconfident, cocky character. He adopted a General Douglas MacArthur–style smoking pipe, carried a swagger stick, and made sure his three stars were clearly visible on his baseball-style campaign cap.

At the start of the operation, American commanders were peeved because Tri held back his advance by a day. He told them, "The omens from a fortune teller favored a slight delay." In Vietnam too, generals listened to soothsayers.

General Tri's troops moved out in force early on April 30. And perhaps the oracle was right. Tri surprised the Americans with his rapid and successful advance. Within a few days his forces drove 40 miles into Cambodia, encountering resistance but quickly gaining the upper hand in fighting.

Less than a year later, General Tri's luck ran out. He died when his command helicopter crashed on takeoff from Bien Hoa Airbase, Vietnam, northeast of the capital.

From a purely tactical point of view, Nixon's offensive made sense: take the war to where the North Vietnamese thought they were safe in "neutral" Cambodia. Cut their supply lines. Destroy their stores of weapons.

At the time, my colleagues in Saigon mocked Nixon's claim that the "incursion" would destroy COSVN (the communist Central Office for South Vietnam) in Cambodia. The US administration portrayed it as a massive North Vietnamese command and control center supplying troops with logistical and armament support for cross-border operations.

The CIA, however, had long advised military planners that "there are no COSVN installations as such." A report declassified in 2007 noted that instead, "COSVN components are spread out and dispersed throughout eastern Cambodia near War Zone C."

Still, the offensive did disrupt North Vietnamese supply lines. It bought the Americans a six- to nine-month lull in major Vietnam combat, allowing Nixon to continue his drawdown of troops as he had promised during his election campaign. United States troop strength dropped from about 334,000 in January 1970 to about 157,000 by the end of the year.

Short-terms gains, however, paved the way for long-term disaster. Nixon's orders spread war deep into a country which, despite the North Vietnamese occupation of sanctuaries and American bombing, had largely escaped the full brutality of the Vietnam War.

The American and South Vietnamese offensive did not surprise North Vietnamese commanders. Captured COSVN documents show they had been preparing for an assault since April 20.

Hanoi's troops retreated further into the interior. At the time of the incursion, Hanoi propaganda leaflets boasted more than one million Cambodians living in communist "secured zones."

On May 7, Nixon issued orders preventing commanders from sending US ground troops beyond 19 miles into Cambodia. He also ordered everyone out by the end of June.

The South Vietnamese had no such restraints. They pushed deeper and remained in Cambodia for an additional month, supported by American bombing.

Again I drove to Cambodia. Border controls had disappeared. It immediately became clear to me that the continued invasion would create an even greater crisis for Cambodia.

Khmer refugees told me of bombing raids hitting their villages. I watched as Saigon troops under General Tri engaged in a wave of looting.

Near Svay Rieng, Cambodia, I saw South Vietnamese troops tearing apart abandoned Khmer homes. They piled their trucks high with stolen food, appliances, and small farm vehicles. They hauled the stash back to Vietnam.

The combination of South Vietnamese behavior and American air attacks intensified ordinary Cambodians' hatred for the new war and for the "invaders."

Consistent propaganda efforts by communist forces molded the thoughts of millions of rural Khmer. "The Americans and their Vietnamese puppets" were the enemy. They brought war to Cambodia. The pampered elite in the cities who backed General Lon Nol and Sirik Matak conspired with the enemy and must be regarded as enemies as well. From May to July 1970, the roots of radicalism, displayed so horrifically five years later, were planted.

■ ■ ■

On the American home front, what was perceived as an "invasion" of a "neutral" nation ignited an immediate and bloody reaction. Half a world away, I felt little of the fallout. In those days, following events in the United States while abroad depended upon crackly shortwave radio reports on the VOA or the BBC World Service. Local armed forces radio provided hourly news bulletins but for obvious reasons did not dwell on war protests at home.

The anti-war movement back at home swelled. What little congressional war support that remained evaporated. Widespread student demonstrations culminated on May 4, 1970, in the tragedy at Kent State University in Ohio. Local National Guardsmen opened fire during demonstrations, killing four students and wounding nine more.

■ ■ ■

Nixon's incursion impacted me personally in two ways. Without Nixon, I later told Sinan, we would never have met. Without Nixon, this Asian studies student turned radio news reporter would never have plunged across the Cambodian border on my first combat mission.

That mission proved a tragicomedy of errors from the word go.

Having reported briefly on the South Vietnamese offensive to the south, I wanted to join American forces inside Cambodia at the Fishhook to the north.

I enlisted my new friend Bill Dowell in the effort. Dowell, a University of North Carolina at Chapel Hill history graduate, had all the Vietnam knowledge I lacked. He came to Vietnam with an impressive array of credentials. In 1968–69, he served 18 months in the army attached to a provincial advisory team in An Loc. An Loc sat on Route 13, a key access road from the north to Saigon and less than 20 miles to the Fishhook of Cambodia, where we were now trying to go. After his army discharge, Dowell—with his fluent French and degrees in comparative languages as well as Asian and Russian history—returned to Vietnam as a freelance reporter.

Dowell and I secured seats on a helicopter out of the airbase at Cu Chi heading for Cambodia. Not long before dusk, we settled into an American Fire Support Base on the Cambodian border. Thousands of these temporary artillery bases were built during the war.

It was an early lights-out as we were to be up at dawn. We slept with our boots on, though there was little sleep that night. Every 10 or 20 minutes or so, the camp erupted in a cacophony of outgoing artillery fire. Dowell called them "Mad Minutes." The enemy must be out there. The Mad Minutes would keep them on their toes.

At dawn I was sleepless but impressed by something that would be ordinary anywhere else. This firebase had readied for artillerymen and the troops going on patrol an impressive hot breakfast: bacon and eggs, pancakes, and toast and jam, buffet style.

I dug in. What was it Napoleon said? "An army marches on its stomach."

A few minutes later the helicopters arrived. We were to accompany a First Air Cavalry colonel to see how the "incursion" was going.

With the doors of the UH-1 "Huey" detached, a two-person flight crew, two gunners with their M60 machine guns facing outward, and five passengers, including the colonel and me, flew off into Cambodia.

We headed out over an area where the Cambodian provinces of Kampong Cham and Kratie come together. We approached Memot and banked right in the direction of the town of Snuol.

Heavily forested areas and large tracts of rubber plantation spread out beneath us. Beginning in 1927, under French colonial rule, Vietnamese and Khmer labor had cleared the land and planted nearly 30 square miles of rubber trees in this area. Latex cultivation produced 52,000 tons and brought in nearly half of Cambodia's $85 million export revenue in 1968–69. The war ensured there'd be little rubber production for nearly a decade.

Our army pilot was an expert at "contour flying." There was nothing quite like the thrill of skimming along at high speeds just a few feet above the tree line. The maneuver also made the chopper less vulnerable to ground fire.

Then came the sharp crack of AK-47 fire. A North Vietnamese soldier below us was either very good or very lucky. We weren't hit, but nearly so. The pilot quickly pulled the Huey into an upward spiral, climbing what seemed to me straight up.

Nobody had told me that consuming large breakfasts and flying across Cambodian rubber plantations infested with North Vietnamese defenders were not necessarily compatible activities. As the helicopter lurched upward my insides lurched downward. The next thing I knew, scrambled eggs flowed steadily toward the colonel's freshly shined boots.

Dowell later recalled, "The colonel lifted his feet off the floor to avoid getting soaked. The absurdity of the situation struck me as a perfect metaphor for the war."

I flew on many helicopter missions over the next five years. I never liked them. I learned one important lesson: Fly when you must on a near-empty stomach. I would never lose my breakfast again.

When I recounted my story, Sinan was kind enough to suppress her smile at least for a minute so she could offer some soothing words to ease my discomfort.

Welcome to Cambodia.

6
War, Love, and Tattered Diaries

1971

INSPECTING TATTERED OLD DIARIES nearly fifty years later can be revealing, sometimes for all the wrong reasons. What you thought was so important then is not recorded. And sometimes what you sought to hide or to forget is.

Extraneous bits of paper, important and not so important names and name cards, and newspaper cuttings stuff my diary from 1971. It provides one page of notes a day for the year. I would jot down my schedule, a few observations—occasionally astute, more often banal. On some days there is just a blank page with a heading at the top: "Phnom Penh" or "Saigon." The tattered diary reveals that on Christmas Day 1970 and New Year's Day 1971, I remained working at my desk at Saigon's Passage Eden.

It reveals that after one year in Asia, I had a new interest in the zodiac and the Lunar New Year. The Lunar New Year, or Tet in Vietnam, came early in 1971—January 27. The date ushered in the year of the pig. Of the twelve animals of the Zodiac, the pig happens to be mine. I am known as a "fire pig." The Vietnamese say he is "ambitious, perseverant, but impatient."

Impatience, I think, became the most important of those traits. With impatience came restlessness and infidelity.

■ ■ ■

Early in January, the Saigon government announced there would be a ceasefire for Tet. I looked forward to my first Tet in Vietnam. I bought presents for Vietnamese friends, assembled a bunch of red envelopes for their children. I wondered if Hanoi and Saigon would really respect the ceasefire. The record of honoring ceasefires instilled little confidence. The memory of the devastating offensive of "Tet '68" remained on many people's minds.

My diary tells me that on January 11, I briefly encountered President Nixon's latest emissary from Washington, who arrived to assess the war's progress.

I drove out to Tan Son Nhut Airbase to hear the assessment of Defense Secretary Melvin Laird after his four days in the country.

The sprawling American Military Assistance Command headquarters sat next to the military and civilian airport. A gaggle of perhaps a hundred men and women crowded into an airbase departure lounge to shout questions.

Laird had come to see that Nixon's plan to pull out American troops from Vietnam proceeded on schedule. Nixon had linked troop withdrawal with what he called "Vietnamization," ensuring that South Vietnamese troops were up to the task of defending their own country.

Laird predictably said, "Vietnamization is proceeding very smoothly."

As I listened, I nudged my way forward to place myself in the secretary's line of sight and got him to call on me. My mind was on Cambodia as I was keen to get back there.

"Mr. Secretary. The military situation next door in Cambodia continues to deteriorate despite last year's incursion. What does the administration plan to do about it?"

"I am actually very impressed and encouraged by the progress the people of Cambodia have made in facing up to the communist threat," replied Laird. "We will watch the Cambodia situation very closely."

He declined to answer whether deterioration would prompt new US action or would impact troop withdrawal.

As it turned out, the Americans were very worried about Cambodia.

General Lon Nol flew to Saigon several days later. Laird had directed the top US military brass there to outline Washington's concerns to the Cambodian leader. Both Americans and Cambodians would have to step up efforts against the communists.

On Thursday evening, January 21, Lon Nol flew home.

The next day, North Vietnamese forces attacked Phnom Penh's international airport at Pochentong, pounding it with rockets and mortars. Khmer Rouge sappers infiltrated the airfield, blowing up aircraft and facilities. The small Cambodian air force was decimated.

Early Saturday, January 23, I raced down Route 1 from Saigon.

With me rode one cucumber-cool veteran reporter and one just as nervous as I was. Dan Southerland of the *Christian Science Monitor* was the senior among us. If he was concerned about the journey ahead, he didn't show it.

Riding shotgun, Ralph Blumenthal of the *New York Times* clutched a pair of binoculars and nervously scanned the road ahead for trouble.

I sat somewhat sullenly in the back seat of the beat-up Peugeot. Eight months plying this route to the border had erased my youthful bravado.

The stretch east and west of Svay Rieng I thought most dodgy. Speed normally provided an advantage. Our driver, however, wisely slowed down before a long open stretch of road. Just ahead, an army land mine sweeping operation was underway. Always good to wait and go in after the mine sweepers, not before. A lot of vehicles had been blown up around here.

Once we reached the ferry crossing at Neak Leung, we figured we had it made. Route 1 beyond that point was usually safe. We waited a good 45 minutes before the crossing.

While waiting for the ferry, Southerland and I set out looking for a bowl of bai sach chrouk, sliced pork marinated in coconut milk, rice, and chicken broth on the side.

"What about it, Ralph?" I asked, a bit too cheerily. "Some Cambodian food?"

"No thanks. I'll stay here and watch the car."

Blumenthal planted himself next to the car and consumed a can of US Army C rations he had brought from Vietnam. Southerland and I pulled up stools at a nearby food stall and began to eat.

Before long, a group of smiling Khmer children gathered to watch two foreign curiosities.

Now I had a most objectionable quirk in those days. In part to distract me from jangled nerves, I carried a small red-and-blue metal kazoo. I couldn't play a proper instrument but I could hum. So out came the kazoo to serenade the children.

"Sok Sa-bay! ... ummmmm—nnnnn—ummmmm." I'm not sure what the tune was. The kids certainly didn't. The young crowd grew larger.

Southerland persuaded me to focus on finishing my pork and rice and get back into the car. Playing a twentieth-century Pied Piper with a kazoo did little for Khmer-American relations. And advertising that there was a trio of slightly crazed Americans on the road to Phnom Penh may not have been the best survival strategy.

■ ■ ■

We made it to Phnom Penh without incident. I parted company with my traveling companions and headed off to my room at the Hotel de la Poste. Shortly thereafter, an explosion rocked the city's electric power control office.

I managed to get a car to survey the damage and then raced out toward Pochentong to learn what I could about the destruction of both military and civilian aircraft.

Soon I was bounding up the stairs of the old PTT to file my radio stories on the decimation of the tiny Cambodian air force and the increasingly precarious situation in and around the capital.

■ ■ ■

Phnom Penh had changed dramatically since my first arrival nearly nine months ago. The attacks in the city marked the war's escalation.

A steady flow of refugees fleeing the advancing North Vietnamese, American bombing, or Phnom Penh's sporadic military offensives swelled the size of the city.

A day or so later, I took a pedicab (we usually called them "cyclos") to the sports arena that once Sihanouk optimistically dubbed the "Olympic Stadium." It had begun to house refugees. Families tried to recreate homes they had been forced to flee. I got out my small film camera and recorded some of the desperation around the field.

Mothers without milk fed children without clothing. Soon, for the first time in its history, international relief agencies began arriving in Cambodia to help care for the hungry and homeless.

■ ■ ■

The demand to file stories on my first day back in Phnom Penh put to one side my deeper reason for wanting to be there. To see Sinan.

Just after sunset, I hailed a cyclo driver. He peddled from the post office past the Lycée Descartes, hanging a left on Monivong Boulevard, and on to a four-story apartment building next to the Esso station.

So as not to attract too much attention, I quickly but quietly climbed the stairs to the top floor.

This was Sinan's place. Unusual for a single Khmer woman, she had an apartment of her own. Sinan had left her sister's family home in early 1969. As her income working at SONATRAC grew, independence from a stifling family environment seemed possible.

A simple single room contained a comfortable living area, what Americans used to call an "efficiency." A curtain separated the sitting area from a large bed. A small attached kitchen and a bathing area completed the amenities. Sinan's windows, protected when she wanted by large, sturdy metal shutters, looked out over the city's main north-to-south thoroughfare.

I knocked on the bolted metal door. No one was home. Recovering from my disappointment, I left a note. "I am back. Might you have dinner with me tomorrow evening? La Taverne? At 7?"

La Taverne provided a convenient meeting place. It sat next door to the Hotel de la Poste and just across the street from the post office. Most people dined in the large outdoor area at the front. I chose a quiet table inside to the rear. Sinan's lessons of last year in social etiquette had not been forgotten. Discretion remained important in our relationship.

I arrived early and ordered a drink. I didn't have a long wait. The sun was just setting, and out from the brightness of the doorway Sinan appeared. The tensions of my day evaporated at once. I stood up and, forgetting all about discretion, embraced her perhaps a bit too tightly. She neither resisted nor admonished me.

"I was really surprised to get your note," Sinan declared, her unforgettable smile staying fixed on me as she sat down.

We settled in and talked for awhile before ordering.

"How did you get here from Saigon?" she asked. "The airport is closed."

"I came by car."

"I know it wasn't your first time, but you must be more careful these days."

She paused to think about her own situation. "You know, I haven't been out of Phnom Penh for nearly two years, not even to see family in Kampong Cham. Je pense—I think with this war, I'll never leave the city."

Each night that week, when we met, Sinan listened patiently to my war stories. She would often lapse into silence, trying to comprehend what was happening to her country.

A few days later I went to the US Embassy for a briefing by the ambassador. Emory Swank had arrived in Phnom Penh about five months before. He provided a realistic appraisal of the Cambodian crisis.

That night, after filing my story, I read Sinan my notes: "The enemy's first major rocket attack against Phnom Penh destroyed nearly all the Khmer air force. The attacks threw everyone off balance. Lon Nol now would have to abandon war in the countryside and use most of his forces just to protect the cities, especially Phnom Penh."

"You realize, Sinan," I warned as gently as I could, "that unless the Americans intervene, I mean, unless they put much more into this war, that Cambodia has no chance?"

She nodded. "But surely the Americans will, won't they?"

"I am not sure Nixon will, can, or even wants to," I replied.

Sinan remembered an old quotation from Sihanouk referring to Cambodia's helplessness as it faced the bitter war next door involving the Americans, Russians, and Chinese. "When elephants fight, the ants must stand aside."

At the end of January, Pochentong Airport reopened. I said my goodbyes and promised to return. The next day I flew back to Saigon.

■ ■ ■

In Phnom Penh in 1971, five young women lived in a bubble.

Through much of that year and into 1972, they formed a dynamic quintet often inseparable on weekends. Sinan, Saorun, Vann, Khoeun, and occasionally Arun maintained a constant whir of Saturday activity.

For this remarkable group of unconventional "city girls," the dangers of the war that swirled around them either did not exist or were ignored.

Phnom Penh remained a very pleasant place to be.

Fast friends, the quintet had something important in common. They were outsiders in their own society. They were all either married to or involved with Western men.

In short, they were "polluted," set apart from conservative Khmer society. The white skins of their lovers made them social outcasts.

Saorun's marriage to a French anthropologist and Khoeun's to a French businessman put them in a slightly more respectable category than the others.

France had ended its colonial rule of Cambodia in 1954 quietly. Generally, Khmer harbored none of the resentment toward the French that their Vietnamese neighbors did. The Vietnamese had fought a long, bitter war against the colonials. The Khmer also did not boast the sense of superiority that Hanoi's leaders felt after General Vo Nguyen Giap's humiliating defeat of French forces in 1953 at Dien Bien Phu.

San Arun, who adopted the American name "Sandy," split from French traditions as well as from the monarchy headed by Sihanouk. She identified herself as one of the new antimonarchists and joined early the Khmer Republic army in late 1970. The communists would soon denounce the government led by General Lon Nol as the "American puppet regime." Arun entered the new world where Americans supplanted the French as the most important people to know.

"Back in those days, there was great enthusiasm for the new Khmer Republic," Arun told me some years later. "Young people like me were happy to serve. Students from the universities saw a future in a new 'Republicanism.' I guess we were pretty naive."

"But you were lucky, you got out before things got too bad?" I asked.

"I met an American. Went to Thailand to live and then on to America. By 1972, I was out of the war. But I always wanted to come back."

Arun returned to Cambodia in 2000 from Long Beach. Again she wanted to serve, this time to help pick up the pieces after the war. To work for the rights of poor Khmer women.

"My family was grown. Unlike Sinan, I never suffered the pain of being trapped. I thought I could do some good in the government's Ministry of Women's Affairs, so I returned."

Vann was the odd one out.

She had no connections to the French and little education. She arrived in early 1971 from a rural village, landing a job at a local Phnom Penh hair salon. Looking back on the carefree days of 1970, she singled out Sinan, who brought her into the club.

"Sinan welcomed everyone," Vann told me when we met years later. "Wealth, education, background never got in the way of friendship. She wanted only kindness and most importantly honesty. She embraced everyone."

Saorun, the high school teacher and wife of the French anthropologist, balanced raising two children with, as she put it, her "club de filles." With her high spirits and boundless energy, family never held her back.

While Sinan often organized nights out, as the oldest of the women, Saorun usually became the leader of the pack.

"I was also the only one of us with a car," Saorun remembered. "I had a Volkswagen Beetle, painted yellow. There were not too many of them in Phnom Penh at that time."

On a Saturday night, five young women would squeeze into Saorun's Beetle. "There were always weekend parties," Saorun said. "Even when there were none, I got that Volkswagen out. We all packed in and just went out for a joy ride, all around the town.

"Careening around the city was of course a lot easier back then than today. We had no traffic jams in Phnom Penh in the early 1970s. We tried not to think too much about the war."

Later the city fell victim to near-daily rocket attacks. Some struck near the Central Market, a short walk from where Sinan lived.

"One evening we were driving around," recalled Saorun. "We were laughing and telling stories of the week before when a rocket crashed into the street just behind us. It really wasn't that far away. We stopped chattering at once. I stepped on the gas. We looked at each other. And we started laughing again. This time, the laughter was prompted by nerves!"

A year later Khoeun emerged as the most responsible of the group.

She was the first of the club to sound a warning. Each of the members, she said, should make plans to leave Cambodia no matter how hard it would be.

"I knew soon after Sihanouk was overthrown that things could not remain the same. War changed Cambodia forever." Khoeun told me in 1975, "Our little club could not last for long. We really had to leave."

By 1973, both Khoeun and Arun chose love of a man over love of Cambodia.

A French engineer and businessman, Paul Rigaud took Khoeun and their family first to France and then in 1974 to the relative safety, Khoeun thought, of Saigon, Vietnam.

Saorun remained the incorrigible optimist. Of course, she had a French husband as an insurance policy for her family.

As for Vann, she continued to remain close to Sinan right up to the fall of Phnom Penh. Vann, as she told me years later, "made a mistake of love."

"I met a young American. He was an aircraft mechanic named Jimmy. We began to live together, over near the Sukalay Hotel on Monivong Boulevard."

Jimmy worked as one of a small band of American civilians who serviced the fledgling "commuter" airline industry in Cambodia.

Barely a year after the war started, North Vietnamese and Khmer Rouge battlefield success made roads impassable, the countryside often inaccessible. Only the provincial capitals (and not all of them) remained under the control of the Phnom Penh government. A small fleet of planes kept the Khmer Republic together—barely. The aircraft kept the cities connected, kept them supplied, allowed them to survive. Jimmy kept the planes flying. And Vann relied on Jimmy.

Unfortunately for her, reliability was not Jimmy's forte. He began to drink.

"Jimmy never abused me. He just could not be counted on to help me. I was still with him in 1975 when the Khmer Rouge arrived. I never left him. I always remained an optimist."

So too did Sinan. She tried to push out of her mind the more dire predictions about Cambodia's future. Life remained good as she looked forward to the return of a young reporter from Vietnam.

■ ■ ■

Returning to Saigon on January 29, 1971, my attention shifted quickly from Cambodia to Laos. United States troop movements were reported in the northern sector of South Vietnam—in I ("Eye") Corp, as it was known.

In the office, Juliette Suong busily phoned around, working her Vietnamese military contacts. She alerted Visnews Hong Kong that something was up.

Vu Hong Lien stopped by with reports that South Vietnamese (ARVN) troops had moved west in I Corp from Quang Tri, Hue, and Phu Bai, heading toward the Lao border.

The following day, as my diary recalls, the military imposed a news blackout. We were forbidden from reporting any information about US or Vietnamese troop movements. The embargo was lifted on February 4.

Pressed by Nixon and Secretary of State Henry Kissinger, military planners had put together a follow-up to the Cambodian incursion a year earlier. This time South Vietnamese troops would target North Vietnamese concentrations in Laos.

Two ARVN divisions, more than 16,000 men, assembled for the assault. They'd be backed by nearly 10,000 US forces in support positions. Americans would remain on the Vietnam side of the border. More than 700 helicopters and more than 2,000 fixed-wing aircraft moved in for the action.

There were several goals.

Once again Nixon needed to buy more time to pull troops out. To defuse ever-increasing opposition to the war, he promised an additional 50,000 men and women home by April.

Secretary Laird told his assistant secretary of defense that it was more important now to get out than to win. That is not what he told their South Vietnamese and Cambodian allies.

For the first time in the long war, a full-scale assault on the nucleus of Hanoi's infiltration supply corridor in Laos not only would buy time but might seriously cripple the communists' strenuous efforts to send troops and material to Vietnam and Cambodia.

The joint command targeted a small town in the Lao province of Savannakhet—Tchepone (sometimes spelled Xépôn). US intelligence identified it as an important Ho Chi Minh Trail junction point. Here the trail met old French Route 9 extending from the Lao panhandle east through the mountains across Vietnam to the coast, ending just north of Dong Ha.

Much has been written about the Ho Chi Minh Trail: for those who have not traveled to that remote region, images emerge of a gigantic, jungle-covered highway, down which flowed vast quantities of war materiel from northern Vietnam through Laos and Cambodia.

Of course, the Trail was not a thoroughfare. It consisted of a large, complex network of dirt roads, paths, and transport points spread out at a day's march from each other. Tchepone was the center of one key transit position for what was called Base Area 604, about 40 kilometers or 25 miles west of the border.

Since 1961, the Trail had put into place impressive assets: 630,000 troops, 100,000 tons of food, 400,000 weapons, 50,000 tons of ammunition. South Vietnamese divisions now planned to wipe out vast stores of war supplies, destroy troops and training bases, and interrupt the entire supply chain.

The Vietnamese named the operation Lam Son 719.

History provided inspiration for difficult tasks. In 1418 the great Vietnamese leader Le Loi launched the Khoi nghia Lam Son from his home in northern Vietnam. The Lam Son Uprising fought a mighty Chinese force. By 1418, the Ming Empire conceded defeat.

Some 553 years later, the South Vietnamese would not have such fortune.

■ ■ ■

I found myself scurrying from place to place from the start of the offensive. On February 8, I filed stories while trying to negotiate transport north to see some of the action. I finally got a seat on a flight to the airbase at Quang Tri.

For the next three weeks, I filed from places that I could not have found on a map the year before. I traveled to see ARVN forces in Lang Vei and Dong Ha and to see Americans in Quang Tri and Khe Sanh.

I was spooked by my visit to Khe Sanh on February 27. This was the location of one of the longest and largest battles of 1968; the indecisive encounter dragged on for six months and took nearly 6,000 casualties, including 274 American deaths. The base had been abandoned for three years.

In the previous two months, a major effort put Khe Sanh back in action again. Sitting 10 miles from the Lao border, it became a key staging area for the operation. My first day there was marked by the shock of seeing so many helicopters return carrying so many dead soldiers from Laos.

I interviewed returning helicopter pilots. Antiaircraft fire along the border, they said, was fierce. Of 300 US choppers committed so far to the drive, they told me, more than 50 had been lost. South Vietnamese pilots too sustained increasing ground fire as they crossed the border in support of the ground assault.

Over forty-five days, helicopters flew more than 160,000 sorties. More choppers were shot down in that time than during any other comparable period in the long war.

On March 6, in the largest helicopter assault of the war, 276 Huey choppers ferried two battalions of ARVN troops into Tchepone. They conducted a search-and-destroy mission for two days. In the view of South Vietnam president Nguyen Van Thieu: "mission accomplished."

Late on the 9th, I left Quang Tri and flew back to Saigon.

That morning, over the objections of American commanders, President Thieu ordered an immediate withdrawal from Laos. It was not an orderly one. Stanley Karnow of *Time* magazine wrote, "The retreat quickly devolved into a rout."

Hanoi prepared for the enemy's retreat. It reinforced positions and maintained sufficient strength to attack beleaguered ARVN units all along their rugged Route 9 exit route. Poor weather hampered air support.

It would not be the last time that President Thieu, overruling expert advice, would order a precipitous retreat that would lead his army and his country to disaster. Dragging on till March 24, Operation Lam Son 719 ended in ignominy.

Military historians analyzed the failures of Lam Son 719. Overall, they argued, the interdiction plan was sound. They attributed the disaster to critical failings, mainly in leadership. Political infighting had long hampered the appointment of strong South Vietnamese commanders. The Vietnamese relied too heavily on American air power and US advisers to call in air strikes. Weather remained a consistent impediment to effective air operations. And the army, which performed well on the flat terrain of Cambodia, became overconfident. Confidence soon disappeared as they faced the harsher conditions of Laos.

As it turned out, the operation had three lasting impacts: Washington now doubted the ability of the Vietnamese to go it alone, Saigon leaders began to seriously doubt the planning and commitment of the Americans, and once well-motivated South Vietnamese soldiers suffered a demoralization from which they were not to recover.

Lam Son 719 resulted in more than 7,500 casualties on the South Vietnamese side and perhaps as many as 13,000 among communist forces. More than 200 Americans lost their lives, many trying to secure the road to Khe Sanh. Among American casualties were top-notch helicopter pilots.

■ ■ ■

I broke off watching the Laos campaign to return to Cambodia on March 15.

Back in Phnom Penh again, no rockets or mortars greeted me this time. A temporarily secure airfield welcomed Air Vietnam 680 as it glided into Pochentong at 9:30 in the morning.

During this visit, I said to myself, Sinan would come first.

We dined at Le Venise, one of her favorites. Run by a nearly always cheery Italian couple, it had been serving pretty respectable Venetian specialties for about ten years.

Sinan and I sipped Italian wine. I proposed a couple of toasts to upcoming anniversaries.

"Quels anniversaires, Jim?"

"Well, first, coming up in just about one month, will be your birthday on April 20."

Sinan smiled. At least I remembered.

"And then—three months from tonight will be the first anniversary of our first dinner together!"

"Well, that is a long time off, Jim. J'espere ... I hope you will be back with me long before then!"

She smiled again, but not as brightly this time. I raised my glass.

Yet raising a glass to life in Phnom Penh seemed strained. It had been one year since the Khmer Republic was established, an anniversary not many were celebrating.

Lon Nol had suffered a stroke. People talked constantly about his health.

"I think his illness will make things worse," Sinan observed. "I hear it's affecting his mind. Did you know he makes his decisions depending on what fortune tellers say?"

I did. But perhaps to make Sinan feel better, I told her that a number of Asian leaders did that.

The "Marshal," the title Lon Nol preferred, appeared to be losing his grip on reality. He descended into a mystical world of psychics and mediums. He could not accept the country's true military situation or the rising levels of corruption that undermined his government. He placed blame solely at the feet of North Vietnamese invaders. He ignored warnings of what would prove more dangerous: the rise of a strong, ruthless, indigenous Khmer insurgency, trained by the Vietnamese.

Signs of Lon Nol's fragility had been there from the start.

Only three months after the coup d'état, the Americans sent a delegation to Phnom Penh to bolster the new regime, which had pledged to help the US in Vietnam. White House National Security Council adviser Alexander Haig headed the group reporting to Henry Kissinger.

Haig, in a memo to Kissinger, described an emotional, unstable Lon Nol. Near the end of a two-hour meeting during which Lon Nol pressed Haig for more military assistance, the general, according to Haig's account, "broke down and sobbed. He got up and went to the other end of the room until he regained his composure."

The next day, I wrote a short analysis report.

"After one year of war," I wrote, "Vietnamese communists dominate the countryside. Their main focus is still winning the war in Vietnam. But they also want to rebuild their supply lines in Cambodia's sanctuaries. They seek to keep General Lon Nol off balance so he with American help can do little more than protect Phnom Penh and a few provincial capitals. In that objective right now, Vietnamese communist forces seem to be doing very well."

Later, I read my one-year report to Sinan. After I finished, she looked particularly sad.

I quickly changed the subject and her spirits brightened.

As the second year of the Khmer Republic began, an optimism prevailed among Khmer that astounded me. In Sinan and her friends, I found a simple, a cheerful naivete, an unwillingness to accept bad news.

Perhaps optimism is rooted in Buddhism. Does karma provide a defense against pessimism? Perhaps it was simply part of an "it cannot be helped" mentality.

I was not alone in my perplexity. Emory Swank later said, "Cambodians had a boundless, almost child-like, confidence in the United States. They never really comprehended the limits of American engagement. It seemed inevitable that they and most Khmer would soon feel badly betrayed."

■ ■ ■

On March 20, 1971, I went back to Saigon.

I promised Sinan I would return for a longer period to mark the Cambodian New Year on April 11. I knew the holiday was important to her.

On April 23 Sinan sent me a letter.

She typed her letter in French on her office typewriter. I stuffed it in my diary and later tried not to look at it. For it was evidence of a broken promise, in fact of more broken promises to come.

"Depuis plus d'un mois que je ne t'ai pas vu! Comment vas-tu-la-bas? Ici a Phnom Penh, je pense sans cesse a toi ... "

For more than a month I have not seen you! How are you doing there?

Here in Phnom Penh, I constantly think of you. I looked forward to hearing from you.

Before I left for the Khmer New Year, I telephoned several times the Hotel de la Poste. I checked at the briefing. I was always told "No, he has not come." Before we separated you told me you might return to Phnom Penh on the 11 of April to spend the Khmer New Year here.

As I write this letter, I do not know exactly where you are. Are you in Saigon or Hong Kong? I am waiting anxiously for your letter so that I can answer you.

> I thought that you had forgotten me. But this day was one of great excitement. I have just received a telegram in which you extended best wishes on the occasion of my birthday. I wasn't sure you would remember. I am very touched and I thank you ... infinitely of your thoughts.
> When will you return to Phnom Penh? I hope soon. And that I'll see you again.
> Come as soon as you can. I embrace you with all my heart, dear Jim. Fondly S. Sinan

■ ■ ■

The tattered diary reveals changes in my life in 1971.

First my career was about to move on. On Sunday, March 21, I filed my last report for Metromedia Radio. That one-year analysis piece on Cambodia would my last.

On Monday, I bid farewell across a shaky phone line to colleagues in Washington and New York. The little network—which if people knew of it at all was through their one big station, WNEW New York—was shutting down. We were all in search of new jobs.

I was lucky. Almost at once a new opportunity appeared.

In those days NBC had an active radio network. They needed stringers—part-time reporters. With the encouragement of correspondent George Lewis, I landed a regular gig, filing daily for NBC News.

I cleaned out my desk out at the Visnews office and moved two floors upstairs to NBC News in the Passage Eden.

On April 2 I took my place for a slot in the rotations at the JUSPAO radio room to file my first reports with the signoff "NBC News, Saigon."

The prospects of a new job elated me. I was about to work for one of the big three American networks … even if it was as a stringer. I had a flashback to Worcester at age 16 and WNEB, when the foreign correspondents I heard on-air conjured up adventure in faraway places.

Yet working for a big network meant I would have less control over my life. I would not be calling the shots. I could no longer just fly off or brave the road to Phnom Penh anytime I wanted. I didn't tell Sinan this—but inevitably there would be less time for her.

Reflected in the tattered diary, another change becomes apparent: a secret I kept from Sinan.

As the year wore on, Sinan's name appears less in the diary and another woman's appears more.

Karen. A smart, aggressive, attractive Chinese woman, born in Guangzhou, raised in English schools in Hong Kong, entered my life. I met Karen on a short visit to Hong Kong at the Visnews office where she worked.

NBC News kept me in Saigon. Karen visited me there. Our relationship deepened.

I told neither woman of the other. My honesty and fidelity became as tattered that year as my old diary was to become.

In midsummer I returned to the United States for a month. I had not seen my family or friends since I left for Japan at the end of 1969. I went to Massachusetts. And to ensure that my work with NBC News remained on track, I paid my first visit to 30 Rock: the RCA Building headquarters of NBC in New York.

Curiously, the moment I set foot in the States, I wanted to get back to Asia.

In the summer of 1971, a war-weariness had settled in America. At social gatherings, people would say, "Oh, you are out in Vietnam and Cambodia, are you? Must be tough. What's it like?"

Then, if I began to answer in some serious way, I would see them drift off.

"Can I get you another drink?" Or they would interrupt. "You must be homesick? You've been away so long."

Well, the fact was I was not homesick at all. I couldn't wait to get back to the war!

I continued to write to Sinan. I wanted to know if life in the Phnom Penh she had introduced me to still had its attractions despite the battles erupting around her. I described how busy NBC kept me. Assignments in Vietnam would make it unlikely that I could return to Cambodia very soon.

In September, Khmer Rouge terrorists launched a series of attacks in Phnom Penh. Two Americans were killed and thirteen wounded while playing baseball near the US Embassy. If the Americans could not even protect their own in Phnom Penh, what hope was there?

I wrote to Sinan again. She should start thinking about ways she might leave Cambodia, at least until things improved, something I thought would not likely happen.

On December 18, I finally boarded a Royal Air Cambodge flight to Phnom Penh for my last visit of 1971 and my first since March. NBC had commissioned a series of reports. They wanted to see if I could get out of the capital. How much of the country was now under communist control?

Before I departed I told Karen about Sinan.

"You need to make a clean break," advised Karen. It was not advice actually; it was an order.

Back on Monivong Boulevard, I very slowly climbed the stairs to Sinan's fourth-floor apartment for a meeting I did not wish to have.

Much to *my* surprise, Sinan voiced no surprise.

"After my birthday, when you didn't return for eight months, what was I to think? You were gone. You wanted to move on. Your career? Another woman? Mais, I knew ... quelque chose avait change ... something changed ... C'était dans vos lettres." A certain chill in my letters had given me away.

I ended our goodbye with one of the oldest lines in the book. "Can we still remain friends?"

"Peut-être," she replied with a pained smile. *Perhaps.*

"I will write," I said in a pathetic farewell.

Some months later, a letter arrived from Paris. It came from Sinan's friend Khoeun, who had moved to France. I had not yet met Khoeun but had corresponded with her.

Khoeun's letter had the tone of an older, protective sister. She wrote in anger. Sinan felt a sense of betrayal. She was hurt. "How could you act that way?" she asked. "You led Sinan on. You raised her expectations!"

She ended the letter with words that could have had a broader meaning: "We thought you believed in commitment. Once you resolved to do something, you would not just up and leave."

■ ■ ■

I soon left Phnom Penh to see as much of the country as I could. I traveled to Kampong Speu, a provincial capital southwest of the capital. The road was safe for about 50 kilometers before descending into no-man's-land. Just to the north, I visited a small refugee center of 400 families. The farmers here fled from the neighboring province of Kandal.

Kandal by December 1971 had become a base area for the insurgency. US bombing began to take its toll among the civilian population.

Carpet-bombing targeted large swaths of rural Cambodia. In places, the pocked landscape looked like Swiss cheese. Refugees fled north and west.

The farmers and villagers I talked to expressed a painful mix of anger, helplessness, and resignation. As a result of the bombing, one older woman told me, young men of her village had fled to join the resistance, to oppose "American imperialists and the puppet Lon Nol clique."

Until bombing was halted by an act of Congress in mid-1973, the United States provided from 30,000 feet an effective propaganda and recruiting tool for the communist Khmer Rouge insurgents.

▪ ▪ ▪

I ended the year exploring two very different realities of Cambodian life: the pampered urban elite and the hardworking Khmer who lived in the heart of the nation's rice basket.

Back in Phnom Penh on Christmas Day, I attended a party hosted by then 28-year-old Princess Bopha Devi.

Having just reported on Cambodia's rural poverty, I struggled to accept the opulence of the gathering. An elaborate buffet supported generous servings of wine and champagne. Much of the party chatter focused on the days before the "Lon Nol Republic." Some members of the royal family attended. Surprisingly, there seemed no attempt to disguise contempt for the most important absent member of the royal family—Norodom Sihanouk, who remained in Beijing after his ouster. People here referred to him as "the communist prince" in the pocket of the Chinese.

"What about Sihanouk?" someone asked. "You know, I have a copy of some of the films he made. We should watch them."

"Which ones?"

"I think its *La Joie du Vivre* from 1968. Or maybe *Crepuscule*, 'Twilight' in English. Sihanouk won the Golden Apsara Award at the 1969 Phnom Penh International Film Festival for that."

"Of course he did. It was his film festival." Laughter.

Not once during the gathering did the conversation turn to war and the desperate conditions across the country.

Bopha Devi struck me as an extraordinary beauty. She was Sihanouk's daughter by the first of his six wives.

She carried herself with grace befitting not only a princess but the lead dancer of the Royal Ballet. The photographs of her early dancing days, ten years before, displayed an even more striking person than the woman before me.

Sinan had told me about the princess. She had been a schoolmate of Saorun's.

"A smart and very engaging girl," Saorun later recalled. "Because of social standing our relationship after graduation was not as close as I would have liked. Bopha Devi became quite protected."

I no doubt broke protocol at the gathering. When I had the chance to meet her, Bopha Devi asked me what I did and what I knew about Cambodia. Perhaps a bit too forcefully I began talking about the refugees I had seen in Kampong Speu. The princess seemed surprised. The war to her remained distant. Ballet remained her passion. She sought to stay away from politics.

I soon drifted away. At this gathering of the privileged, I emerged feeling I had visited an alternate universe.

On December 30, I flew northwest to Battambang. I discarded the idea of driving up Route 5. The road was open sporadically in late 1971. The 180 miles to the northwest could take anywhere between five and eight hours if I managed to avoid an ambush. Instead I flew on one of those little planes that Vann's partner Jimmy serviced.

Battambang ranked as Cambodia's second-largest city and served as the provincial capital to the nation's rice basket. I wanted a glimpse of what Cambodia might have been before the war—a comparatively quiet rural nation, trying to stay out of conflict, able to feed itself and export a modest amount of rice.

As 1970 began, Cambodians cultivated nearly 9 million square miles of paddy. They produced 2.5 million tons of rice, perhaps half of it from Battambang. By the end of 1971, war had stopped production on 2 million square miles. For the first time, Cambodia received rice supplies from the outside, 58,000 tons in 1972.

January to March is the normal rice harvest season here. A 5-mile ride out of town revealed the fertile, verdant rice fields and farmers with abundant crops of sweet potatoes, corn, and cucumber.

The bustling city of Battambang near my hotel seemed home to small gangs of black marketeers. They traded in luxury goods smuggled in from Thailand, the border less than 74 miles away. When Khmer Republic troops could be spared for escort, the goods flowed down Route 5 to the capital, where they would be available for those who could afford the inflated prices.

On New Year's Eve 1971, after a three-hour drive by taxi, I found myself in the Thai town of Aranyaprathet. On New Year's Day I arrived in Bangkok, where I could write my stories for NBC Radio.

■ ■ ■

On January 5, I returned to Saigon. NBC was happy with my reports from Cambodia, but more important assignments in Vietnam would occupy me in 1972. I would watch the fate of Cambodia as closely as I could, but I would not return to Phnom Penh for three years. Romantically, my relationship with Karen would grow. We would travel around the world together and try to settle down in America. Then nearly as quickly as it grew, our attachment to each other sputtered and died. My restlessness outstripped any other emotion.

Sinan would become what she described later as a "distant friend."

7
MED Team C

FORTY-YEAR-OLD DECLASSIFIED PENTAGON REPORTS can make for tedious reading. In the case of the "end of tour" reports of Brigadier General Theodore Mataxis in 1972 and Major General John Cleland in 1974, however, they provide fascinating background to the world into which Soc Sinan entered in late 1972.

The two generals portray rather sad and futile efforts to provide Cambodia something it had never had and should not have needed: a well-equipped fighting army. The generals in turn commanded something called the US MEDT-C, the United States Military Equipment Delivery Team Cambodia.

Just before Sihanouk was deposed, Cambodia maintained a haphazardly organized 32,000-man army. Highly corrupt, this personalized army, of which Sinan's father was a part, fought off small-scale internal rebellions and gathered kickbacks from the North Vietnamese for transporting rice and weapons. The air force consisted of fifteen aircraft. It was derisively described as "the Phnom Penh Royal Flying Club." Most of the pilots were members of the royal family.

Four years later in February 1974, "FANK," as Marshal Lon Nol's army was called (the French acronym for the Forces Armées

Nationales Khmères), had bulked up to more than 253,000 soldiers and more than 100 aircraft. The durable training/counterinsurgency, single-engine aircraft T-28, first manufactured in 1949, became the staple of the Khmer air force. All of these new assets were funded by more than $225 million in US aid.

The MEDT-C struggled to provide arms and train Cambodians to use the hardware and to effectively manage troops. Sometimes they succeeded. Often they failed. It was too much, too fast, against a more determined and more formidable enemy.

The Team also struggled against an American Congress which did everything it could to make the mission impossible. As General Cleland even-handedly put it, the US Congress sought to "prevent further growth of a US commitment which would drag our nation even more deeply into a difficult situation."

First, Congress limited the number of Americans who could be in Cambodia to fewer than 200. While it authorized the MEDT-C to deliver weapons, it banned it from "advising" the Cambodian army. Finally, on August 15, 1973, Congress ended any US combat air support to the Cambodians. All US bombing stopped.

Still the team's numbers grew from 13 in January 1971 to 113 at the end of 1972. About a third of the team stayed in Saigon or Bangkok ready to fly into Cambodia on temporary duty, or "TDY." Although they were not "military advisers," they gave advice to the Khmer on how to weaponize and organize their armed forces. Drawing fine lines remained a consistent feature of the Indochina war.

■ ■ ■

Into this confusing world of military intrigue entered a still-curious, smart Khmer woman seeking, very frankly, something different, and something to get her mind off the rather reprehensible reporter who had disappointed her and then disappeared.

Sinan's pain subsided somewhat by late 1972.

Saorun and Vann and her other friends continued to be a source of diversion. There were those outings, wild nighttime rides around Phnom Penh. Despite the war, SONATRAC remained in business and continued to employ Sinan.

Vann's partner Jimmy told Sinan about occasional parties at which some eligible American military men might be found.

"See you Saturday night?" asked Vann hopefully.

Sinan joined in hesitantly at first.

■ ■ ■

One evening Sinan was introduced to a tall, thin older man—at least a dozen years older than she was. His name was Walter Herbert. With his close-cropped hair and strong, angular features, he presented a stark contrast to the young, shaggy, feckless reporter she had once known.

Herbert seemed mature, settled, steadfast, responsible. He reminded her of a kinder, gentler, understanding version of her father, Commander Soc Sonn. Walter served as the senior financial officer for the American military team.

Sinan called Walter "Major Walt" or "the Commander," *Le Commandant* in French. That's how a Cambodian immigration document described him when, with Walter's help, Sinan applied for a visa to the United States in 1973.

Later Sinan reflected on her first impressions of the MEDTC, introduced to her by Walter.

Through *Le Commandant* I came to know the American Military Equipment Delivery Team Cambodia staff.

They were housed in beautiful homes and traveled around a lot, providing support to the Khmer army. They were military but wore plain clothes, dress pants, short sleeves, shirt and tie. They only put on uniforms for special occasions to inspect Cambodian troops.

They traveled sometimes in groups in small vans or jeeps painted green or black.

Some MEDT-C lived in a three-story compound on the main road which connected the city to Pochentong and the small military airfield there.

The compound was located between the school of art L'École de Beaux Arts and the Cambodian Cabinet Ministry.

I used to see them, often with bar girls at restaurants around the city. But when the rockets began to fall and Khmer communist agents started throwing grenades in bars and in movie theaters, I seldom saw them leave their compound.

Most Khmer I knew thought the Americans lived like kings.

Many Vietnamese, Chinese, and Khmer wanted to work for them. Khmer men wanted to be security guards for them. Khmer were paid about $20 a month. Khmer women wanted to be with them.

Born in 1935, Walter Herbert had had a long army career. He was assigned to Phnom Penh in late 1972 for a one-year tour.

"I was introduced to Major Walt through a friend—Colonel Bob Barnes—who told me the team came to Phnom Penh to teach Lon Nol's soldiers how to fight." Sinan wrote some years later. "Bob said we needed to understand strategies of war and how to use the equipment being given by the United States."

As senior financial officer, Walter was charged with a task that grew increasingly futile. He prepared budgets, tracked funding, and tried to ensure the Pentagon's money was spent wisely.

As General Cleland put it, "audit staffs were overwhelmed by the task of 'finance verification' as the size of the Khmer Republic's armed forces increased by nearly tenfold."

Soon Cleland, the MEDT-C, and Walter faced "phantom payrolls" and "flower people."

The fact was that the troop strength of 253,000 was phony. "Phantom" soldiers appeared on rosters. As many as 100,000 nonexistent soldiers enabled Cambodian unit commanders to draw extra pay and pocket the proceeds. "Flower people" were servants, bodyguards, and friends who had no real military function but whose pay came out of the padded payrolls. The payrolls, of course, were being met by Washington. Untangling and stopping the waste soon became the full-time work of Walter and his team.

■ ■ ■

In his short time in Cambodia, Walter fell quickly in love.

Denny Lane, Secretary of the General Staff and General Cleland's French language officer recalled an extraordinary woman. "She caught the eye of a number of the MEDT-C men," Lane said later.

Four decades later Walter had trouble speaking to me of the young woman who had so captured his heart. In 2017, Walter had been happily married for forty years to Davi, another Khmer woman. They had one son together.

I phoned him at his office in Washington. I had met Walter only once, in June 1975. He had good reason to resent me and my influence on Sinan. Yet he was friendly, engaging.

When I probed more deeply his thoughts about Sinan, there was a long silence. Walter's voice broke. Then—"Sinan was a troubled soul," he recalled sadly, "but I was enchanted by her, I was infatuated."

In 1973, Walter took Sinan to the United States on a scheduled visit to Washington to present his MEDT-C budget to Pentagon seniors. Sinan visited his home in Brooklyn, New York, that August. His sister recalls being taken with "a shy, but exceptional Cambodian woman."

Sinan got her first taste of "the Big Apple." She liked New York, though she found the crowds oppressive. She visited Washington, DC. thought she might return. She left behind a few of her possessions for safekeeping.

After she returned to Cambodia, Walter spent much of the next year trying to persuade her to leave Phnom Penh and settle down permanently in Washington.

It was complicated. They talked about marriage at the end of Walter's one-year tour in 1973. Sinan remained uncertain. After she returned from America, she wrote her friend Khoeun that she could not make up her mind.

Walter's thoughts of marriage were a mixture of deep affection and guilt. He felt sorry for her. How would he feel if Sinan failed to leave Cambodia?

From his perspective inside the US Embassy and at the Pentagon, he knew better than most that both Sinan and Cambodia were living on borrowed time. He knew people like Sinan—with her background—would be high on the communists' list for elimination.

Walter wanted to make sure she got out. Although thousands of miles away in Washington, he made all the arrangements.

Against all logic, through 1973, 1974 and into 1975, when I arrived, Sinan continued to vacillate.

8

Dress Rehearsal for the Final Act

IN JANUARY 1972, I immersed myself in work. I asked NBC if I might expand my output. If NBC could not elevate me to a staff position, would they allow me to freelance for others?

"No to staff. Yes to others," New York said. I added National Public Radio to my strings. In Hong Kong, I approached the magazine *Far Eastern Economic Review* about further freelance work. The editor of *FEER* agreed.

My old friend and university roommate, Jim Russell, first suggested in 1969 that I might consider going to Vietnam. He had done a stint in Indochina and now had begun work at NPR Washington.

NPR would accept analysis pieces and feature stories about the South Vietnamese, whereas NBC News usually commissioned impossibly short 40-second "spots" about American troops. NPR permitted me to write the occasional analysis piece on Cambodia from Saigon. Public radio then did not have the budget for another reporter in Phnom Penh.

■ ■ ■

At the end of March, the biggest story so far in my fledgling career dropped in my lap.

The largest battle of the war erupted. It would prove in many ways a dress rehearsal for the final collapse of South Vietnam three years later in April 1975.

▪ ▪ ▪

February 1972 began as a pretty quiet month. Communist attacks on Saigon's positions were down. Much global attention focused on China. President Nixon was due to arrive in Shanghai on February 21. I wrote a piece for NPR on the possible impact of China rapprochement on the war in Vietnam.

Nixon pursued multiple strategies. He pursued diplomacy with Beijing. Would the Chinese assist in advancing a peace agreement with Hanoi? Would Nixon-Kissinger diplomacy with both the Soviets and the Chinese produce a reduction of armaments flowing to North Vietnam?

Nixon continued to withdraw troops. In January about 130,000 American forces remained in Vietnam, a quarter of what there had been in early 1969. By May 1972, the number dropped to 69,000. Among them the actual number of "combat" troops stood at fewer than 6,000.

Despite the humiliation suffered a year ago by Lam Son 719 as Saigon troops retreated from Laos, the US administration still trumpeted "Vietnamization." South Vietnamese forces must be ready to continue their nation's defense on their own.

Meanwhile, Nixon intensified bombing of North Vietnam. Between February 13 and 17, I filed repeated stories on the increased air war. Intelligence reports suggested a significant buildup of Hanoi's forces.

US officials predicted a major offensive. But no one knew exactly when. The Tet holiday seemed likely. US bombing would do what it could, in the words of the day, to "interdict" the arms supply routes, forestalling a 1972 Hanoi campaign. The air force coined a peculiar euphemism for some of the intensive bombing. They were called "protective reaction strikes." When Hanoi's Russian-provided SAM (surface-to-air missile) batteries proved effective, the US would retaliate with massive bombing raids.

The Vietnamese New Year holiday, Tet, began February 14. South Vietnam braced itself for a North Vietnamese offensive. It didn't come. Everyone breathed a sigh of relief.

February slid into March. Still no major combat. I flew to Hong Kong for what we used to call "R and R"—rest and recuperation. I returned to Saigon on March 12.

Nixon's drawdown continued. Just before my return, the 101st Airborne Division, the last ground combat division in the country, departed.

On March 21, I lunched at the old French Cercle Sportif Club and marveled at how quiet things were. I noted in my diary that communist insurgents near Phnom Penh staged a major artillery bombardment, killing more than one hundred civilians, the heaviest attack on the city since the war began two years before.

I thought again of Sinan. Not knowing how Sinan would receive my words, I wrote instead a note to her friend Khoeun in Paris. "How is Sinan doing?" I asked. Again I warned of the obvious, the war was closing in. Had Sinan given any further thought to leaving Cambodia? Although we were no longer lovers, might Khoeun at least let Sinan know I was still around and willing somehow to help? I received no reply.

I walked back to the NBC bureau in Saigon's Passage Eden, but my thoughts were elsewhere.

■ ■ ■

NBC News had downsized its Saigon bureau since the height of the war in 1967–70. Two staff television correspondents remained, as well as a few radio stringers such as myself. The downsizing reflected a waning interest in the war, particularly now that the focus was on Vietnamese actions. With few American combat troops in the field, major operations that put US soldiers at risk, New York management thought, were concerns of the past.

In late March, George Lewis, the senior correspondent in country, and his wife Janie went on vacation. The second correspondent, Art Lord, confined himself to Saigon as his wife Susan expected a baby. Their daughter Sharon was born on April 7.

George and Art had good company in taking much-needed breaks. The US ambassador to Vietnam, Ellsworth Bunker, flew to Kathmandu to see his wife, a diplomat in Nepal. The American commander, General Creighton Abrams, planned a vacation with his family in Thailand. Earlier, in January, Defense Secretary Melvin Laird, who refused to believe intelligence reports, told a congressional committee that a large communist offensive in 1972 "was not a serious possibility." NBC bureau chief Bob Toombs looked forward to a quiet Easter.

He was not to have one.

What we did not know then was the vast extent of Hanoi's buildup and the timing of its use. Fresh supplies of Russian and Chinese armaments poured into the North in the final months of 1971. MiG aircraft, new SA-7 heat-seeking missiles, and increased artillery assets arrived in steady shipments.

Hanoi would introduce a level of tank warfare not seen before. Soviet T-54s and Chinese PT-76s had been readied for the task.

Hanoi's planners, including General Vo Nguyen Giap, called the 1972 general offensive Operation Nguyen Hue. As with most Vietnamese campaigns (North or South), the name honored a historic national hero and his heroic victory. The Emperor Quang Trung (also known as Nguyen Hue) surprised and defeated a Chinese army near Hanoi in 1789.

The arms bonus for Hanoi came because of Nixon's China visit. Not wishing to alarm its wartime ally, Beijing dispatched new weapons as reassurance of continued support while Chinese leaders pursued its new diplomacy with the United States. Not to be outdone by Beijing, Moscow pledged more support to Hanoi, including Russian military advisers.

Hanoi's politburo discussed three objectives: take territory to improve their bargaining position at ongoing peace talks in Paris, embarrass Nixon as he began his campaign for reelection, and destroy Nixon's goal of "Vietnamization." Based on the performance of South Vietnamese forces in Laos, Hanoi saw the ARVN as a pushover.

Operation Nguyen Hue would be fought on three fronts. The largest operation in the far north would steamroll down Quang Tri Province and Military Region One, what the Americans called I Corp. Units would then attack from Laos and Cambodia into the Central Highlands. A third front would be opened from rebuilt and expanded Cambodian sanctuaries north of Saigon and push south through the towns of Loc Ninh and An Loc.

Hanoi launched what Americans would call the "Easter Offensive" at noon on March 30.

Hanoi did something not done before. In the past, all attacks came from infiltration points in the west, from Laos or Cambodia. This time Hanoi ordered three army divisions, 30,000 men, backed by heavy artillery straight across the Ben Hai River, across the DMZ—the internationally recognized demarcation line between North and South Vietnam. The massive force aimed to blitzkrieg down Highway 1, take the town of Dong Ha, move on quickly to the provincial capital of Quang Tri, and plunge further south to the city of Hue, which had suffered greatly in the communists' 1968 Tet Offensive.

The days of guerilla war were long gone. A traditional ground invasion at its most audacious was planned.

Confusion reigned not only at the NBC bureau but apparently at ARVN and MACV headquarters as well.

At the end of day one, a string of South Vietnamese firebases along the DMZ as well as bases to the west along Route 9 came under intensive artillery bombardment. The brunt of the attack fell on units of the ARVN 3rd Division. A recently formed outfit, it found itself under attack in the middle of a troop rotation. The 3rd Division had never trained against a conventional armored invasion.

At the end of day two, Good Friday in the Christian world, the North's artillery reduced villages near the DMZ to rubble. The towns of Dong Ha and Cam Lo came under assault. A stream of desperate refugees with whatever they could carry took to the roads and fled south to escape the onslaught.

■ ■ ■

On Saturday, April Fool's Day, NBC News finally mobilized *its* troops.

NBC was well staffed with some of the best camera shooters in the business. Vo Huynh and his younger brother Suu, Le Phuc Dinh and sound tech Cung, and Yasuda and Yashiro (known as the Y boys) from Japan were all true veterans.

As for reporters this day before Easter Sunday, NBC came up short. Late in the day, Bob Toombs realized he had no staff correspondents to provide coverage for NBC television. He turned to a long-haired, 24-year-old radio stringer suited up in impossibly wide lapels tailored to a sweaty made-in-Saigon shirt. Baggy bell-bottomed jeans hung from his hips.

I sat in the corner of the NBC office.

I had just gotten off the phone with a US colonel named Lawford and a Vietnamese information officer named Lieutenant Colonel Bo. They were at the Phu Bai air combat base 8 miles southeast of Hue. I wasn't having much luck getting information.

"I don't know," said Bo from his office 57 miles south of the action, "but there's heavy fighting between our forces and the communists who attacked us right across the DMZ. Our firebases are holding."

Toombs suggested I put down the phone. "Need to press you into service, Jim. Can you take a charter to Quang Tri first thing in the morning?"

"Sure, what time?" I replied, with the unquestioning confidence only youth provides.

"0700, Tan Son Nhut. You better go pack. Get some sleep. I've already sent the Y boys as well as Dinh, Cung, and Vo Suu north to Hue. Vo Huynh's on standby. They'll meet up with you on the ground. Need you to get us something for Sunday's *Nightly News*."

As I agreed, I realized I had never done a television news story before. I had shot some 16 mm film but had never been in an edit room and knew nothing of the difference between writing for television and writing for radio or print. This was a hell of a way to get on-the-job training.

Slight delay. Wheels up just after 8 on the Continental Air Services twin-engine Beechcraft Baron. Both Continental and Air America operating charter services out of Tan Son Nhut earned a good deal of money from the American TV networks on pretty dicey missions.

The destination this time: Quang Tri airfield—35 kilometers (22 miles) south of the no-longer-demilitarized zone.

I carried my usual backpack, kit, clothing, and a helmet. My essentials included my sturdy Olivetti, a Sony TC-45 cassette recorder, and a 35 mm Praktica still camera made in Dresden. For this trip I jettisoned my Canon Scoopic 16 mm film camera. Too much stuff. Besides, some of the best cameramen anywhere were waiting at the other end.

A couple of hours later the little plane swooped out of the clouds onto what seemed an impossibly small air strip.

"A near-miss landing," I wrote in my diary. "Ed, the pilot, dodged holes from artillery strikes as he touched down."

Engines running, Ed made no attempt to hide the fear on his face and ordered me to go. I scrambled out of the aircraft.

As I did, he shouted, "Don't expect me to pick you up!"

I waved. Within minutes he was airborne again.

A short time later a rocket slammed into the runway. A few more artillery rounds like that and the airstrip would be unusable.

The Quang Tri combat base sat just to the east of Route 1. Running as fast as I could with all the junk strapped to me, I made a beeline toward the highway.

I was confronted by an incredible crush of refugees streaming south.

Old and young. Mothers carrying their babies. Men leading their oxen and cattle. An old woman hauled all her possessions in two baskets held aloft by a bamboo pole over her left shoulder. They walked. They ran. At the sound of gunfire they scurried to the side of the road, sometimes diving for cover.

Among the civilian refugees were hundreds if not thousands of ARVN soldiers. Abandoning their weapons, they deserted their positions and joined the exodus.

I pulled out the camera, started snapping pictures. The Associated Press, which had offices next to NBC in Saigon, had armed me with some rolls of Kodak Tri-X Pan film.

On Monday morning, April 3, the Springfield, Massachusetts, *Union* fronted one of my uncredited refugee pics. My parents in Worcester would see it but not know it was mine. The headline read "North Vietnamese Tanks Advance, Situation Viewed as 'Grim.'"

But I saw no North Vietnamese T-54 tanks that day. They were 30 miles north, moving in my direction.

Things were certainly "grim" though. During my first hour on the ground, artillery batteries fired twenty rounds of incoming.

I quickly sought refuge in a storm drain under the highway. There had been no recent rain and the gulley was mostly dry. This seemed to me the safest place to be while I collected my thoughts and wiped off both the sweat on my brow and the tears that welled up in my eyes.

The tears rose from the sight of the human misery all around me and from the increasing panic within me, which asked, "What should I do next?"

I looked around me in the storm drain. Four or five ARVN soldiers had joined me. They were laughing. I offered them some cigarettes. Through laughter one expresses fear and nervousness. These were clearly not among Saigon's bravest fighting men.

I did not know it at the time, but as I arrived at Quang Tri airfield, the boldest communist attack of the war since Tet 1968 had entered its fourth day.

Much of the defense of South Vietnam's northern border had collapsed in those four days. Ten fire support bases strung along the DMZ had been either overrun or hastily evacuated.

Virtually the entire 3rd ARVN Division—nearly 10,000 men comprising three infantry regiments, artillery, mortar, and engineering elements—had died, had been wounded, had surrendered, or (like the boys with me in the storm drain) were on the run.

At this point more than 80 percent of the ARVN Division's artillery passed into the hands of the enemy.

As I hunkered down in my under-the-road bunker, 9 miles north of me, remnants of the 3rd ARVN, reinforced by South Vietnamese marines, held the line at Dong Ha—just.

The marines and a courageous US Marine Corps adviser briefly halted Hanoi's armored assault. That marine, with the extraordinary skills of an acrobat, scaled the girders of a bridge. He blew a key route across the Cua Viet River.

Summoning what little courage I had, I emerged from my shelter and looked around to see the sad procession of refugees continuing to head south. I snapped a few more pictures. I got out the recorder to get some sound and voice a short description.

Then—I thought it a mirage at first. I saw two M151 utility vehicles, the only two jeeps on the road heading north, in defiance of all common sense. A most welcome sight. The NBC camera cavalry had arrived in the form of the Y boys and Le Phuc Dinh.

I didn't need any encouragement to jump on board.

The next few hours involved a mad scramble for vision. Dinh raced north to see how close he could get to the front line.

The Y boys and I witnessed an extraordinary scene developing just across the road, 4 miles north of the provincial capital of Quang Tri.

The Ai Tu command post, HQ for the 3rd Division and the northern defense operations, was being evacuated—at least most of it.

It was not an orderly withdrawal. We filmed from the road as American advisers ignited a bonfire of battlefield maps, intelligence reports, and other materiel. They shot holes in trucks and drained one of the larger water towers. A US Chinook helicopter flew into position to ferry them out. Only a small American tactical team would remain behind.

We learned later that the commander of the 3rd, Brigadier General Vu Van Giai, ordered a retreat south to what he thought would be the safe citadel of Quang Tri City, out of range of North Vietnamese 130 mm artillery fire.

What was supposed to have been a simple transfer of headquarters turned into a melee lasting into early morning on April 3. ARVN officers and enlisted men scrambled to leave. An American adviser later said, "Radios were left on and simply abandoned, maps and classified materials lay where they were last used ... complete bedlam existed."

Included in the retreat were nearly 150 men of the American advisory team. Some of them were those we filmed without knowing precisely who they were.

Advisory Team 155 comprised one of the last teams of military advisers attached to ARVN forces. These advisers proved critical in the months ahead as the Saigon troops clawed back their territory.

Within hours of Hanoi's assault on March 30, American advisers directed naval gunfire from destroyers off the coast. Poor weather made air strikes difficult at first. As skies cleared, the advisers proved indispensable in pinpointing targets for air strikes. More than once they rallied hesitant South Vietnamese commanders.

On Sunday, April 2, Garrick Utley presented NBC *Nightly News*. A new voice led the broadcast.

"We have just received by satellite," said Utley, "pictures of the South Vietnamese retreat."

I began my first of what turned out to be more than 3,000 network television reports over the next thirty years.

> The French used to call this Route "the street without joy." Somewhere between ten and twenty thousand desperate people are fleeing southward down the highway to escape a North Vietnamese advance.
>
> It's nearly 20 miles from here to the DMZ, and some of these people have walked almost that far. Behind them they have left devastation near the towns of Cam Lo and Dong Ha. They were right in the path of a North Vietnamese drive to cut off the northernmost province of South Vietnam.
>
> Nobody—Vietnamese or American alike—has seen such a civilian refugee crisis since Tet 1968.
>
> The refugees seek the safety of Quang Tri City—where there may be no safety.
>
> One tragedy is the civilians abandoning their homes. Another is that the army is abandoning its bases. The South Vietnamese army is in full retreat.

The piece ended by questioning whether the South Vietnamese would continue to cut and run or would rally and counterattack, proving that Vietnam could stand on its own and in doing so show that Nixon's words about "Vietnamization" were not simply hollow ones.

■ ■ ■

For me the Easter Offensive would also see my first "near miss." I would cover war, conflict, and other dangerous situations many times in the years ahead: Vietnam, Cambodia, China, Afghanistan, Lebanon, Iraq, Bosnia, Somalia, and South Africa. I never liked it and was never much good at it.

Still, there is nothing quite like the adrenaline rush when you survive a particularly hairy combat situation.

On Wednesday, April 5, Dinh, Cung, and I headed north from Hue, through the city of Quang Tri toward Dong Ha. Small clumps of sand, a few larger dunes, and speckles of uneven tree growth dotted the area east to the sea and just west of Route 1. It formed a treacherous pocket.

We stopped.

We left our cars and drivers behind and advanced cautiously on foot.

Moving slowly forward , I came across a group of eight of my colleagues. Every one of them had far more combat experience than I. Every one of them cowered in the sand.

A phalanx of bao chi (Vietnamese shorthand for newspaper reporter) consumed by curiosity and devoid of common sense crept forward.

After a few minutes, some of the group moved on. I remained to the rear. Fox Butterfield, interpreter-photographer Nguyen Ngoc Luong, and war veteran Rick Brummett moved farthest ahead.

They suddenly found themselves surrounded on one side by South Vietnamese marines and North Vietnamese army regulars on the other.

They hit the ground.

Butterfield told me later he was so close to enemy lines that he could hear the Hanoi soldiers shouting to each other.

A round of mortars came sailing in. Brummett was hit by shrapnel fire, Luong was slightly wounded.

A short distance behind, I shoved my head into the sand.

The battle erupted around us. I thought of Bernard Fall. This was his *La Rue Sans Joie*. Would my end be like his?

Suddenly what I thought was a B-40 round sailed over my head. It seemed like I could actually feel it brush my helmet.

Within twenty minutes or so—it seemed like hours—the firefight ended. The North Vietnamese withdrew, the South Vietnamese (at least for the moment) retained control of the road to Dong Ha. I stood up and brushed sand off my baggy jeans.

Later we advanced with a company of marines. These were angry men, angry at this enemy intrusion. They had just taken back a position held by Hanoi troops.

I accompanied my friend Ron Moreau. Moreau, a *Newsweek* stringer, possessed something rare among reporters—fluency in Vietnamese. Moreau had arrived in Vietnam (as did a half dozen of the best Indochina specialists anywhere) attached to IVS, International Voluntary Services, a nonprofit organization focused on developmental projects.

As we mounted a small dune, Moreau spotted the marines beating a North Vietnamese prisoner of war unmercifully with rifle butts. I looked on, disturbed but lacking the courage to intervene.

I heard Moreau shout in Vietnamese. He had interrupted an act of revenge on a lone POW. The marines stopped.

I will always remember the moment for two reasons. Moreau displayed extraordinary decency and bravery. And up until that time, I had never seen a Hanoi soldier up close.

∎ ∎ ∎

April proved a dangerous month for journalists in Quang Tri Province. The setbacks for South Vietnam were one thing. But in the little world of war reporters, Operation Nguyen Hue took its toll. Alex Shimkin, another Vietnamese-speaking stringer and IVS veteran, got caught behind enemy lines and was killed. Terry Khoo, a Singaporean shooter for ABC News, died when he found himself in the wrong place amid constantly shifting battle lines. Veteran NBC News cameraman Vo Huynh barely escaped death with a serious injury to his neck.

■ ■ ■

A few days later on April 10, after my stories were filed, Bill Corrigan, head of foreign news at NBC New York, sent a telex message to NBC Saigon. "Tell Laurie we appreciate the manner in which he filled a serious hole we had which we hope is on the way to solution. Regards and good luck to all."

I stayed on for most of April covering the battle for Quang Tri, retreating for overnights in Hue, 35 miles to the south. Soon more-seasoned correspondents joined me. I was no longer needed "to fill the hole," as Corrigan put it.

The two other fronts in the offensive became active: one north of Saigon, the other in the mountainous central region. After I spent a few days in Saigon, NBC flew me to Pleiku to cover action on that second front in the Central Highlands.

On May 1, South Vietnamese troops lost the battle for Quang Tri City. Hanoi gained a major psychological victory. It would be five long months before Saigon forces took Quang Tri back. Relentless use of American bombing slammed the North Vietnamese forces.

Hanoi had overextended its forces. Opening three fronts against South Vietnam was two fronts too many. Saigon rallied and decisive American air power doomed the bold North Vietnamese invasion.

Still General Van Tien Dung, the commander of Hanoi's "People's Army," studied the mistakes. He learned the weaknesses and strengths of his enemy. He bided his time. Three years later, he would implement a very similar scenario. He would do so at a time when the government in Saigon could no longer summon unlimited weaponry and most importantly the air power of the Americans. For Hanoi, Operation Nguyen Hue proved an excellent dress rehearsal for the final act.

∎ ∎ ∎

By 1973, I needed a break from war. What I thought was a near-death experience in Quang Tri affected me more than I thought it would. I left Vietnam. I returned to the world of freelancing for anyone who would have me. I had an informal understanding with NBC New York that if I wanted to return later, I could.

En route back to the United States, I traveled across South Asia to Europe, reaching Paris just in time for the January 27 signing of the Paris Peace Accord. It was formally called the "Agreement on Ending the War and Restoring Peace in Viet Nam." It did neither.

I stood outside the Hotel Majestic on the Avenue Kléber as groups of Vietnamese youth hoisted flags of the National Liberation Front (NLF), known to most as the Viet Cong. The agreement signed by Henry Kissinger and Le Duc Tho satisfied no one I knew. My Vietnamese and Khmer friends feared the worst. Cambodian peace had no place in the deal. A very imperfect ceasefire began on Sunday, January 28.

In Paris I briefly met a man named Bui Huu Nhan. He served as a spokesman for the talks, working for Nguyen Thi Binh, the foreign affairs minister of the Provisional Revolutionary

Government or PRG (what we used to call the Viet Cong). He would soon be sent back to Vietnam.

In my diary for Sunday, January 28, 1973, I wrote, "Ceasefire: a treaty has been signed. The war has ended for Americans. They will get prisoners of war back from Hanoi. The main objective. But the war will continue for the people of Indochina."

Arriving in Washington in early April, I decided to return to academic life. I completed work on a degree, work that had been interrupted when I flew to Japan. NBC Saigon earnings provided me enough cash to take my mind off the search for an immediate assignment.

After a few months, the *Far Eastern Economic Review* offered me more work. My old friend Russell Spurr, who had run the Visnews office in Hong Kong, was now managing editor of the *Review*.

Under the byline "James Laurie" (I thought Jim was too informal for such a respected publication), I wrote regularly for *FEER* for a year and was appointed "Washington correspondent."

I tried to keep my eye on Cambodia. Among those I interviewed for the *Review* was Lon Non, the younger brother of Marshal Lon Nol. "Le Petit Frere," as he was known, had a fearsome reputation for brutality, incompetence, and being a disruptive influence on his brother.

At the urging of Emory Swank in Phnom Penh, he had been shipped off to Washington as a Cambodian "ambassador at large."

I recalled a dinner with Sinan in 1970. She called Lon Non "un sale individu," a dirty or nasty individual. She knew him for his sinister looks—dark glasses and thin mustache. He was a known enemy of intellectuals, students, and teachers. Sinan advised me in a conspiratorial voice, "Lon Non, you know Jim, will *eliminet* anyone who challenges his brother."

When I met him, Lon Non had cleaned up his image, shaved his mustache, learned some English, and wanted to go back to Cambodia.

He voiced repentance for past behavior, but when I told him that many in Phnom Penh did not particularly want him back, his eyes hardened. He looked sternly at me and snapped, "I'd like to know who those people are!"

■ ■ ■

War in Cambodia became most deadly each year during the dry season. Combatants could move more easily.

Sitting in Washington, I was surprised that the Khmer Republic had survived as long as it had. Lon Nol's government seemed in near-constant turmoil.

By January 1973, on the communist side, Khmer Rouge units had assumed much of the fighting. They no longer relied on their Vietnamese allies at the front lines. The Khmer Rouge grew from 5,000 fighters in 1970 to a brutally effective force of more than 40,000.

In early 1974, the Khmer Rouge launched a dry season offensive from both the northwest and south on Phnom Penh. The communists came within 3 miles of Pochentong Airport. The city withstood increased shelling. By March, the communist offensive stalled. Again the Khmer Republic held on.

An American relay of C-130 transport planes carrying rice and ammunition from Thailand helped keep Cambodia alive. Even more importantly, the Khmer navy managed to keep the Mekong River supply route open to Vietnam.

In November 1974, people in Phnom Penh braced for the next dry season.

Each day at the small apartment where I lived and worked on Nineteenth Street NW, I scoured the *New York Times* and its coverage of Vietnam and Cambodia.

On December 15, the *Times* quoted now former ambassador Swank. "The war has lost all meaning," he said.

The article pushed me to take action. I needed to return. For those I knew in Phnom Penh, the war certainly had meaning.

Just before Christmas, I called NBC New York and volunteered my services. "How about a short-term contract to return to Cambodia? Is there a 'hole to fill,' Bill?"

Bill Corrigan said he'd consider it. I should come to New York and talk. "Let's meet after the holidays."

I grew increasingly anxious.

I broke up with Karen. She suffered my constant restlessness in Washington. She wanted to settle down, start a family. She knew I did not. Later in 1974, Karen met and married a more stable, steadfast man from Boston.

From a distance, I watched Cambodia crumble. My thoughts turned again to Sinan. Old feelings, old passions flooded back. This was not a time for delay. I needed to return.

9

Collapse: Part 1

IN FEBRUARY 1975, Corrigan kept stalling. He was looking for a "hole for me to fill." It took a lot longer than I wanted to find that hole. Finally at the end of the month, I could wait no longer. I bought myself a cheap ticket to Saigon through London and Paris. I cobbled together several freelance assignments. Corrigan said NBC would pay me $100 a day "if you get there in time."

For years I had seen the advertising in the window of the Air France office on the ground floor of the Caravelle Hotel on Tu Do Street. "Direct service Paris-Saigon-Paris."

Air France had offered services to colonial Indochina since 1933. In those days "a flying boat" would depart Marseille. Seven days later you would be sipping pastis on Saigon's la rue Catinat. In 1975, the journey was considerably shorter, and I preferred gin.

On Sunday, March 9, after a short stop at the NBC Saigon bureau, I arrived in Phnom Penh.

Seated next to me on the flight was a mixed Vietnamese French woman named Viviane Chapuis. Viviane, dressed for the heat of Phnom Penh in a light, pastel frock and looking as if she were about to attend an afternoon tea party, was flying in to see her Khmer fiancé.

His name was Suor, she told me. Yem Guech Suor served as a physician, a surgeon at a Cambodian military hospital. Viviane wanted desperately for Suor to return with her to Saigon and take that Air France flight back to Paris.

I told Viviane I too had a friend in Phnom Penh. We resolved to get those we loved out. The end was near.

A few rows back sat a TV crew from ABC News. Irv Chapman and his crew wore helmets with flak jackets at the ready. Viviane and I looked back. We felt positively naked.

On landing I saw good reason for Chapman's caution. Pochentong no longer was the sleepy airport I flew into a few years earlier. It suffered occasional attacks then, but now fierce and frequent artillery fire struck daily. Passengers disembarked and ran a gauntlet of sandbag installations to reach the terminal building.

Senior NBC News correspondent Jack Reynolds had held the fort as sole reporter in Phnom Penh for more than a month.

I was here to "fill the hole" again.

Reynold's nerves—everyone's nerves—were frayed. Since the first of the year, artillery from Khmer Rouge positions across the Mekong River rained indiscriminately on the center of the city.

Unlike most other news agencies, NBC chose not to base operations at Le Royal (renamed the Hotel Le Phnom). Instead we were at a grittier hotel on the main street of the city. NBC and ABC occupied much of the Monorom on Boulevard Monivong. It stood closer to the Central Market and closer to danger. On March 3, a rocket tore into the sidewalk just in front of the hotel. A young woman bled to death at the hotel entrance.

I took a room facing a side street. The windows and small door to the balcony were carefully sandbagged. I peered through the cracks to see a limited view outside.

The hotel also stood closer—only a four-minute run—to the apartment still leased by Soc Sinan.

• • •

Upon arrival, I immediately reached out to Sinan.

Apart from one handwritten thank-you in 1974 for a birthday card I sent, she had not written since Christmas 1972. I last visited her when I delivered my pitiful "can we still be friends" message. Again, I climbed the familiar stairs to the fourth-floor apartment and left a note.

To my pleasant surprise, she had not cut me off. The next day a note arrived at the Monorom. Dinner was fixed for Wednesday, March 12.

She arrived looking exactly the same as two years ago. Despite our estrangement, feelings came pouring back.

Life had moved on for both of us.

She told me—though in very little detail—of her relationship with the MEDTC financial officer and her love for a man she referred to as "Le Commandant." She had enjoyed her month in New York and Washington in 1973.

Walter wanted to marry her. He certainly wanted her out of Cambodia.

"Le Commandant," she said, "is a good man."

When his tour with the MEDTC ended, Walter tried his best to stay connected from Washington.

Sinan guarded her privacy, her secrets well kept. Knowing that I was on delicate ground, I did not want to pry.

She simply said, "Walter has asked me to join him in Washington. He sends me a telegram nearly every week."

"So why aren't you there?" I asked, a note of incredulity in my voice. "You know things are getting very bad here. The end could come anytime. When it does it will come with very little warning."

Sinan turned evasive. "I don't know. I have things to do here."

"Like what?" I tried to keep my tone as neutral as possible.

"I want to get some silver jewelry finished. The silver work in Phnom Penh is very good, wouldn't you agree?"

"Yes, it is. But don't you know how dangerous things have become? I am back because everyone says these are Phnom Penh's last months or even days."

"I know, but we went through this kind of scare last year during the dry season and survived."

"Yes, but it's different now," I argued. "I have just flown in from Saigon. Things don't look good there. South Vietnam looks pretty unstable. If Vietnam is in danger, you're in even greater danger."

Sinan's eyes darted away from mine. "Well anyway, I told Walter I would fly to Washington after the Khmer New Year. I want to be with my family in Phnom Penh for the New Year on April 14. You remember how important the holiday is, don't you?"

A flicker of recognition. I remembered the strong if sometimes naive woman I had known three years ago. Sinan had a stubborn streak. I would wait a few days and try again.

∎ ∎ ∎

Whoever controls the Mekong controls Cambodia's capital.

A big difference now from previous dry seasons was that Saigon and Phnom Penh forces could no longer control the river. The Americans helped ship about 80 percent of Phnom Penh's supplies up the Mekong from South Vietnam. The airlift into Pochentong presented a second lifeline. But aircraft from Thailand could not match the volume on the river. On January 26, 1975, the last large river convoy made its way from Vietnam up the river to the Cambodian capital.

∎ ∎ ∎

As before, actions in Washington and Hanoi were about to determine the fate of both Cambodia and South Vietnam.

On February 14, one of my stories appeared in the *Far Eastern Economic Review*.

> American financial support for the wars in Cambodia and Vietnam are disappearing fast. A U.S. Congressman has filed a lawsuit charging that the Ford Administration was violating the law in giving direct military aid to Cambodia.

President Ford, I wrote,

> was engaged in an effort to scare Congress into voting an additional $300 million for Vietnam and $222 million for Cambodia in military aid for 1975. Previously Congress had approved $700 million for Saigon and $275 million for Phnom Penh.

And I reported a warning from Vice President Nelson Rockefeller:

> "If we don't receive funding, and the communists take over and there's a million people liquidated, then we know where the responsibility will lie."

Unknown to me and most foreign analysts, the communist politburo in Hanoi was debating their options as I wrote my story. The politburo saw President Ford as a weak leader. Nixon's resignation in August 1974 on the eve of impeachment, Hanoi reasoned, removed the element of unpredictability in American leadership. The United States, Hanoi concluded, would not reenter the war. The communist leadership put into motion a plan to reunify Vietnam by 1976, by force.

Commanding general Van Tien Dung moved south. The Paris peace treaty would be put aside for the sake of "reunification." Dung would test South Vietnamese resolve in the mountains of the Central Highlands. He launched Campaign 275 on March 3.

On Sunday, March 9 (the day I arrived in Phnom Penh), Vietnam became the lead of NBC *Nightly News*.

Hanoi decisively violated the Peace Accord. In the Central Highlands, about 100 miles south of where I reported on the second front in "the dress rehearsal" of 1972, the communists closed in on a place called Ban Me Thuot.

Today Ban Me Thuot is a comparatively sleepy city, known for its coffee growing. Then, it was a significant military target and gateway to central South Vietnam. Hanoi attacks closely followed the 1972 playbook. But this time there were no American advisers, no American air support, nothing from the United States to save South Vietnam.

Within two weeks, after ferocious fighting, South Vietnam's President Nguyen Van Thieu ordered what proved to be a disastrous retreat. The ARVN fled in panic. Communist troops cut the country in two. The end of the Republic of Vietnam was in sight.

If Vietnam was in trouble, Cambodia didn't stand a chance.

Days after the start of Campaign 275, a further blow came in Washington. Congress was about to take both Cambodia and Vietnam off life support. Ford failed to muster the votes for more money to stave off defeat—if only for a little longer. Congress years earlier had blocked any further bombing support for Cambodia.

On NBC Tom Brokaw reported what many refused to believe. "If US aid is not forthcoming and Phnom Penh falls," Senator Dewey Benton (Republican from Oklahoma) told Brokaw, "a bloodbath will follow." Brokaw quoted Secretary of State Kissinger as saying negotiation was not possible.

Everyone seemed to be talking about "bloodbath." Even California congressman Pete McCloskey, a longtime opponent of the war, wanted to give Cambodia just a little more time. McCloskey proposed enough funding to maintain support until the wet season in June—and only until then. He suggested June 30 as a final cutoff date for military assistance. At least Cambodians who might face certain death would have more time to leave.

As McCloskey put it:

> We caused a nation of seven million people to lose many lives. We created hundreds of thousands of refugees. We could not have a greater sense of guilt to any nation in the world than what we have done to these poor people. It is for that reason, that sense of guilt, that causes me to think we owe them the best chance of keeping the most number of Cambodians alive.

The congressman's idea went nowhere.

The next day, Tuesday, March 18, I reported for NBC *Nightly News* on the fifth anniversary of the ouster of Sihanouk by Lon Nol and supporters. There were of course no anniversary celebrations.

I ventured out to an island in the Mekong to see the remnants of the Khmer Republic's Naval Riverine Patrol. They could no longer keep the river open. Near the front lines, I interviewed tired, hungry refugees who after so much suffering wanted only peace.

The ring of fire around the capital grew tighter. Khmer Rouge artillery attacks on the city increased in frequency and deadliness.

• • •

Telegrams arrived from Washington nearly every day in March urging Sinan to leave.

Still she resisted.

She was well aware of the city's deterioration. She now mocked the rich people continuing to stage cocktail and dinner parties. She watched wealthy Khmer and Chinese leave the city, flying off to Paris, Bangkok, or Hong Kong.

"The wealthy Khmer are getting their children to France," she told me.

She had not seen her own father, now retired General Soc Sonn, in some time. A well-founded estrangement remained, yet she spoke of him with concern.

"Our family is large, comfortable, but not rich. While many others sold their property to leave, we don't want to."

Sinan's father now lived on a military pension. He supplemented his income serving as an adviser to one of the small local airlines for which Jimmy the mechanic worked.

Sinan told me her father had no intention of leaving. "No foreign nation, my father says, could give him what he loves about Cambodia—'food, language, religion, customs.'"

General Soc Sonn looked forward to his 63rd birthday.

Years later Sinan wrote about her concern too for her older sister, Sithan, with whom she wanted to spend the New Year holiday. "My oldest sister cut back her lifestyle. There were no more servants. She cut back meals for the family. Instead of three dishes, they made do with two. Everything was just too costly."

• • •

On Saturday, March 22, I took Sinan to dinner, for the first time with journalist colleagues—a terrible mistake.

It was a farewell gathering for some reporters who were leaving Cambodia. I am not sure why I invited Sinan. Perhaps I thought if she saw hardened reporters preparing to leave town, it might encourage her to do the same.

But this was no ordinary dinner.

One of two popular diversions among foreigners in Phnom Penh at that time were Saturday nights at Madame Chantal's villa, where attractive Khmer women would serve clients long pipes of opium. Carefully separated in discreet sitting rooms, diplomats, businessmen, and journalists would smoke the night away—into oblivion.

La Pagode restaurant on Monivong offered another diversion, the one we attended: Saturday night couscous dinners. The chef generously laced the traditional Moroccan dish or maybe onion soup with what foreigner clients referred to as the alternative "Khmer Rouge," particularly strong hashish, extract of the cannabis plant. To most, the unique seasoning resulted in only a mild high, enough to relieve the stress of war, at least momentarily. I failed to realize the impact might be very different for the uninitiated.

True to character, Sinan never reprimanded me for taking her to such an event, where she really did not belong. Yet she remembered. Years later she sent me her diary:

It was a goodbye party on the second floor of a popular restaurant. Quality French wine and champagne and toasts all around. But Jim failed to warn me of the hashish cooked in the food. I knew of course in Cambodia, marijuana, hashish, and opium were easy to grow and cheap to buy. Lots of the men on the MED Team used it. It was fun … but not for me.

Just before dessert, I fell and slid under the table. I was so embarrassed. I could not even walk. Jim quickly picked me up and took me out of the restaurant. Dizzy, overcome, confused … I should have seen in that party an omen. If I didn't think more clearly, my future would be in doubt.

■ ■ ■

About a week later, the routine task of filing a television story for NBC took an unusual turn. Our routine was to wrap the film we had shot that day, add a recorded voice narration, place it all in shipping bag, and race it to Pochentong Airport. In the days before videotape, before digital cards, before the internet, all network stories were edited from 16 mm film. Neither Phnom Penh nor Saigon had processing labs or satellite uplinks. Film was processed, edited, and transmitted to New York from Bangkok, Hong Kong, or Tokyo.

If I had any hope of making the air, I must get newsfilm on a plane to Bangkok.

I was late. Inexperience puts limits on speed. A C-130 cargo arrived from Bangkok carrying food. It would carry passengers out to Thailand. With film bag in hand, I rushed onto the plane. In those days, airport security made no attempt to bar a rather crazed foreign reporter on deadline.

I spotted someone willing to "pigeon" my story to Bangkok. I made the handoff. As I turned to the rear door, I heard a loud, sickening thud. I raced to the C-130's exit.

An artillery round had hit the runway. The plane began to taxi to takeoff. I couldn't stay aboard. I had work to do and a dinner planned with Sinan!

The rear cargo door remained open. As the pilot pushed the throttle forward, I jumped.

I landed well but hard, about 10 feet down, and in doing so I sprained my right wrist. Disguising pain and embarrassment, I handed off the "pigeon" information to the NBC producer at the Monorom Hotel and headed down Monivong to see Sinan.

"You did what?" she asked, concern and sympathy written on her face.

"I jumped out of a plane."

Seeing my swollen wrist, she took charge. The next thing I knew we were seated at the office of a local Chinese doctor she knew. Sinan always knew how to take care of other people. If only she would take care of herself. The doctor had my lower arm encased in a cast in no time.

Sinan and I laughed about my clumsiness.

Meeting the Chinese Khmer doctor made me think of Viviane Chapuis, the woman on the plane, and our pledge to evacuate from the city those we loved.

The next day, I looked in on Viviane and Suor at their small apartment not far from the Central Market on Street 136.

Suor was a handsome, smart, soft-spoken Khmer. He had just come back from a grueling day at Preah Monivong military hospital, north of the Wat Phnom.

Every day proved a grueling one for the people there. Given the limited facilities, medicines, doctors, and nurses, the hospital was overwhelmed. Suor voiced a deep commitment to care for the war wounded. He had graduated from the University of Phnom Penh's school established as the Royal College of Medicine after the French left in 1953.

In 1970 there were about 520 physicians in Cambodia—about one doctor for every 2,000 people on average. Such numbers were not unusual for a poor country. Twenty-nine hospitals with nearly

7,000 beds served the nation. Seven hospitals were in Phnom Penh.

After eighteen months of war, only thirteen of twenty-nine hospitals were still open. Yet war casualties increased demand for beds by uncounted numbers.

After the Khmer Rouge took charge, the number of Khmer physicians dropped drastically. About 500 practiced in Cambodia in 1975. Four years later, the radical communist purge would leave only forty-five Khmer doctors in the entire country.

Viviane was clearly worried. To get Dr. Suor out of Cambodia would not be easy. Cambodia needed doctors. Suor and Viviane needed papers. He was on active duty. Viviane would work relentlessly on behalf of Suor, though she would ultimately fail.

■ ■ ■

Like many others, Sinan was confused by what she heard about life in rural areas. Khmer Rouge brutality, she would discover, had been practiced in the countryside for three years. In the capital, Sinan listened to radio broadcasts of Sihanouk from Beijing. The figurehead president, the friendly face of the communist-led movement, lured his countrymen into a false sense of security. Sinan wrote later that she was among those fooled:

> I had not been to the countryside in a long time. Most of the areas like my home village were occupied by the communists. I knew my mother's family was still in Thlok Chhreu, but we had no contact.
>
> Sihanouk confused us. He was on the radio—supporting the Khmer Rouge. He said all would be well. Should we listen to Sihanouk? The Lon Nol government banned listening to "communist radio." We did it anyway.

Sihanouk had charisma. A popular leader and the only one most of us had known. Old people loved him like a God. They listened when he spoke. His speeches fascinated me. Sihanouk said life was good in the "liberated zones." There, food was cheap. A kilo of pork sold for two riels. Here in the city—a pork kilo would cost 2,000 riels. Maybe life under the Khmer Rouge might not be so bad after all.

Sinan's faith in Sihanouk and her vacillation puzzled me. After a while I began to see it as she did. She loved Cambodia. To separate from it, she would have to abandon a lifelong lover.

Sinan feared the increasing artillery barrages. A few weeks earlier a rocket had landed outside her apartment building, killing a small boy.

One day I gave her the key to my room at the Monorom. With its sandbagged windows, it might be marginally safer than her apartment.

I came back late one evening and found her studying an older analysis piece of mine in the February 21 edition of the *Far Eastern Economic Review*.

She smiled and said, "You see. You wrote it here. There's hope!"

I saw nothing hopeful in my 3,000 words.

I introduced *Review* readers to Ambassador John Gunther Dean and his hopes for a "controlled solution." Dean, a veteran diplomat, had served in Laos in 1972. He'd been given some credit for brokering an imperfect but lifesaving three-party coalition government. Dean, I wrote, was brought in as a "peacemaker" to replace "a discouraged Emory Swank."

I doubted Dean could repeat his Laotian solution. Conditions were clearly different. In Cambodia "bitterness between the two sides will not permit a Laos-type settlement," I wrote.

I reported how Dean had recommended that Secretary of State Kissinger engage with Khmer Rouge leader Khieu Samphan. Dean felt that, as a member of the politburo, he would have more clout within the communist leadership. Previously US officials had reached out only to Sihanouk. Kissinger ignored Dean's idea, although he had two opportunities to meet Khieu Samphan in North Africa and central Europe.

I ended my piece noting that not much had changed in Indochina. Either by granting aid or by withdrawing assistance, United States policy makers determined the fate of millions of people, as they had been doing for more than a decade. "Life or death in Indochina," the top line on the story read. "Washington calls the shots."

Two weeks after I wrote the piece, I met Ambassador Dean at his residence. Much to my surprise, he praised the article. At least I had outlined what he was trying but failing to do.

■ ■ ■

On March 19, John Chancellor introduced a piece on Wednesday's *Nightly News*. I had Sinan in mind when I wrote it. I showed her the script, though we had no way of seeing the report in Phnom Penh.

Introducing my story, Chancellor said, "Many citizens in the Cambodian capital still behave as if there were no war at all."

I then described a society in denial. My narration covered pictures of university classes meeting as normal, dance and cultural events, and the elite playing tennis or relaxing by the pool at the Cercle Sportif.

I could not believe that in a place under daily attack, mired in misery, and faced with so few prospects, people could possibly display such optimism.

Major Walt continued to use all his influence to get Sinan out. On March 31, he pulled off an extraordinary feat.

John Francis McCarthy, consul at the US Embassy, known to friends as "Black Jack," took his pen to immigrant visa document number 590938 in the name of "Soc Sonan."

If she would just use it now! The immigrant visa was stamped valid until midnight on July 31. Her passport was valid until May 7. She was all set to go.

On April 7, Colonel Bob Barnes raced from the Embassy to Sinan's Monivong apartment. One of Walter's best friends, he had also fallen in love and married a Khmer woman. He had got her on a plane to Washington a few months earlier. Now Barnes begged Sinan to leave with him that very day. Walter had made all the arrangements. Sinan made her excuses. She still would not go.

"And what about my family?" she told Bob.

"I like my life in Phnom Penh. I want to be with my sister for the Khmer New Year. Please, Bob—what difference will seven days make?"

Bob shook his head in astonishment.

"You'll regret your decision, Sinan," Bob scolded. Colonel Barnes left for Pochentong. He boarded his flight to Bangkok alone.

Sinan now was not only stubborn but confused and tormented.

The evening after Bob departed, she sat with me as I pounded away at a news story. She was sullen and unusually quiet.

I looked up from my typewriter. "What's wrong Sinan?"

She recounted her encounter with Colonel Barnes and then suddenly blurted out. "Do I really love Walter?"

An unspoken reality sat in front of her. An unreliable reporter after three years away had flown back into her life. I may not have intended it, but my return had clearly caused doubt, confusion, and pain.

"Sinan," I replied with perhaps a bit too much sternness, "please, whatever your feelings for Walter, don't decide now. Get to America. Decide there. He's done so much to arrange for your departure. Don't delay. We don't know what's going to happen here. It is time to leave!"

She remained quiet, lost in thought. I got up, embraced her.

"I better go home." Sinan turned and left, making her way along the familiar route down Monivong.

I returned to my typewriter.

■ ■ ■

American aid flights still arrived daily from Bangkok. The US sent in 500 tons of rice each day.

In early March, the US Embassy handed out a "USSAG FACT SHEET":

> The United States Support Activities Group, 7th Air Force, Nakhom Phanom Royal Thai Air base in conjunction with the Military Equipment Delivery Team, Cambodia ... are conducting one of the largest airlifts since the Berlin Airlift in 1948–49.
>
> Working around the clock, the personnel are assisting in providing approximately 1400 short tons daily of ammunition, rice, general cargo and fuel.
>
> Although not as large as the Berlin Airlift which averaged about 600 flights and over 5,000 tons daily, the Cambodian airlift, with daily rocket attacks ... has provided an additional challenge to the commercial and contracted pilots who fly the daily missions.

■ ■ ■

On April 10, 1975, Vietnam led NBC *Nightly News*. Much of its half hour focused on Indochina.

John Chancellor read the first lead-in:
> South Vietnam's army is putting up its stiffest resistance since the North Vietnam offensive began. The army is holding fast to Xuan Loc, a city northeast of Saigon. As Don Harris reports, fighting is heavy on the highway between Xuan Loc and a nearby town.

After six minutes on the fighting in Vietnam, Chancellor turned to Cambodia.
> In Cambodia, the Khmer Rouge have moved to within 2 miles of Phnom Penh airport. Insurgents have steadily shelled and rocketed the airport, effectively causing suspension of US food and airlifts yesterday for five hours. The situation on the front north of capital city is critical. Jim Laurie reports.

I reported from my visit to the front lines just the day before, where Cambodian troops fought, still holding the Khmer Rouge back:
> Here on what's called the "north dike" the Khmer Rouge have breached Phnom Penh's perimeter several times this week. In this attack they broke through lines and set fire to a refugee camp before being beaten back. Some experts believe the final assault on the capital could come through this north dike. Government troops are still holding on—shoring up the lines as best they can.

After my report ended, Chancellor went on to introduce a report on Vietnamese orphans from Saigon arriving in Seattle.

He then turned back to Cambodia. Tom Brokaw came on camera reporting on President Ford's upcoming "State of the World" address. The speech, billed as "the most important address of his presidency, would deal," said Brokaw, "with humanitarian and military aid to Indochina."

Chancellor also read what to many were surprising results from a public opinion survey. "A new NBC News poll tonight reveals that a majority of Americans blame Congress for the military reverses now being experienced in South Vietnam."

■ ■ ■

I thought I was prepared for the end of the Cambodia war. I was not.

The morning before my last day in the country I visited the US Embassy. Word of any evacuation plans would be relayed to reporters at the Royal Hotel. Notice, I was told, might be short. I should have bags packed.

I picked up the latest US military attaché office handout, this one dated April 11, 1975. Typed in all in caps, its first page read:

With the defense perimeter of Phnom Penh steadily shrinking, Government forces yesterday, April 10, launched a number of aggressive actions and scored considerable success against communist forces, inflicting, at the same time, high communist casualties.

… the high point of action was at 1630 hours … communist forces, however, remain within three and one half kilometers north of Pochentong airfield … in other actions around the Capital, there was little change in the positions on both sides.

The embassy note concluded by reporting the American airlift of supplies to the capital had resumed. The memo was the last the American Embassy issued.

■ ■ ■

Late on the night of April 11, NBC producer Tom Corpora attended a meeting at the old Hotel Le Royal. I did not attend.

Instead, I had an early dinner with Sinan. I told her the embassy would be making an announcement soon. "Be ready," I told Sinan. Heng, the worried and always helpful NBC driver, took Sinan back to her apartment on Monivong.

I went to bed early. After midnight, Corpora woke me with word. April 12 would see an early start. Washington ordered the American Embassy shut down and all personnel out. The three US networks would go with them.

Diplomats, journalists, key Cambodian political figures, and well-connected friends were asked to "assemble at 0800 hours."

A dozen large helicopters from ships in the Gulf of Thailand aimed to complete their mission by 10 a.m. The embassy would close. Anyone who chose to remain in Phnom Penh would do so at their own risk.

The address by President Ford had made it clear—more support for Cambodia would not be forthcoming. Without the daily airlift of American supplies from Thailand, no one knew how long the Khmer Republic could hold out.

That night saw little sleep at the Monorom. I resolved I would be up at dawn and race down Monivong Boulevard to Sinan's apartment. I would give her a few minutes to pack her things. Then I would whisk her to the American Embassy. To the helicopters. I was certain we could find McCarthy. He had signed her papers. With her connections and mine, there would be no trouble finding her a seat on one of the aircraft.

A little after 6, I looked out my window, peering through the sandbags on the balcony.

A familiar face was attending to his motorbike below. Steve Heder, a fluent Khmer speaker and a stringer for NBC News, was preparing to give away his motorcycle to a Khmer friend.

A student of Khmer Rouge behavior in rural areas, he had advised me weeks ago to make sure I got Sinan out the country.

He shouted upstairs. "The evacuation is on. Things don't look good."

Steve, who would go on to write some penetrating scholarly work on the Cambodian communists, could not have understated things more.

Things did not look good.

I was packed. Two bags contained all my belongings. I borrowed one of the NBC cars. Heng drove me to Sinan's apartment.

Two steps at a time, I bounded up to the fourth floor. The apartment was shuttered. I banged on the metal grating. No answer. I banged again.

Where was she? How could she not be here? I told her to be ready. A choking feeling welled up in my throat. What should I do? I had to be at the embassy by 8.

I pulled out an old business card. I scribbled on the back.

"Sinan—We must leave Cambodia. The Embassy has been ordered out. You must—go. Please get to the Embassy by 10 or get to Bangkok. I will be there."

With conflicted emotions and a sickening stomach, I ran down the stairs, jumped in the car, and headed off to the American Embassy.

Corpora and a two-man camera crew were there ahead of me.

The crew, O'Reilly and Riley, were burly part-time firefighters from Los Angeles. While they had landed in Cambodia only ten days ago, they had the nerve and the street smarts of an experienced team that has been through Los Angeles race riots and California forest fires. For me they were a reassuring presence.

Stan Riley, the sound technician, a few days earlier had presented me a gift: a recording he had made of Khmer "pinpeat" music, similar to what the Javanese call gamelan. Proof that in wartime there still could be great beauty.

His partner, cameraman Dan O'Reilly sensed my distress. My failure to find Sinan shattered my nerves. My inexperience as a television reporter compounded things. Prodding me, O'Reilly steadied me as I struggled to deliver a few words to camera while open trucks pulled away from the embassy. The trucks carried a few hundred diplomats, journalists, and invited Cambodians, making their escape from the increasing chaos of Cambodia.

In silence we made our way a few blocks to a primary school behind the US Embassy.

US Marines secured the schoolyard as a landing zone. One by one, the CH-53 "Sea Stallions" shuttled in and out, carrying people off to a carrier in the Gulf of Thailand.

At the edge of the schoolyard, Khmer children lined up to watch. I was astonished. No one tried to breach the marine security perimeter. No one tried to rush the choppers. The children stood quietly watching what must have been an incomprehensible scene. Big men in helmets, their rifles at the ready, anxiety on their faces, shouted at others to hurry, to run to helicopters. Ambassador Dean became so nervous about an incident marring the evacuation that on the advice of his military attaché, he asked

Marine commanders to order the Marines on the ground to keep their M16 magazines empty.

As it turned out the Khmer, children and adults alike, remained fatalistically calm. Their gaze turned upward as the Americans pulled out.

■ ■ ■

Although I had no way of knowing, Sinan watched the dramatic evacuation from a position less than two blocks away.

The night before, after Heng dropped her off, she took a cyclo to Saorun's home. The once carefree yellow Beetle driver needed someone to comfort her and look in on three-year-old Eric.

"Saorun and Eric were very much afraid," Sinan later said.

A photograph of a smiling Saorun in front of her new house, which she had bought in 1974, betrays none of the tension in the family.

Her husband had left for Bangkok, taking their older child with him. Saorun and Eric stayed behind.

Their new home sat four blocks from the US Embassy.

Hearing the commotion, Sinan left the house and walked down the street to get a better view of what was happening. She wrote later what she saw.

I walked along the Avenue of Liberty. I saw a Cambodian friend of the Commander. "The embassy," she shouted to me, "is leaving."

A large crowd stood in front of the marine guard house. Most of the people were from the neighborhood nearby.

As helicopters flew overhead, most of the crowd across from the embassy remained calm. They were not anxious to leave.

Just after 10:00 I noticed a man from the embassy come out and board what appeared to be one last truck.

I knew the man. Walter had identified him a year ago as the CIA station chief. Walter said he would be the last man out. Once he was gone, it would be over.

After the last helicopter disappeared over the tree line, a round of artillery crashed into the embassy area from the east side of the Mekong.

Sinan ran to find shelter.

I kept running. Back to Saorun's house. Streets were now empty. Then I heard more rockets … dropping like rain. Saorun was crying. Eric was hiding in a cupboard.

It was noon. We had lost our appetite after what we had seen that morning. I remained at Saorun's house for much of the afternoon.

■ ■ ■

On board my helicopter, a wave of guilt swept across the aircraft. Hardened journalists, diplomats, and military men shed tears. I was not the only one who had left people behind in a nation we loved.

Neil Davis sat with his CP-16 camera cradled in his arms. Sullen and depressed, he did not attempt to raise it. In the five years I had known the always active Davis, I had never seen him like this. He had developed close ties in Cambodia after moving to Phnom Penh.

Neil told me later, "I just could not bear leaving the city. It had become my home. So many friends left behind." He took few of his possessions from his apartment on Monivong, where he had lived for three years. Devastated, Neil stared blankly ahead.

Almost by reflex, and no doubt to take my mind off what was happening, I pulled out my small film camera. I aimed it out the window of the CH-53, leaning down to get a last shot of Phnom Penh.

The golden steles of Phnom Penh pagodas, glistening in the morning sun, fast disappeared beneath the rotor blades. I put the camera down, slumping into my seat.

■ ■ ■

The United States dubbed the evacuation Operation Eagle Pull. Marines handed out one-page safety instructions: "General Procedures. No Smoking. Keep your seatbelt fastened."

The cheerful Madison Avenue tone at the top of the brochure irritated me:

WELCOME ABOARD MARINE HELCOPTER INC (Flight 462)

Non-Stop to the Gulf of Thailand

You are aboard the most sophisticated helicopter in the world—the CH-53.

The Pilots and Crew of this aircraft are the most professional and highly trained known to man. We hope you enjoy your flight. Estimated time en route to the Gulf is 1 hour and 10 minutes... For the Pilots and Crew of HMH-462 we say again: WELCOME ABOARD.

We flew to the USS *Okinawa*, an amphibious assault carrier ship fitted to carry twenty-six helicopters. I jumped off the chopper onto the ship's deck.

I looked around the deck to see other landings. There were some Khmer among them. Might it be possible? Might Sinan have gotten on a helicopter without me seeing her? She knew Black Jack McCarthy. Where was he? Maybe he got her onboard. Maybe, just maybe.

I spotted a glum Ambassador Dean in suit and tie, American flag folded in his arms, disembarking another helicopter. He looked as miserable as I felt.

As soon as I was assigned to ship's quarters, I began to write my NBC piece. I summoned every bit of concentration.

I concluded with this:

> The Americans clearly prepared for the worst in this evacuation. The fear of panic as seen in Vietnam was uppermost in their minds. As it was, the Cambodians took this evacuation as they have taken the whole five-year war ... with fatalism and resignation. After five years, the US leaves the Cambodians to work out their future without American help.

One of the ironies of NBC and television news in 1975 is that my report, which producer Tom Corpora skillfully dispatched to Bangkok for satellite transmission, did not make it onto NBC *Nightly News* on April 12.

April 12 was a Saturday. In those days, before 24-hour TV news channels and heavier competition, the three networks broadcast no Saturday evening newscast. NBC Radio news aired my reports as usual.

My last television report from Phnom Penh on Friday, April 11 described the Cambodian government's disappointment with President Ford and his failure to get more aid from Congress. I noted that while the military situation remained critical, the Khmer Republic army was still staving off communist forces advancing from the north. They would fight on, I wrote.

By Monday, Cambodia was news no longer. Chancellor led Monday's *Nightly News* with debate within the Ford administration on how the *next* evacuation should be carried out—evacuation of Americans from Vietnam.

US Marine commanders had prepared for a helicopter evacuation of about 600 people from Cambodia. They were meant to include 146 Americans including Khmer with US citizenship, 444 Cambodians and other nationalities.

The actual name list revealed many more could have gone but didn't. Operation Eagle Pull rescued 84 Americans and only 205 Cambodians and other nationalities. At least another 239 Khmer, including Sinan, could easily have gone.

Dean offered seats to all the prominent Khmer Republic leaders who remained. Prince Sirik Matak, who led the plot against Sihanouk in 1970, declined the offer, as did the acting Cambodian Chief of State, Prime Minister Long Boret, who remained behind with his wife and baby daughter. "Marshal" Lon Nol had resigned and left Phnom Penh for Hawaii on April 1.

Only the little-known Saukam Khoy, the acting president for twelve days, and his family joined the evacuation.

As one of his last acts before the Americans departed, Sirik Matak addressed an emotional letter to John Gunther Dean. The letter, written in Khmer, French, and English, haunted Dean for the rest of his life.

Dear Excellency and friend,

I thank you very sincerely for your letter and for your offer to transport me towards freedom. I cannot, alas, leave in such a cowardly fashion.

As for you and in particular your great country, I never believed for a moment that you would have this sentiment of abandoning a people which has chosen liberty. You have refused us your protection and we can do nothing about it. You leave us and it is my wish that you and your country will find happiness under the sky.

But mark it well that, if I shall die here on the spot and in my country that I love, it is too bad because we are all born and must die one day. I have only committed the mistake of believing in you, the Americans.

Please accept, Excellency, my dear friend, my faithful and friendly sentiments. Sirik Matak.

Sirik Matak, Long Boret, and others would within a few days be executed by the Khmer Rouge.

On the *Okinawa*, I stared, trying to be inconspicuous, at a small huddle of Khmer keeping very much to themselves. I looked carefully. Sinan, of course, was not among them.

Where had she been? Why wasn't she home? What would happen next?

■ ■ ■

At Saorun's house, the afternoon passed gloomily.

Around 3, there seemed to be a pause in the rocket attacks. Sinan said goodbye to Saorun and kissed Eric on the cheek. They agreed they would try to see each other for Khmer New Year less than a week away. Sinan made her way cautiously back to her apartment on Monivong.

As Sinan reached the fourth floor, a neighbor came out of the door of an apartment two doors down.

"Where have you been?" she asked. "Your American friend came by looking for you this morning. We did not know where you were. He came in a Mercedes-Benz. He looked very worried. He left something for you."

Sinan wrote later:

When I opened my apartment door, I saw it lying on the floor. A simple business card from Jim. On the back he wrote:

"Sinan—We must leave Cambodia. The Embassy has been ordered out. You must go ..."

When I held his card, my hand was shaking. Tears began streaming down my face.

10

Khmer New Year

Saturday evening, April 12, 1975—Phnom Penh

SINAN RECALLED,
I was now very much alone in my fourth-floor apartment. After an hour or so I dried my tears and calmed down. Jim was gone. Walter's embassy friends were gone. I had not listened to any of them. I had to come to grips with reality.

My head was filled with a mixture of sadness, loneliness, and fear.

■ ■ ■

When I dined with Sinan early Friday evening, April 11, she seemed focused not so much on war but rather on Khmer New Year. We talked at length about the importance of it to her.

I became irritated when she said she had to pick up on Monday some handmade jewelry she ordered for the holiday.

"You mean you would risk staying here when it is getting more and more dangerous every day—just for some jewelry? You must be ready to go, Sinan."

Perhaps my tone was too harsh. She paused for a long while.

"No, it's not just my bracelets. It's my family. I want to be with them for the holiday. Just a few more days. I can leave Cambodia right after Choul Chnam Thmey."

I shook my head. I just wasn't sure there was time.

In her denial of reality, Sinan, like many city Khmer, fell back on family, on tradition, on Buddhism, on ritual. These were constants that surely would survive no matter who came to power in Phnom Penh. Everyone looked back on simpler times and a better life. Choul Chnam Thmey was part of that: the Khmer New Year.

The Chinese and Vietnamese (Lunar) New Year in late January or February each year was a celebration of the moon. Quite distinctly, the Khmer New Year, Choul Chnam Thmey—celebrated as Songkran in Thailand and under other names in the "Indianized" states of Southeast Asia—focused more closely on Buddhist traditions. The three days marked the end in mid-April of the harvest and the start of the rainy season. The New Year began on day one as a family occasion, with a big dinner and gifts for all. Day two provided a day to pay respects to parents and grandparents. The celebration ended on day three with Buddhist rituals, including the washing and cleansing of Buddhist statuary.

Sinan would take the risk. She would mark Khmer New Year on April 14 in Phnom Penh.

■ ■ ■

On April 14, I sat in my room at Bangkok's Trocadero Hotel on Surawong Road. I ignored the festival in Thailand. I had flown in the day before from the *Okinawa*.

I turned the radio to the BBC World Service, listened and wondered. Might Sinan find a way to Thailand? Perhaps on a Cambodian military helicopter? Walter had friends among Cambodian officers. How about Vietnam? Sinan knew her friend Khoeun Rigaud now lived in Saigon. I remained in touch with Khoeun. I had not forgotten her letter scolding me for my infidelity in 1971.

■ ■ ■

The BBC reported that Premier Long Boret had formed a new government of generals and planned to fight on. American diplomats in Bangkok still tried to reach out to Norodom Sihanouk in Beijing seeking a ceasefire. There seemed an unwillingness to believe that Sihanouk had no influence over events on the ground.

A dozen or so journalists remained in Phnom Penh, including five Americans who chose not to join the embassy helicopters. Among them was Sydney "Syd" Schanberg, who filed for the *New York Times*. The British journalist Jon Swain, whom I met in 1971 when he worked for Agence France-Presse, now filed for the *Times* of London and stayed as well.

All the dispatches spoke of an eerie calm among "fatalistic Cambodians." Long Boret met reporters on April 14 and even sounded optimistic. He declined to join those who condemned the Americans as cowards, defeatists, and guilty of betrayal.

I found it difficult to believe the city could hold on much longer. Food, fuel, arms had been stockpiled, but how long could they last? Wounded soldiers and refugees crammed into all the city's hospitals. I wondered about Dr. Suor. Was he still patching up poor soldiers under arduous conditions? I knew that Viviane had returned to Saigon without being able to obtain Suor an exit permit.

■ ■ ■

On Khmer New Year's Eve, Sinan tried to prepare for the holiday. Phnom Penh authorities lifted a curfew late in the afternoon.

People needed to go shopping. We Khmer were always optimistic even at the worst of times. We still hoped to have a feast.

I went out to the Market Orussey, a short distance away. I bought some rice—about 15 pounds. Just in case. Many shops were closed. Those that were open sold food at high prices—whatever they could get. I walked home and tried to sleep.

Monday, April 14

The first day of Choul Chnam Thmey arrived. Dawn promised a clear and shiny day. New Year's Day, the happiest day of the year. I was up early and when I went out and looked at people's faces—I could only see sadness and worry in their eyes.

I roused myself to go to my sister's house. I put on a traditional Khmer dress and walked out to the boulevard hoping that some public transport would be working. None was.

I found a cyclo. The driver charged me three times the normal fare. I did not mind.

I arrived at my sister Sithan's home at 10. All my sisters and brothers and their children were there. Amazingly, they had already prepared a New Year's meal. Good, bountiful food for this special occasion.

Before sitting down to eat, we wanted to go out to pray at the Temple of Sras Chak. My mother's ashes were kept at that Buddhist temple, deposited there some twenty years before. We must pay our respects and pray to the spirits of my mother and our ancestors.

Suddenly, my brother-in-law said he had just heard a bulletin on the radio. It warned of more rocket attacks. Going outside would be impossible. We never made it to the temple.

Instead we prayed at home and dined together. To me the food did not taste good. I was too upset and worried about the future of all of us—especially the children. I looked at them. They were simply playing and laughing. Their parents asked them not to be too noisy.

None of the family spoke one word about leaving the country. They were resigned to their fate.

As dusk approached, my sister asked me to stay the night. I politely refused and said I must get back to my apartment.

I made my way slowly home a bit after 3:00. Khmer Rouge rockets began to slam into the city again.

A cyclo driver charging four times the normal price took me home, driving through near-deserted streets. I felt sorry for the cyclo man. He had to work on a very dangerous day to make a living. He took a big risk. I admired his courage.

Tuesday, April 15

The next day of the New Year is usually a day of celebration. A day to go out with parents or grandparents. But this year, the city re-imposed the curfew. Few people went anywhere.

I walked down one flight in my building to visit Srey Peo's apartment. She was a very attractive girl in her early twenties. I liked her. She was married to a man at least double her age. Her husband was an editor at the Ministry of Information.

Srey Peo was joined by a few friends in her small apartment.

She told me that nearly all the information on Phnom Penh radio for the last few weeks was false. The end was coming soon but the ministry would not admit it.

She and some of her friends, she said, were not worried. When the Khmer Rouge took over, there would be family reunification. Most people had relatives in the countryside or in provincial capitals.

Srey Peo said people were happy there. They would be free to go to the "liberated zones" where their family members were.

I thought about what people were saying. I thought that anyone in the Lon Nol army would face trouble. And Srey Peo's husband with the ministry, surely he would not be safe. The Khmer Rouge—I thought—would show no mercy to the regime they had defeated.

April 16 would be the last day of the New Year's holiday. No one would be going to pagodas. Prayers to Buddha would have to be done at home. Most people would remain indoors.

I picked up the English radio station from Vietnam. It reported the war there was intensifying. As to Cambodia, Saigon radio said "the insurgents" had Phnom Penh surrounded and the defenses of the city had begun to "collapse."

■ ■ ■

While Sinan struggled with her New Year's plans, I remained in Bangkok searching for any war news I could get. I met colleagues evacuated from Phnom Penh. We monitored the radio. We shared a gut-wrenching gloom. A number of us who had left behind Khmer friends and colleagues frantically and unrealistically tried to organize a rescue. I added Sinan's name to the list of those in need of evacuation.

For three days starting from April 13, a C-46 transport plane from Thailand flew over Phnom Penh trying to determine whether it was safe to land at Pochentong. It was not. A colleague at ABC News, Frank Mariano, argued emotionally that something must be done. He had served in Vietnam as a helicopter pilot. "I'll take a chopper in to rescue our friends myself."

In the end, of course, nothing could be organized, nothing could be done. It was too late. Mariano and I and others were crestfallen.

We heard the news in Bangkok late in the morning of April 17th. Advance units of the communist insurgents entered Phnom Penh around 9:30. Premier Long Boret resigned. Three governments in three weeks had dissolved. The Khmer Republic established in March 1970 disappeared.

In early afternoon, a brigadier general went on Phnom Penh radio to announce the surrender. He asked soldiers to lay down their arms.

Later on the 17th I heard reports of the first victory broadcasts on Phnom Penh radio. One message came from Khieu Samphan, the man mentioned before as the subject of Dean's recommendations to Kissinger to engage with the Khmer Rouge leader, rather than only Sihanouk. Khieu Samphan, identified as "commander-in-chief," delivered a message to the city.

Khieu Samphan was a name that some among the capital's elite might have known. He stood for elections in the early 1960s to represent a district in Kandal called Saang. In the mid-1960s, Sihanouk drove him out. Khieu fled to the rural north to join other communists. Like others in the insurgent movement, Khieu studied in Paris in the late 1950s. He received his PhD after writing his thesis on how Cambodia must break from global capitalism and rely on "autonomous economic development."

Khieu's statement appealed for calm. The appeal might have been reassuring except that words of an unidentified voice who spoke next were not: "We enter Phnom Penh as conquerors. We have not come here to speak about peace or to talk with the traitors of the Phnom Penh clique."

Soon the Khmer Rouge rounded up all remaining former government leaders.

Among them, I learned later, was Lon Non, "Le Petit Frere," whom I interviewed in Washington in 1974. He returned to Cambodia but did not join his brother when Lon Nol fled to Hawaii. Instead, Lon Non tried to form a small rebel unit and join the Khmer Rouge. The new rulers would have none of it. When he surrendered, he was very soon shot dead.

If there are ghosts at the American Embassy in Phnom Penh today, they are likely to include Lon Non, and perhaps Sirik Matak and Long Boret.

The "new" embassy was built in 2004 on the site of the old French Cercle Sportif. The Khmer Rouge used the club as execution grounds for the remnants of the Lon Nol era. Those who surrendered were killed within days. The bloodbath in Cambodia had begun.

■ ■ ■

Soc Sinan, meanwhile, waited.

On the night of April 16, I felt very exposed in my top-floor apartment. It was raining rockets again. I had no bunker to hide in.

At midnight I heard helicopters again. It sounded like it was over near the Olympic Stadium.

The helicopters Sinan heard were those of the last commander of Khmer Republic forces, General Sak Sutsakhan, his family, and colleagues. They boarded the very last flights out of Phnom Penh to Thailand. They were supposed to be joined by other officials and their families, but the others never made it.

It was a very hot night in the hot season. But somehow I felt cold, a chill. I sat in my apartment with my music, my radio, and my books. What next?

Trouble—yes—but it would not affect me. I was an ordinary person. The Khmer Rouge would not harm me. Besides, we were all Khmer. We were all Buddhists. We were not Vietnamese, Thai, or Lao—people from the outside. Buddhism was a peaceful religion. We believed if we harmed someone, we would be punished, if not in this life, then in the next. There had been no bloodbath when Sihanouk left and the new government came in 1970. Yes, I told myself—difficulties in the beginning, but things would return to normal under a new government as it had in the past.

Thursday, April 17

My apartment was on the top floor in building 602 Monivong. It provided a good location for seeing what might happen next.

It faced the boulevard. An Esso gas station stood to the north and Okha In Street to the south. To the rear—some larger houses owned by wealthy Khmer. From my apartment across the gas station, I had a good view to the north with no tall buildings nearby.

I got up early and turned my radio to the Saigon station, which had news every hour.

They reported that the Khmer Rouge were on the edge of Phnom Penh. I also heard that half of South Vietnam had fallen to North Vietnamese forces and that President Ford was still trying for money for military aid for Vietnam.

I turned to the Phnom Penh radio station. Nothing. Things must be very grave.

At 9:30, I could not contain my curiosity. I put on a sarong and a long-sleeve blouse and walked down to the street toward an old movie theater. Some boys on bicycles approached me. Khmer Rouge troops, they said, had reached the Chinese hospital on Monivong. Others were approaching from the Temple Preah Put Mean Bun. That meant they were less than half a mile away.

Ten minutes later I saw them, my first sighting of the Khmer Rouge ever.

Most were in dark-brown uniforms. When some people cheered them, they did not smile. They stared at us with big round eyes. They seemed so young. Boys. They looked very serious. Some had black trousers with rubber belts. Long sleeves, black hats, the type the Red Army wore in China.

On their feet were the sandals made from car tires just like the ones I read the soldiers of North Vietnam wore.

Around their waists, a clutch of grenades. Over their shoulders—Chinese AK-47 rifles or in some cases even American M-16s, which I guessed were taken from the dead bodies of Khmer Republic soldiers.

The Khmer Rouge walked from side to side down the boulevard. They shouted in Khmer—"Long live the brave revolutionary forces of Kampuchea," "Down with the American imperialists and their running dogs."

As the Khmer Rouge came down the street, small crowds grew thicker. A few peddlers entered the street selling Pepsi-Cola and ice. I bought some and started walking back home.

As I crossed Monivong Boulevard, more Khmer Rouge entered from the south.

I walked up the stairs. I was tired and upset. I was a few days away from my 27th birthday but I felt much older.

I had never been this upset before in my life—not even when my grandparents who I loved very much died or when my mother died.

I placed my battery radio on my lap. I sat. I could hear the chanting outside. I peered through the window slats at the Khmer Rouge victory.

How could the Khmer Rouge have gained victory so quickly? All I wanted to do was to enjoy the start of the New Year. Then I would have left the country. With Jim. Or go to Major Walt. Or maybe with Saorun and Eric.

I was so selfish to think only about myself. I wondered what Saorun was doing now and little Eric. I had not seen them since before the New Year.

I sat alone and burst into tears.

A few minutes later—I stopped crying. I said to myself, I must face reality. There is no way to avoid the Khmer Rouge. They are here.

It was nearly 10. I looked out. More people were standing on their balconies looking at the parade of Khmer Rouge on the avenue below.

I got up walked down to the third floor to see the Reine family. They too were standing in the balcony. By now we saw tanks and armored personnel carriers come down the street. The Americans—the MED Team Cambodia—had given them to Lon Nol's army. Now they were driven by the Khmer Rouge.

Children were happy and smiling. Older people showed grief on their faces.

Srey Peo's husband put on the radio. Revolutionary music. Then an announcement:

"Old employees of the radio station should return to work."

Srey Peo's husband, who had worked at the Ministry of Information and Broadcasting, wanted to stay with his family. He would not return to work.

The voice of the "head Buddhist monk" of the nation then came on the radio. He said that "patriots should remain calm and stay in their houses."

Then back to revolutionary music.

I watched also as people began to react to the Khmer Rouge.

Before the arrival, many people wore colorful clothing. After they arrived, people had changed to simple white and black.

Looking down, I saw a Khmer Rouge soldier waving his hands from the gas station, beckoning the people above to come down to the street.

I hesitantly moved down the steps again, bringing with me my small portable radio.

I listened to the news from Saigon, the FM station in English. It said as of 9 this morning, the Khmer Rouge had taken all of the capital and controlled all of Cambodia.

I turned the sound low but unfortunately not low enough.

"Who has that radio on, listening to a foreign language?" I heard a man shout in an angry voice.

I turned around and saw a young man in his early twenties, wearing black clothes, a Chinese cap, Vietnamese sandals, and a large watch on his wrist.

"If you don't turn that off and listen to Angkar's order, Angkar will seize your radio."

He then aimed his rifle at me with a disdainful, nasty look.

It was the first time I had come face to face with the anger of the Khmer Rouge. It was also the first time I heard a new frightening word: "Angkar."

I obeyed. Shivering, I returned quietly to my apartment.

11

Angkar

A BOLD HEADLINE SPREAD ACROSS the front page of the *New York Times* read, "Phnom Penh surrenders to rebel forces after offer of ceasefire is rejected."

"Rebel forces": exactly who were they? Conditions in the Cambodian capital were such that in April 1975 very few—including Sinan, myself, and most city residents—knew much. The Lon Nol government portrayed them as hard-core communists under the influence or control of the Vietnamese communists in Hanoi.

We knew much about the Vietnamese communists and how they would behave. Their leaders were accessible in Hanoi. Many of us had met with Vietnamese communist officials in Paris or even in Saigon after the 1973 Paris peace treaty.

For the most part, contact with Khmer communists did not exist.

Most people knew only their figurehead—Norodom Sihanouk. Ousted from power with a death sentence hanging over his head, Sihanouk determined in 1970 that he would maintain at least the illusion of relevance. At Beijing's urgings, he cast his lot with the communists.

The only other person some in Cambodia had heard of was the "socialist" professor at the University of Phnom Penh in 1959,

Khieu Samphan. Khieu had stood for elections as a deputy in what passed for a National Assembly in 1962 and 1964. When he emerged from hiding after 1970, it was into top positions within the Khmer Rouge.

Leading radical communists such as Pol Pot, whose name later became synonymous with genocide, were unknown to us in the early '70s.

While Sihanouk provided the public face of what was soon renamed (without a sense of irony) "Democratic Kampuchea," power on the ground rested with the cadre enforcing the commands of what most people referred to as "Angkar."

Sinan had not heard the word before, but she would hear it often and learn to fear it now. Simply translated, "Angkar" or "Angka" meant "the organization." It comprised the governing body of the Communist Party of Kampuchea. The high organization, or politburo, was called Angkar Loeu. For months the names of the members of the politburo were kept secret. On the day of Phnom Penh's "liberation," the only faces of Angkar Sinan saw were those of distrustful young soldiers. As Sinan wrote later:

It was clear looking at these young soldiers that they did not trust us at all.

They walked back and forth and stared. They shouted at people. They called on everyone to bring out and turn in guns or military gear. "Angkar orders you turn in all weapons."

I saw people place rifles, military gear in the middle of the street.

At 3 p.m. exactly, I saw a long procession of people, walking north to south. They carried their belongings on their backs and on their heads. Some had mopeds, some slowly moved push carts. Some had children in small trolleys. They pushed them slowly along.

I looked around. Suddenly even my neighbors were leaving their homes. Many had already packed their essential belongings. Everyone was leaving!

I descended the stairs to the sidewalk again.

I saw a Khmer Rouge with a loud hailer.

"The Americans are going to bomb the city," he announced. "You must get out of the city. You will be gone for three days. Do not take many things. Take rice for yourself, some cooking pots, and mats to sleep at night. That's all! Angkar commands it!"

Many people could not find their family members. The end had come too soon. Government workers from the old regime had no time to return to their wives and children.

The Khmer Rouge repeated their warnings. "Everyone must leave. American airplanes are coming soon. Leave quickly before it is too late."

I listened. But I was confused.

A book I had read about China's Cultural Revolution came to my mind. I also remembered Major Walt's warnings, that the Khmer Rouge were extreme in every way. They could not be trusted.

I decided I did not believe Angkar. I wasn't going anywhere.

I returned to my apartment, closed my window and shutters, and lay down on my bed.

I thought back on all the wonderful times I had had in the city.

Saorun, Khoeun, all the friends. The life I had built since childhood when my grandfather brought me here from Thlok Chhreu.

I liked my job at SONATRAC. I liked the American people I met. I had very few worries. I knew now, I was selfish. I ignored the poverty of my city and my country. I had to adjust to a new reality.

I turned on my cassette player and listened to some French chansons that were my favorites. Then I listened to my American music. "San Francisco" sung by John McKenzie: "If you're going to San Francisco, be sure to wear some flowers in your hair."

It was to be the last time I would listen to my music.

Lying down, I just stared at the ceiling.

Around 4 p.m.—I decided to venture out once more.

I saw my neighbor Bopha leaving with a few bags. Her mother asked me to go with them. They said they were obeying Angkar but would be back in a few days. I thanked them for their kindness but said I was going to stay and look for my sisters. Mme Reine prepared to leave with her husband and children. Everyone looked upset.

I held Mme Reine's hands. She looked deep into my eyes with affection. She said, "I may never see you again, but whatever happens may the spirit of Buddha and the angels of the eight corners always be with you."

On street level, I walked a few blocks south on the street and then turned back. So many people were leaving. A steady stream. How could all two million people in the city be on the road?

Before I could return to my apartment, I was confronted once more by a Khmer Rouge soldier.

"Why are you walking north instead of south?" he demanded.

Again I lied. I would become good at telling lies. "I must pick up my daughter before I leave the city!"

He saw how upset I was and let me go.

It was getting more and more difficult to sneak around as the soldiers were stationed on every corner.

I ran up the stairs to my apartment as fast as I could.

A Malay family that lived down the hall was packing. They said they were going to the French Embassy. They had heard thousands of foreigners and Khmer were going there for protection. They suggested I go but that I must get there before nightfall. I wished them luck and hurried to get inside my apartment.

As night fell—it seemed only three of the twelve apartments on my floor were still occupied. Myself and two others. Each retreated into our private worlds.

I ate a little food, I turned on a big fan, I lay down again.

At 8 p.m. … April 17, with the sound turned down, way down, I listened to the Voice of America.

I kept the shutters closed, lights off. I did not want the KR to see me. I tried to sleep.

■ ■ ■

In Bangkok, I continued to monitor Cambodia as best I could. The last international news transmissions from Phnom Penh went out a little after 1 in the afternoon from the old post office (PTT) where I used to file my radio stories. The PTT did not open again for more than four years. The Hotel de la Poste and La Taverne, where Sinan and I had often dined, across the street never reopened.

■ ■ ■

On Friday, April 18, hiding in her apartment, Sinan finally began to pack her belongings. She carefully placed three suitcases on her bed and began sorting clothes.

I put a silk sampot, dress pants in one. I arranged more practical country clothing in the second. I put all my French-made clothing in a third valise.

As the sun came up, I looked out the window.

People still streamed down the Avenue leaving town. Some even walked their pigs. I saw people on hospital trolleys with tubes of serum still clinging to their bedsides being pushed along.

No one seemed to pay attention to anyone else. Everyone appeared consumed with their own crisis.

I saw a line of Buddhist monks. They were being forced to march out of the city from the temples. What was happening? We were Buddhists. We did not mistreat monks!

At 3 p.m., Bopha returned. She had left yesterday.

"I must get more food, mats, and mosquito nets," she cried. "The KR soldiers lied. We reached the outskirts of town at Kbal Thnal and were told to keep going. You will never go back, the family was told. I had to sneak back. I must return to my family, to help them."

I shook myself back to reality. I continued to pack. I sorted through my mail. I had a full drawer of letters, most from Walter—my "commander" whom I did not obey.

I selected a few important letters. I must throw the rest away. My life depends on it. If the Khmer Rouge find these letters from a foreigner, an American military man, I'd be doomed.

I put them all in a large brown bag. I looked outside and quickly raced down the stairs to street level. I ran around the back of the Esso gas station. I remembered there was a wide drain for refuse at the back. I quickly got rid of the bag, the letters, the memories. I looked around to see if anyone noticed. No one had.

I raced back upstairs. It was 5:00.

I saved a few items and carefully hid them among my things.

I kept my school diploma, my entry visa to the United States, an air ticket, a reference letter from SONATRAC, a few pictures of America, my old Larousse French dictionary, and the business card from Jim, on which he had written that last note to me.

Then—I got carried away. I wanted to keep my favorite books.

I packed another small suitcase.

My father had written a book in French called *Life Is for Struggle*. It portrayed his military career and his strict outlook on life.

A small book by Dale Carnegie in French, *Comment se faire des amis, l'art de reussir dans la vie*. And one by his wife, *Comment aider son mari a reussir dan le travail.*

Now I had five suitcases. I know, too much! But what do you save of your life?

I looked out the window. On the second day after the victory of Angkar, the city had died. After dark, it was a city only of sounds.

Electricity still operated but there were few lights.

At about 9:00, I could hear soldiers moving about in the big houses next to my apartment building.

I could hear the soldiers, breaking things. Destroying, tearing things up. I heard a window shatter. Then I heard laughter. They burst into song—revolutionary songs.

Occasionally I heard shots fired. I think into the air.

They also broke into a neighbor's car that had been left behind. A white Renault. Somehow they managed to start it and I heard them just driving around near the gas station.

I tried to eat. I tried to sleep. Most of all I just tried to keep quiet.

At night, I decided I would use only one small candle on the floor. I would not cook in the kitchen nor add spices to my food. The odors could attract attention. When I flushed the toilet early in the morning, I was afraid I would be heard. I lived this way for one more day. Prisoner in my own apartment.

■ ■ ■

On Sunday, April 20, as she wrote later, Sinan's situation suddenly changed. She had defied Angkar's orders. She had remained in her home while most people left the city. The soldiers began conducting a house-to-house search. They broke locks and doors, wantonly destroyed property, and stole what they thought might be useful. They waved their AK-47 assault rifles left and right, up and down as they walked down the streets.

As the Khmer Rouge shot the bolt on the door and entered her apartment, Sinan cowered by her bedside and feared she would soon be dead. Two soldiers aimed their rifles at her head.

I was in that world just in between life and death. I prayed to be spared.

They shouted—"Put your hands down. Don't pray to us. There is no prayer in revolution. We are all equal! Why are you still here? Everyone else has left, evacuated to the countryside."

Overcome by fear, I tried to concentrate. I tried to answer their questions.

I said I was ill. "I just got out of hospital a few days before liberation. I hoped my family might pick me up."

They listened but kept their rifles on me.

They asked me where my husband was. I said he had left me and gone abroad. They grilled me on my illness. I then thought of something.

I had had an operation a few years back. There was a scar on my abdomen.

So I said I had had serious surgery and showed them the scar. They clearly did not know a new scar from an old one.

They seemed to have a moment of pity and then launched into an attack on my "husband."

"You must be a rich capitalist. Otherwise your husband could not go abroad. The poor cannot afford to go anywhere. They only work. The capitalists just get rich."

I made no reply.

They finally put their rifles down.

I looked at the soldiers. I made an observation that was to help me later. The soldiers did not wear the same uniforms.

While both wore what we called Vietnamese sandals, they were different in other ways.

One was younger and wore long black cotton trousers with a rubber belt. He had a black long-sleeve shirt and wore a Mao Zedong–style hat.

The older soldier wore military green, not that different from that worn by the old Lon Nol army. He had a dark-green Chinese hat.

The young soldier dressed in black was about 18 years old. He spoke with an accent common to the southwest of Cambodia. He had little education.

The older soldier dressed in green was perhaps 25. He seemed to have some education, but I could not place his accent.

I later learned that the black uniformed Khmer Rouge were from the southwest region. Originally from Kandal, Takeo, or Kampot, these young soldiers were known for their cruelty and were considered the most pure in communist ideology.

Those dressed in military green were from the eastern region—east of the Mekong River. They were considered better educated, more tolerant.

The one in the black uniform did most of the talking, most of the threatening. It was clear he was the one who could shoot me.

When I thanked him for not shooting me, he said, "Don't thank us, thank Angkar. But you and your kind must pay for being slaves of imperialists."

The young man in black suddenly turned and left my apartment to batter down the next door.

Then I asked the soldier in green, who seemed slightly kinder, about the instructions of Angkar.

"I was told that the people would have to leave the city for only three days," I said. "But now it is day four and no one has returned?"

He did not admit those instructions were lies. He simply said, "Angkar wants to make people feel more comfortable in leaving their homes. In fact all people will have to resettle in the countryside and grow rice. People in the city had life too easy for too long. People in the country had to hide in bunkers, leading miserable lives under the constant bombardment of the Americans and their B-52s."

"We have expelled the US imperialists," he said. "Now it is your turn to work for the revolution."

I asked him if I could stay here and wait for my sisters. He said, "Your sisters cannot come here. Everyone is outside the city. They will not be allowed back in."

Then he asked, "Where is your hometown?"

I told him it was Thlok Chhreu in Kampong Cham Province.

"Leave the city," he advised. "Try to go there, where you may have relations."

"Go, take everything you can. Don't leave things here. You will never come back to this apartment again!"

I quietly asked more questions. Who could stay in the city?

"Only revolutionary soldiers and officials of the new Angkar government."

I said I was a secretary in a national corporation. I could help.

He said simply, "According to Angkar's plan, we are not to use anyone from the old regime. We will train our revolutionary patriots to be better workers than those of the old feudal and imperialist regime!"

"You better leave soon. You will become a farmer for the rest of your life. Pack and leave now," he warned. The soldier in green then turned around. He disappeared through my broken door.

I now knew I had to get out. I heard the soldiers break more doors, more locks. I peered out my broken door. I saw them looting whatever they wanted—watches, radios, cassettes and players.

I had delayed as long as I could.

I repacked once more. Took a small pack and stuffed the best of my jewelry, some foreign currency which I had hid inside the water tank in the toilet, and a few of my most important letters and documents.

I looked at the five suitcases I had already packed—days ago. I wondered how I could carry them.

I walked to the ground floor to look for a cart or a trolley on which to put my bags.

Next door was a pharmacy. There were a dozen Khmer Rouge soldiers seated on the pharmacy counter. They had turned on the fan. They were laughing. Boasting of a brand-new radio and a motorcycle they had stolen.

They looked at me strangely. I was bold. I told them I was looking for a cart to carry things out of the city.

One of the more senior-looking cadre looked around and found a stainless steel medical cart, two shelves, four wheels. He dragged it out and gave it to me.

He told me to help myself to any medicine I wanted from the shelves.

"Everything belongs to all of us, everything belongs to the people."

He repeated, "Take what you need. You'll be traveling to the liberated zone. You'll need these things later on."

So I grabbed the most common medicines—aspirin, calamine lotion, tetracycline, B_{12}, vitamins. All the labels were in French. None of them could read the labels. I am sure they didn't know what I was taking.

When they saw me take off the shelf some French toothpaste, they laughed. I guess Angkar did not believe in using toothpaste.

On my way out, the young cadre who had found me the medical cart called me over.

He noticed I was wearing jeans. They weren't fancy but certainly looked "Western."

"From now on, do not wear that kind of trouser," he ordered me sternly. "You must wear the right clothes. Don't destroy our culture."

I pushed my cart back to the apartment building, to the bottom of the stairs. One by one I brought down my five suitcases and small backpack from the fourth floor.

I walked back up to my apartment for the last time.

I found in a drawer three incense sticks. I arranged my mother's picture on the small table by my bed. I lit the joss sticks. The trace of smoke glided upward. I prayed to Buddha. I looked at my mother and prayed for her help, prayed for her blessing.

12

Vann, Saorun, and Eric

LESS THAN A MILE and a half north of where Sinan cowered from two Khmer Rouge soldiers, three days of dramatic and ugly scenes turned uglier.

In the late afternoon of April 17, Angkar commanders decided to shut down the hotel once known as Le Royal.

Large white flags and red crosses adorned the front of the old French-built hotel.

More than a thousand people were holding out there. With nowhere else to go, much of the foreign community gathered as the International Red Cross and other humanitarian workers struggled to care for hundreds of war wounded, both soldiers and civilians.

The Geneva-based International Committee of the Red Cross declared the hotel a neutral zone. Elsewhere, in other wars, such an ICRC declaration offered protection.

The radical communists did not respect neutrality. The Khmer Rouge recognized neither the ICRC nor the diplomatic rights of foreign embassies. Armed Khmer Rouge soldiers rampaged through the hotel compound.

They forced all Khmer citizens out. At gunpoint, these too joined the mass exodus to the countryside.

The foreigners in the hotel compound decided to seek the security of the French Embassy further along on Monivong Boulevard. Some Khmer went with them. A sad procession walked north.

Jon Swain for the *Times* of London, who arrived a few days earlier on the last commercial flight in, wrote, "An unthinking madness was taking over."

Syd Schanberg of the *New York Times* saw from the walls of the French Embassy a "peasant revolution." As he gazed outward he realized "the Khmer Rouge are turning Cambodian society upside down."

As of April 18, nearly 2,000 people crammed into the French Embassy. Sinan's friends were among them.

Vann, the hairdresser Sinan had befriended, pushed her American airplane mechanic lover to go to the embassy on April 18.

Overcome by the chaos and brutality they were seeing, Jimmy began to drink heavily. Realizing the life he loved was coming to an end, he consumed anything he could get his hands on. He fell into a drunken stupor. Vann gathered all Jimmy's things, found his American passport, awakened him, pushed, and cajoled. The two struggled to the gate of the embassy late in the day.

Vann, however, had an additional problem. She and Jimmy had lived together for nearly five years but never married. Vann, a Khmer, had no marriage certificate, no American citizenship, no papers, no passport.

Without hesitation, Khmer Rouge cadres split up couples, split up families, showed little concern for orphaned children. Absent foreign passports or the right papers, the communists forced the expulsion of any Asian-looking person from the embassy. French diplomats could only voice feeble protests. The "peasant revolution" lacked sympathy for "city people" and cared nothing about diplomatic niceties.

Subterfuge became Vann's only option. With the help of Schanberg, Vann hid in the embassy.

. . .

Sinan's best friend with whom she had spent the night of April 11 nearly did not make it.

Saorun Ellul and her son Eric remained at their new home near the American Embassy. As Sinan braved rocket fire to watch the American evacuation, Saorun hid with her tiny son, seeking shelter in a closet.

Estranged from her husband, Saorun had stayed in Phnom Penh while Jean Ellul took their older son and flew to the safety of Bangkok a few weeks earlier. Saorun told Jean what Sinan had told me. She wanted to stay in Phnom Penh for the Khmer New Year.

On the 17th, Khmer Rouge troops marched by her house. Within 24 hours Angkar ordered everyone in the neighborhood out at gunpoint. She gathered up Eric, their French passports, and what food and clothing she could quickly find. Saorun packed everything into the little yellow Volkswagen Beetle, the car in which she, Sinan, and their friends had so happily cruised around the city a few years earlier.

Late in the day, Saorun raced first to find her parents and two cousins who lived nearby. With the terrified group inside, she slowly began driving northward, out of town in the direction of Route 5 toward Battambang. At times her way was blocked either by other desperate people on foot or bicycle or by soldiers waving AK-47s menacingly.

As she drove, she watched the "revolutionaries" loot once-beautiful Phnom Penh, street by street, house by house.

On the outskirts of the city, the little Volkswagen sputtered and stopped. Saorun had run out of gasoline. Her family began to push the car forward with all their possessions inside, slowly, ever so slowly.

Saorun watched those around her—a horrific procession leaving the city. Later she told me she thought of them as "walking dead."

She kept thinking, where would they go? Where could they find a safe place to stay? Eric fidgeted in her arms.

Suddenly out of nowhere appeared a young man on a red motorcycle. They were nearly 4 miles north of the city.

Saorun's days as a much-loved schoolteacher then yielded an unexpected result.

"Teacher, Teacher, is that you?" the young man shouted.

Saorun could not remember his name, but the face seemed familiar.

"I was in your class many years ago! Don't you remember?"

"Of course," Saorun replied, without really remembering.

"Where are you going, teacher?"

"With the people, with everyone else, to the north. Angkar has ordered it."

"But you are French, are you not? Your husband is French, no? Come with me!"

A few minutes of hesitation: Only Saorun and little Eric had French papers. The rest of the family would have to stay and go on to the countryside.

"For Eric's sake, you must go," urged Saorun's mother.

After tearful goodbyes, the family continued on, slowly pushing the yellow car with their belongings inside.

"Hurry," shouted the young student. "We have to go back, back into the city."

Saorun, holding Eric in her arms, jumped on the back of the red motorbike. The student set off, speeding south toward the French Embassy.

As they raced along, it soon became apparent that the Khmer Rouge were erecting roadblocks to prevent reentry.

Saorun's student thought quickly. He drove off the main road and managed to navigate a series of back alleys and narrow dirt paths out of view of the roadblocks and checkpoints. The young man maneuvered his bike skillfully to the northern end of Preah Monivong.

At the embassy gate Saorun recognized Francois Bizot, a French ethnologist who knew her husband. Bizot quickly ordered the gate opened and pushed Saorun with Eric through to the safety of the grounds of the French mission.

With not much more than a nervous smile and hands cupped together in the usual Khmer expression of greeting or farewell, the young man on the motorbike rode off and disappeared. Saorun would never see her student again. She blamed herself for not being able to remember his name. Saorun also lost family members to the "revolution." She was never reunited with her parents after that tearful farewell on the road out of town.

■ ■ ■

By the time Sinan said goodbye to her apartment after her near-deadly encounter with Angkar, a heartbreaking situation had developed at the French Embassy.

The Khmer Rouge began ordering anyone without a foreign passport be expelled from the overcrowded compound.

Saorun and Eric were safe but Vann's decision to stow away under Jimmy's and Schanberg's protection was risky, a risk all agreed was worth taking.

Within a few days, the Khmer Rouge forced most Cambodians out of embassy protection. They separated mothers from babies, husbands from wives.

Supplies ran low in the embassy. The French government put an airplane on standby in Bangkok. Officials pleaded with the Khmer Rouge for landing rights at Pochentong.

The new rulers refused, claiming the airport was not secure. Yet several planes from Beijing with top communist officials arrived at Pochentong during the week.

Eventually, the agents of Angkar arranged to send everyone in the embassy to Thailand in two slow-moving convoys of open army trucks. The Khmer Rouge ordered the convoys to travel backroads and wartime trails to avoid the main highway. Hundreds of thousands of people still clogged the main route to the northwest. Hungry civilians expelled from Phnom Penh trudged slowly forward on a tragic death march toward Angkar work camps.

In the first week of May, after a three-day journey, two groups of refugees including 656 French citizens and 390 people of other nationalities staggered across the bridge at Aranyaprathet to the safety of Thailand. Among them were Saorun and Eric.

And Vann, the stowaway? As the convoy moved out, she crouched beneath the feet of Schanberg and Jimmy, covered by blankets. The all-seeing eyes of Angkar fortunately failed this one time. The cadre never looked under the feet of the Americans.

As with many later survivors of Khmer Rouge genocide, the ability to hide in plain sight proved essential.

When I learned later of the French ordeal, I asked myself what would have happened if Sinan had gone to the embassy. In all likelihood, the American paperwork drawn up by Black Jack McCarthy would have failed to work. The exposure of her

American connections would have put her in more danger—even greater than what Sinan now faced as she finally moved out of her little apartment on Monivong into a precarious future.

13

New Friends

Mid-afternoon, Sunday, April 20, 1975

SINAN STEPPED OUT into the heat of day. Painfully she pushed her pharmacy trolley across the empty Esso station lot. She turned south. She tired easily.

She stopped and looked back at the top floor of her abandoned building. All around her, she saw the agents of Angkar searching every house, every store. Incredibly, four days after the ordered expulsion, at least two million people had disappeared. The streets were largely empty.

I just kept walking and pushed. Soldiers stared at me, surprised that anyone remained in the city.

I learned a lot about the Khmer Rouge that fourth day after their "liberation." I learned they were thieves, they lied, they broke into homes, they took people's things and had no feelings for city people, or perhaps for anyone.

Before their victory, I used to admire their courage and their struggle to eliminate what I saw as a corrupt regime—that of Lon Nol. I used to listen to their radio broadcasts. Through Sihanouk's voice on the radio, they portrayed themselves as reformers who treated people well in liberated areas.

I learned to believe only what I could see. Believe actions not words. I had been a trusting person. I was no longer.

After pushing my trolley awhile longer, I noticed a small medical clinic. The door was open. I peered in. I could see many patients had left in a hurry. Bits and pieces of hospital equipment lay strewn about.

The Khmer Rouge had already been here. They had slashed mattresses and turned things upside-down in each room. Perhaps they were looking for weapons or maybe gold or other valuables. In the laboratory, all the serum bottles were broken. Instruments, needles, catheter tubes were scattered here and there. I could see blood on the floor. It was very quiet.

Then I smelled something cooking. It was nearly 5 p.m. I made a bold decision.

I walked upstairs and discovered two people huddled around some hospital beds pushed together.

A boy of about 12 lay on one bed. He had a tourniquet around his left leg. He had very dark skin, dark big eyes. He looked frightened and confused.

Next to him was woman in her 60s. She was slim with lighter complexion and curly hair. She looked at me with deep sadness in her eyes. I could tell she had not slept for days.

We spoke. She said she was the boy's grandmother. Her name was Kunthea. I told her I lived not far away. She seemed kind and friendly.

I decided to drag my cart into the clinic and stay the night.

I was taking a chance. I simply prayed the same soldiers who found me in my apartment would not find me here.

After I gathered my things, the three of us had dinner. I cleaned up afterwards. The woman seemed glad of the help.

We spoke after dinner. Kunthea had been here in the clinic since April 16. Her grandson's leg had been crushed in a bicycle accident. They lived on the outskirts of the city. Her daughter was supposed to come and pick them up. She never came. I told her that it was likely the Khmer Rouge would not let her. Kunthea looked down. She had no idea where her daughter might be. She told me what happened next. One by one people left the hospital. The doctors and nurses were ordered out. Patients who could walk left because there was no treatment and little food.

With great difficulty Kunthea and her grandson moved from place to place in the clinic. She found rice and meat in a refrigerator on the top floor. They hid. Somehow, they eluded Khmer Rouge soldiers.

There were a few others in the clinic.

A young man, maybe 25, wearing a dark silk sarong and a white T-shirt said his name was Sam Nang. He had a badly injured leg. He told us he was a member of the old city police department. He very much feared for his life. There were two more wounded men on the second floor. Both in bad condition. We were not doctors, but at least we could feed them.

Kunthea was typical of the Khmer people I knew—kind, helpful. The teachings of Buddha, she said, meant we must help anyone in need.

As darkness fell on the 20th, we decided we should not talk anymore. We were afraid of being heard. I put my mosquito net over me and fell asleep in the darkness.

Monday, April 21

Sinan, Kunthea, and her grandson continued to hide out in the clinic. Around noon they were startled by the arrival of ten Khmer Rouge soldiers.

"Why are you still here?" the soldiers demanded.

Each person provided an excuse. Sinan again showed her old surgical scar. The soldiers left. The small group remained.

Again we cooked a meal. We ate silently.

We could hear the Khmer Rouge singing revolutionary songs loudly across the way at a villa once owned by the Indian Embassy.

I used that time to put my small radio up to my ear. While I could, I wanted to hear the 8 p.m. news from the VOA. The news this day was very bad.

There was nothing on the radio about Cambodia. Vietnam was the headline. An angry President Nguyen Van Thieu had resigned. Thieu had been the leader of South Vietnam for more than eight years, since before I got my first job and went to work at SONATRAC. I found what I heard hard to believe.

Tuesday, April 22

My third day at the clinic. One day seemed like a year. I considered myself lucky. I had good company in Kunthea and her grandson.

Two things happened in the afternoon that would change things.

Around 4, another Khmer Rouge patrol came. This time commanded by a young woman of perhaps 19. She marched in looking at me with jealousy and hatred in her eyes. She had her hair cut short, not much different than the men.

"Comrade," she shouted. "How long are you going to keep your long hair? Don't you know that Angkar expects you to cut it? In the liberated zone no one is allowed to have long hair. You better get that cut!"

I just looked her and nodded my head.

After the patrol left, the Khmer Rouge turned off both the power and the water. I was surprised it had remained on for so long.

I discovered there was still much water in a cistern on the fourth floor, enough water to last a month I thought. There was also food and some beer and wine in the fridge. As the power was off, we'd have to eat and drink quickly. I took everything I could to share with my new friends downstairs. I gave some to the wounded men, who did not look like they were improving.

We made the night a special occasion. We found some joss sticks. We lit them and prayed to Buddha and our ancestors. "Please," we prayed, "come help us and destroy the Khmer Rouge regime."

Then we all ate and drank both beer and wine. I actually woke up with a hangover. I would not have beer or wine again for many years.

Thursday evening, April 24

Sinan and her new friends hung on in the Phnom Penh clinic. It became clear, however, that with electricity cut, she and her small group would soon have to move on. After dark, they could hear young soldiers all around them. As if they were at recess at school, the children of Angkar laughed, broke things, and sang revolutionary songs in the old French-built villas nearby.

Then the laughter stopped. Sinan braced herself.

A group of Khmer Rouge women marched into the clinic. They gave us one final warning. We had to leave by tomorrow. There would be no more delay.

Then one of the girls returned with a flashlight. Shining it in my eyes, she demanded I get out of bed and follow her. I had no idea what to expect. My other new friends could stay. I would be their representative.

They told me to dress quickly. I put on a dark blouse with long sleeves. I took a bath towel and wrapped it around my head to cover my still-long hair.

It was hot outside, but I shivered.

There were no lights outside on Monivong Boulevard. Apart from the soldiers' flashlights, the nearly full moon provided the only brightness.

The Khmer Rouge walked me briskly back in the direction of my old apartment. I looked up. In the distance, I could see the door wide open, my old apartment dark.

The soldiers pushed me forward to the entrance of what used to be the Ministry of Education and Culture. This seemed to be a Khmer Rouge headquarters. Inside everyone wore black clothes. Some sat on the floor.

A man of about 30 sat at a desk. He must have been a commander of some sort. He asked me to sit in front of him. He looked Chinese to me, and when he spoke his speech suggested he had some education. He spoke loudly.

"I want to be clear. You and the rest will leave the clinic by tomorrow. It is totally against Angkar's plan for you to stay in the city while millions are already in the countryside. We know we still have enemies in the city. We must clear them out."

He spoke sternly. I sat like a stone in front of him. He asked about my background.

I told him the truth—at least about SONATRAC where I worked. He knew the contribution the company made to the nation's agriculture. I noted that my company had a reputation as a left-wing progressive organization. Two of the members of the company management had joined the Khmer Rouge in the jungle back in the late 1960s. I also mentioned that two brothers of Comrade Khieu Samphan had worked with me.

My stories made no impression. All people were equal under Angkar, he said.

If we did not leave tomorrow, we would be considered enemies.

"We don't need people from the past. We only need those who struggled for the Revolution.

"It will also do no good to hide your background. Angkar has eyes and ears everywhere. We know everything.

"If you were a man you would be dead! Since you are a woman, we have some compassion."

He wished me luck in the liberated zones. I returned to meet my new friends in the clinic. We started to pack again for our departure in the morning.

Friday, April 25

Early in the morning a military truck arrived, but it was not for Kunthea, her grandson, or for me.

Without a word, they went straight to the three wounded men remaining in the clinic, including the frightened former policeman.

The three were taken roughly away. One screamed in pain. I had the feeling the men were being taken to be killed. We never saw them again.

I started reloading Kunthea and her grandson's things with mine in a larger cart I had found at the clinic.

I also thought it wise to salvage whatever rice, whatever food I could from the clinic. We took cooking utensils as well.

We propped the boy on the cart and set off from the clinic.

Two of us pushed the cart together. We decided to go east and try to reach the east side of the Mekong River. We both had been born on the eastern banks of the Mekong. Perhaps we could go to my mother's village of Thlok Chhreu.

Ten minutes later, however, we were stopped at a roadblock.

"The order of Angkar is that you cannot go east. You must go south!"

Phnom Penh was now a ghost city. The people were gone. The once-beautiful homes, gardens, and streets were cluttered with filth and debris. A stench rose wherever we walked. Dead dogs, cats, other animals lay in front of houses everywhere.

We moved slowly. Grandmother Kunthea exhausted quickly and was extremely upset.

By noon we had traveled less than 2 miles from the clinic.

By 4:00 we had reached an area not far from Saorun's house, where we had last seen each other on April 12.

While my traveling companions rested, I ran to see about Saorun's home.

Her house, of course, was empty and in a pitiful condition. The doors and windows, clothes were scattered everywhere. Clearly the Khmer Rouge had been through it floor by floor. It had been such a lovely place. I wondered where everyone went. Did they get out? Where was Saorun? And my favorite boy—Eric?

I stood outside staring. I dared not go in. I again cried silently and returned to my new friends.

We resumed our slow procession, pushing our cart now down Liberty Street, Preah Sereipheap.

Just before dark, we reached the old US Marine Guard House across from the United States Embassy. I was back to where I had been 13 days before. Back to where I might have made my escape and did not.

The embassy seemed occupied by hundreds of Khmer Rouge soldiers. From the way things looked, this must have become an important military headquarters.

There were trucks and cars moving on the street. A few entered the embassy, checked thoroughly by the soldiers.

The road in front which had been a wide four-lane boulevard had been restricted to two. Big trucks formed barricades near the embassy and other cars and trucks were stopped.

My traveling companion took a mat off the cart and put it on the sidewalk next to the marine guard house fence. We struggled to help her grandson off the cart to lie on the mat. Kunthea asked me to look for firewood so she might cook some dinner.

Firewood was not a problem, but water was. I boldly banged on the door of the guard house. A Khmer Rouge woman soldier answered. She allowed me inside to the first-floor kitchen. I filled up my two-gallon canister from a big barrel in the kitchen.

It was a bizarre scene inside the guardhouse. About a dozen women soldiers camped out here. Short-cut hair, black uniforms, country girls perhaps 18 or 19 years old possessed small packs, a few clothes, a mat, a mosquito net.

They clearly had no understanding of the city. They broke the water taps because they didn't understand how to turn them on and off. The same with the gas stove. What they could not make work, they destroyed.

I asked one if I could use the toilet in the building. They agreed and four of them followed me to watch. I couldn't even close the door. One told me she had never seen a toilet before. She was afraid to sit on the seat. They had never used the bathtub either. It all looked disgusting. Everything was so dirty. They'd be better off bathing in the river.

As I took my water outside, I noticed a large washing machine sitting on the lawn. The Khmer Rouge were trying to figure out what it was.

They had ripped it out of a nearby house. The young women opened the machine, looked inside. They turned to each other. What is it? Some thought it was a stove. No one could figure out how it worked. French-made, there were instructions in French on the side.

One soldier stopped me. I put down the water. Can you tell us what it is and how to use it?

I told them I had never seen such a machine before.

Of course I knew exactly what it was and how to read the instructions. I longed to wash my clothes in a washing machine. But I sensed a trap. I realized the Khmer Rouge hated city people, hated people with education. If I knew too much, I'd be in trouble. Besides, in a way, it was my revenge. Let them remain ignorant!

I thought back to 1973 when Walter introduced me to other members of his military team. MED Team members sometimes stayed here at the marine house. Perhaps this was one of their washing machines, which they always preferred to the Khmer way of cleaning clothes by hand.

As I carried my water canister away, I heard one of the girls say "Crazy Akaing [slang for what Khmer call Americans]. Whatever they used this machine for—it's useless. Typical capitalists: they own lots of things, worth nothing!"

After the three of us ate, we spread our mats out and fixed our mosquito nets that we had taken from the clinic.

I could not recall the last time I slept outdoors. Two soldiers walked by and asked us if we wanted to move inside the marine house. They said we could stay with them so long as we were on our way to the countryside in the morning. I thanked them and said no.

I was surprised by their kindness. I was also surprised that we had not been interrogated or searched or threatened since we were expelled from the clinic.

I guess three people—a 65-year-old woman, a poor crippled boy, and I—just did not seem threatening to them.

So we were left alone, left to endure their constant singing of revolutionary songs—especially by the men in the US Embassy across the street.

Saturday, April 26

We were up at first light, preparing the cart for what we assumed would be a long day of walking and pushing.

At dawn a big military tanker truck stopped in front of the embassy. I was able to fill our water canisters.

We started off.

We saw an open-back army truck pass by. Much to our surprise the truck stopped, backed up.

A Khmer Rouge soldier who seemed to be in charge asked if we wanted to ride out of town on the truck.

We had no idea where it was going but we agreed.

The soldiers politely carried all of our things onto the truck. While the woman and I rode in back, they even took the small injured boy and let him ride in the more comfortable cab in front.

The truck started up and drove straight south until it reached the junctions of October 9 Road and Monivong Boulevard.

I thought and hoped the truck would cross the Monivong Bridge heading east. Instead it headed to Takhmau, south of the capital toward the province of Kandal.

I quietly said goodbye to Phnom Penh.

As I saw where we were heading, Kunthea and I asked the soldiers if we might get off. We wanted to head east. I wanted to travel to the place where I was born, and Kunthea now wanted to go to Neak Leung. We both sensed that heading east toward Vietnam was a much better idea than going south or any other direction.

The Khmer Rouge said crossing the bridge, heading east, would not be possible.

Their eventual destination, they said, was a district called Koh Thom, still not far from Vietnam. We both agreed to continue on. I thought for a moment that sticking with the soldiers might give me a chance to escape to Vietnam.

In any event, it was rather comfortable on a truck on the highway. I did not like the idea of pushing our cart, laden with all the luggage Kunthea and I had as well as the injured boy.

As we drove, I saw no civilians, only soldiers and military vehicles.

Then well outside the city, I noticed a small crowd. Civilians camped out under the shade of large mango trees.

None of the adults were smiling. Smoke from cooking stoves arose around them. It was difficult to know what they were waiting for. Would they be admitted back to the city or taken elsewhere?

The truck continued on its way to Koh Thom.

At one point the road ran close to the Bassac River. I saw a horrible sight. Dead human bodies were floating on the water, floating south toward Vietnam. With death all around I worried about disease that might affect all of us. Hygiene did not seem a priority for the Khmer Rouge.

Our truck, which contained the three of us and about a half dozen soldiers, stopped to pick up others. They were much more in need than we were. At least the driver had some compassion.

As the sun rose higher, it got extremely hot in the back of the truck. Late April is one of the hottest times of the year.

One scene haunted me for many years. We stopped for a young woman who had just given birth in the outdoors. She looked very pale. There was blood all over her sarong. She clutched the tiny baby, which cried constantly. Clearly she had given birth along the highway with no medical attention. Flies hovered over her, the blood, and the baby.

By the time we reached the district of Saang, the truck was full. About twenty of us, about a dozen children. We passed a checkpoint.

We started up again and then I heard the driver shout. We had a flat tire. We could travel no further. We would never make it anywhere near Vietnam. Soldiers helped us haul all our things off the truck.

We sat on the ground near a military checkpoint.

For the first time—since I had left my old apartment—we were subjected to a search of our possessions by the Khmer Rouge.

I was nervous at first. But then I could see these young boys were looking for only certain things. One soldier said, "You must be an upper-class Phnom Penh person."

I said nothing. He kept rummaging.

"Do you have any men's watches?" he asked.

I did not. Clearly, these boys wanted watches. They asked that of every city person. I recall seeing the cadre I met in Phnom Penh wearing a big shiny watch. The soldier continued to rummage.

Then he found my Larousse French dictionary, my father's memoirs, my music cassettes. I was foolish to put them all in the same place.

He took them all. He also took some medicine the cadre at the pharmacy had asked me to take.

Then he spotted a stack of Cambodian riels. Currency from the old regime.

He laughed. Took the stack of bills and threw them high into the air.

"There will be no need of money under Angkar," he shouted.

I was lucky. I had hidden my truly important papers among my clothes and underwear at the bottom of two suitcases.

The search complete, we were left sitting alone, uncertain of where to go next.

Around 4:30 in the afternoon, a soldier seemed to take pity on us and offered us some food.

He handed us each two rolls. One contained rice mixed with white and yellow corn wrapped in a banana leaf. In a second roll, a banana leaf was wrapped around a piece of fried dried fish. It tasted good. I thanked the soldier for our first meal since early morning.

"Do not thank me," he replied. "Thank Revolutionary Angkar. This is the way the revolution works. People are not selfish as in a capitalist society. If we have food, and others do not, we share. There are no rich, no poor, everyone is equal."

As night began to fall, the soldier who had given us food asked the three of us where we were going to spend the night.

We said we did not know. The soldier asked that we follow him.

And so on Sunday, April 27th, Sinan and her new friends awoke in a new home. A rural commune in the distict of Saang. Sinan would now have to learn how to live under "Revolutionary Angkar."

■ ■ ■

When she put her ear close to that small transistor radio on the evening of April 21, it would be the last time Sinan would hear a foreign radio broadcast for nearly five years. The shortwave signal of the Voice of America faded in and out.

As Cambodia disintegrated on its route backward to "Year Zero," Sinan learned on the radio that South Vietnam was moving steadily toward collapse. Saigon, thought Sinan, sounded very much like Phnom Penh.

14

Saigon: A Plan

WITH A SENSE OF COMPLETE helplessness, I sat in the comfort of a hotel room in Bangkok listening to the radio.

It seemed incredible that a country could be completely cut off from the outside world in the twentieth century. Yet Cambodia was.

My distress and that of others who had friends in Cambodia deepened. The only comfort I could find lay in the distraction of work.

On April 20, I flew to the Philippines. Roaming through newly established refugee camps at the American Clark Airbase, I wrote of the increasing flood of desperate people arriving from South Vietnam.

Late on April 24, I flew from Manila to Hong Kong. At the NBC office at the New Mercury House in Wan Chai, I joined the man who had helped me set up as a radio reporter in Saigon's Visnews office in April 1970. Just twelve days earlier, I had shared a helicopter with him and others fleeing Phnom Penh.

The Cambodia experience shattered Neil Davis. He left friends behind. His apartment in Phnom Penh remained full of his Indochina memorabilia. His career in Vietnam and Cambodia stretched back to 1963.

Not one to sit around and moan, Davis needed to snap out of it. He must get on to his next assignment.

Davis and I sat down. We put together a plan. Of course, my mentor took the lead. We would return to Saigon. No matter what, we would stay. As we looked at a battle map of Vietnam, we knew clearly that the end could not be very far away. Maybe a few days, a week or two—max.

We resolved we would refuse any American helicopter evacuation like the one we had just experienced. No more "Eagle Pulls," no more USS *Okinawas* for us! We would see the war through to the end, to its inevitable conclusion.

For me, the impact of losing Sinan weighed heavily in my decision. Her friend Khoeun lived in Saigon. I could see Khoeun. Perhaps somehow Sinan would find her way to Vietnam. Perhaps I would be given another chance at her rescue.

In addition, I had great confidence in Neil. Whether over beers in Saigon or at his apartment in Phnom Penh, he had always been generous in educating this novice. He had been a great mentor. In turn, although I did not smoke, I bought cigarettes just so Neil could bum them off me. I never knew him to buy his own.

Neil also had an ace in the hole in South Vietnam. He felt he knew the communists who we assumed would be declaring their victory soon.

The Paris Peace Accord provided a rather unsatisfactory cease-fire-in-place arrangement, where communist and Saigon military units were permitted to maintain control of whatever territory they possessed in early 1973.

A number of the deal's provisions seemed unusual. Among them was that a delegation of the Viet Cong, officially known as the Provisional Revolutionary Government (PRG) or National Liberation Front (NLF), was provided a presence in Saigon.

A nearly 200-member delegation including both northern and southern communist military personnel lived in a tightly guarded compound at a place called Camp Davis. The camp formed part of the sprawling Tan Son Nhut Airbase. It had been named many years earlier after James Thomas Davis, an Army Specialist 4, who was the first American to be killed in the American war in December 1961.

The senior PRG officer at the compound was Colonel Vo Dong Giang. He and one of his deputies, a man we came to know only by his nom de guerre, Phuong Nam (which literally meant "man of the south"), met journalists often.

Neil Davis developed good rapport with both. He enlisted their assistance in visiting "liberated areas" of South Vietnam in April 1974.

Both Giang and Phuong Nam spoke good French and some English. They knew the value of the right kind of media coverage.

In Cambodia, by contrast, there was no one on the communist side to talk to. Media? What media? Those who trusted the media-savvy Sihanouk as an intermediary got nowhere. As Neil noted, "Trust Snooky and get snookered."

■ ■ ■

On Sunday morning, April 27, Neil and I boarded an Air Vietnam flight from Hong Kong. We touched down in Saigon three and a half hours later.

We checked into the Caravelle Hotel. We preferred the Continental Palace across the square for its colonial ambiance. But the Caravelle seemed to offer more security in what we expected could be some difficult days ahead.

I scribbled in my diary just after my arrival. "The political situation is deteriorating rapidly. Militarily, NVA-VC forces are closing in around the capital. It shouldn't be long now."

We assessed the risks and compared our conditions to those in Phnom Penh. The Khmer Rouge had essentially imprisoned all foreigners, including eighteen journalists, in the French Embassy. We might become prisoners in Saigon in a similar fashion, but we doubted it.

Over many years, Vietnamese communists had become skilled at handling foreign media. Hanoi officials had invited journalists like Harrison Salisbury of the *New York Times* to Hanoi. They courted celebrities like Jane Fonda and Joan Baez. They understood the anti-war movement in America. The Khmer Rouge had no such sophistication.

Our biggest worry focused on the South Vietnamese military. Bitter, disgruntled, feeling betrayed, Saigon soldiers might lash out, attack any foreigners they could seize. We hoped Saigon would surrender peacefully and the communists would take the city quickly, forestalling a period of anarchy and bloodletting.

That evening, as soon as I could, I left the Caravelle and walked the few blocks up Hai Ba Trung Street to the home of Khoeun Rigaud in the French residence apartment compound just behind the French Embassy.

Her husband, Jean Rigaud, greeted me coldly. He seemed to harbor a fair amount of hostility toward Americans. No wonder. He worked for a French firm. He had recently moved his family to Vietnam. And now his life in Saigon seemed about to crash down around him.

Khoeun, on the other hand, despite her past reprimand, greeted me warmly. We talked for an hour about Sinan. We voiced the unrealistic hope that somehow Sinan would turn up here and we could take care of her.

Khoeun introduced me to the wife of another French businessman living in Saigon—Amy David. Amy said she also knew Sinan. She invited me to dinner the following night. I accepted the invitation, thanked Khoeun, Amy, and Jean, and ran back to the Caravelle. A curfew had been imposed but was not rigidly enforced.

Neil greeted me with news that had broken while I was gone. The South Vietnamese National Assembly had appointed a new president to lead the nation at a "time of grave crisis."

Heavyset and 5 foot 10, retired general Duong Van Minh was known as "Big Minh." Though out of power, he had been a well-known political figure in Saigon since 1963. Big Minh became the second new president installed since Nguyen Van Thieu bid a tearful farewell on April 21. As he departed, Thieu, who had led South Vietnam since 1967, accused the Americans of betrayal. Minh pledged to seek a ceasefire and ways to restore peace to South Vietnam through negotiation.

As in Phnom Penh three weeks earlier, I felt the time had long passed for negotiation. As if to prove my point, six North Vietnamese rockets slammed into central Saigon that evening. One scored a direct hit on the roof of the colonial Majestic Hotel, with its commanding view of the Saigon River. The suite which the Saigon government used to house visiting dignitaries sustained heavy damage.

Monday, April 28, 1975

Neil and I met in the morning at the NBC office on the fourth floor of Passage Eden and examined battle maps, assessing as best we could the state of Saigon's military position.

Conditions had deteriorated overnight.

Since their successful offensive in the Central Highlands in March, the North Vietnamese army had crushed South Vietnamese units in one province after the next. Saigon forces suffered insufficient weaponry, poor leadership, and low morale.

The advantages which had saved ARVN forces and the Saigon government at Easter 1972 were no longer available. B-52 bombers no longer flew from Utapao. No aircraft carriers sat offshore ready to intercede. No destroyers with their long guns could provide direct fire to any point along South Vietnam's coast.

In May 1972, the air armada at South Vietnam's disposal which beat back the communists included 200 B-52s, four US Navy carrier groups, more than 400 additional fighters and bombers, and the latest technology.

In June 1974, the RVNAF, Saigon's air force, on paper looked strong: 60,000 men and nearly 2,000 aircraft of various type, none of them heavy bombers.

Soon after the Paris Peace Accord both sides engaged in a land grab, with short pauses between fierce battles. South Vietnamese resources became quickly depleted and were not adequately replaced.

While American war financing decreased, Hanoi's allies boosted spending.

Still, the speed of the South Vietnamese collapse surprised everyone, including Hanoi's military brass. I interviewed the North Vietnamese commander, General Van Tien Dung, in Hanoi in 2000.

As late as March 10, Dung told me, he did not expect 1975 would produce "our great spring victory," as he had titled his book. Hanoi's planning had targeted victory for early 1976. Only after Saigon troops surrendered most of the province of Quang

Tri without a fight and retreated from the Central Highlands in near-total panic did Dung realize victory was in reach. The politburo gave the offensive a new name: the Ho Chi Minh Campaign. It then ordered General Dung to take Saigon in time to celebrate the birthdate of their first leader on May 19.

As I looked at the map of Saigon at the NBC bureau, I noted in my diary the immediate vulnerabilities on the outskirts of the city: "the 'Newport' Bridge across the Saigon River, Tan Son Nhut Airport, and the route east toward Xuan Loc," where after a fierce twelve-day battle, ARVN troops had finally given up and retreated to Saigon. Hanoi's troops would now be moving very quickly indeed.

■ ■ ■

Neil and I spent about an hour discussing evacuation plans with the NBC staff. Most of the Vietnamese staff had already departed to the Philippines. I visited several of them when I was there.

Three Vietnamese remained. Anyone who wanted out was flying out. NBC had also rescued its Cambodian interpreter from Phnom Penh, while some other news agencies had not.

Two Vietnamese employees decided to stay. Cung, the sound technician I worked with in 1972, declared he would be all right and would stay at home. Nguyen Van Anh, whom I did not know well but who for many years was the "Mister Fixit" of the Saigon bureau, wanted to stay and work. Able to repair anything from an old Auricon film camera to the old Ford van that NBC used for a crew car, Anh would prove essential to Davis and me in the days ahead. A third employee, the office receptionist who delayed her departure for family reasons, planned to leave soon.

American staffing remained heavy. Don Critchfield produced and ran the bureau. Robert Wiener and David Butler handled

NBC Radio. Television correspondents included Don Harris and Don Oliver. George Lewis and Art Lord, for whom I "filled a hole" in 1972, had returned to Saigon as well. Garrick Utley had just departed for Guam to cover the start of the massive evacuation and refugee drama.

US Embassy officials advised Critchfield to reduce his staff to an absolute minimum. A final American evacuation would start soon.

"Critch" agreed to turn over to Davis and me the keys to the safe and its ample stash of US dollars. Someone at the bureau, I cannot recall who, also turned over to me the keys to a small vehicle which I had always cherished. It was a Citroën La DaLat: named for the beautiful hill station and resort of Da Lat. The French had opened a car assembly plant in Vietnam in 1936. In 1970 they started assembling a version of the "Baby Brousse," a wonderful, open utility vehicle that I loved.

Neil and I kept a low profile. Apart from the NBC staff, we revealed to no one our plan to remain in Saigon.

At about 4:30, I walked over to the Caravelle to freshen up. Given what we had just discussed—that the end was near—it struck me as a fairly quiet late afternoon.

I strolled across to the rear of the Vietnamese National Assembly (the old French opera house), took a left onto Hai Ba Trung and ten minutes later a right at the French Embassy to the home of Amy David and her husband at 6 Phung Khac Khoan for an early dinner. Khoeun joined. Her husband Jean stayed home.

I wanted to maintain my psychological connections to Sinan through anyone who knew her. Amy had left Phnom Penh about three years earlier to marry Dominique David, a French businessman who seemed well connected to the embassy.

The French occupied a unique position in Vietnam. France stationed diplomats in both Hanoi and Saigon. Despite their diplomatic access, I felt they were now peddling an unrealistic scenario for Vietnam's future, similar to the "controlled solution" which John Gunther Dean envisioned for Cambodia.

Jean-Marie Merillon became French ambassador in Saigon in 1973, a few months before the American ambassador, Graham Martin, arrived. The two maintained a close relationship right up to the final days. The French and American embassies shared a common boundary wall. A door through that wall provided easy access for the two diplomats. Merillon floated the idea that France might be an honest broker. Based on the Paris Peace Accord, a way might be found to negotiate a coalition government that would provide Hanoi the eventual unification it demanded but save the Americans and South Vietnamese from a humiliating defeat. Most importantly, it would save lives.

The French helped persuade President Nguyen Van Thieu to leave Vietnam on April 21. The departure of Thieu might open the door to a negotiated settlement.

French optimism may have influenced Ambassador Martin. Overruling urgent advice from his CIA staff and defying orders from Washington, he repeatedly delayed the evacuation. The French pursued peace feelers with Hanoi.

The possibility of a negotiated solution provided an animated dinner conversation at the David home on April 28.

"We should exhaust every possibility," Dominique argued. "The ambassador thinks there is a chance."

"It is far too late," I countered. "A 'controlled solution' is no more possible here than it was in Cambodia. I was there a month ago when the American ambassador floated such ideas. Pipe dreams."

Turning to Khoeun and Amy, I let my emotions get the better of me. "This kind of false optimism led Sinan to believe she could stay in Phnom Penh. It's the kind of thinking that got her trapped."

Silence around the table. Then Dominique added, almost in a tone of mourning, "Oui, peut-être, mais c'est aux deux endroits la faute des Américains." Yes, perhaps, but all of this is the fault of the Americans.

As silence set in again, Amy poured another glass of Bordeaux.

The phone rang. A friend had called Amy to tell her the latest news. Saigon radio reported several aircraft had strafed Tan Son Nhut Airbase, shutting everything down.

With the help of a South Vietnamese pilot defector, Hanoi's General Dung had managed to assemble a small squadron of captured A-37 bombers at the coastal airbase at Phan Rang. Five planes flew south to Saigon. Unopposed, they attacked Tan Son Nhut. They destroyed a dozen planes on the flight lines. South Vietnamese troops scrambled. They cleared the wreckage. The airport reopened several hours later, but only for a little while.

News of the attack provided my excuse to cut short my dinner with Amy, Dominique, and Khoeun. With a curfew in place, I ran carefully down near-deserted streets back to the Caravelle.

The next day—April 29—would be a very busy one.

15

"No One Should Be Afraid"

Sunday, April 27, 1975—Saang District, Democratic Kampuchea

AS I WAS BOARDING my flight to Saigon, Sinan and her new friends, Kunthea and her grandson, began their first day in the rural district of Saang. About 25 miles south of Phnom Penh, Saang rests on the banks of the Bassac River in Kandal Province.

It may not have seemed so at the time, but Sinan had much to be grateful for. She had survived close encounters with hostile Angkar cadres. She had gotten motorized transport at least partway into the countryside. Most of the possessions she had carefully packed remained with her. A Khmer Rouge soldier with some compassion fed them and brought the three into a village named Prek Touch in Saang. The soldier introduced Sinan to a "revolutionary" woman, a "base person" named Yem.

A woman named Yem took us in. She was about 30 years old. She wore her hair cut short just to her ears and wore a long black skirt. Under the orders of the local Khmer Rouge chief, a man she called Comrade Eng, Yem allowed us to stay in her small house built close to the ground and made of bamboo and dried palm tree leaves.

Yem explained she was already caring for two evacuees but they were young and healthy and stayed outside in the open air. We could stay inside where she lived with her small son. A kerosene lamp lit the common living/sleeping area. No furniture, bamboo mats lined the floor.

Yem seemed typical of rural women in liberated areas. She had one child, 5 years old. Her husband, a Khmer Rouge soldier, had been killed during the battle for Saang a few years ago. She could neither read nor write but was politically active in the village. She was trusted by all as her background was "pure," 100% Khmer Rouge.

On our first day, Yem spent hours talking or I should say lecturing us. She was very proud of her late husband. "He died for the revolution!" Prek Touch became a "liberated zone" since just after the start of the war in 1970. Yem had worked in the fields in this area since then.

Yem showed impatience with city people. They were weak of body and weak of mind. City women—with their makeup, their painted nails, long hair, and bright, gawdy clothes that fit too tight—must be condemned.

Geographically, Prek Touch was similar to the village of my birth town of Thlok Chhreu. Both were rich agriculturally. Both sat next to a major river. Mine the Mekong. Here—the Bassac. The rice here was good, as was the corn, soybean, sesame, and a variety of fruits and vegetables.

Most of the people had mixed Khmer and Chinese blood.

Comrade Yem insisted she was pure Khmer. I suspected she had Chinese blood as well. But it was important in Khmer Rouge Cambodia that you be as ethnically pure Khmer as possible.

Yem now proudly served Angkar. She was pleased that Angkar chose her to lead a women's work team and ordered her to look after us.

Yem was always up at dawn preparing rice to take with her as she began her workday. Her child would be cared for by a work team of women 65 and older.

I was left on my own for a while, a chance to take stock of my situation. I dressed in black clothing as close as possible to what I saw people around me wearing. I put a scarf around my head to disguise my hair, which was still long.

I decided to take a short walk to explore the village. There were small houses like Comrade Yem's, but there were also large wood houses covered with red tiles and supported on large round columns. Clearly this village enjoyed prosperity in the past.

As I was walking, I remembered I knew a family from this region. A woman named Hong used to live near my father's house in Phnom Penh. I recalled she said her hometown was Prek Touch. I asked around for the house of Hong's parents.

I went there and much to my surprise there was my father's neighbor Mrs. Hong. We hugged and spoke in hushed voices.

She warned me to be very careful about telling anybody about my background. Keep as many secrets as you can, she advised. "I am lucky, my parents have lived here for some time. Although their house is large, they have been accepted as revolutionaries."

She recommended that I settle down here with her.

I thought about her advice as I walked back to Comrade Yem's place.

We joined Comrade Yem for dinner. I contributed part of my rice from Phnom Penh to her rations.

Angkar gave her a rice ration according to her work with the work team. Since she was a cadre, she got a good allotment.

She complained about the new city women who had been assigned to her. None of them knew how to cut rice. I was annoyed by her criticism because I did not know either.

After dinner I walked to the Bassac to bathe and bring back some water for Kunthea and her grandson.

When I returned to Comrade Yem, a Khmer Rouge security man interviewed Kunthea, my traveling companion. Her grandson watched.

The security cadre then turned to me and asked me about my background.

I kept Mrs. Hong's advice in mind. I answered his questions carefully, mixing truth with falsehoods.

Yem sat next to us, smiling. She encouraged me. "You can always tell the truth to Angkar. No one should be afraid."

I admitted my connection to SONATRAC, for I thought it might be good to mention the "progressive" reputation of the agricultural company.

I said I was from a poor Phnom Penh family.

Of course, I said nothing about my father or my American connections, my journalist friend and certainly not Commander Walter of the MED Team.

The slogans of April 17 still rang in my ears.

"The American capitalists are our number one enemy and whoever has associated with them is also our enemy. They will be destroyed."

Tuesday, April 29

I began to settle into the village of Prek Touch.

But soon a settled life meant boredom. I would scavenge for firewood and bring it back to Yem. I could not read, listen to the radio. No music, nowhere to go. Nothing to do.

I walked to the main road just to see if by chance I might meet anyone from the city I knew. Even on the 29th—there were still people on the road moving slowly south. Not many were allowed to stay, as I was, in Saang District. I was lucky in that regard. I could have been forced further south. Deeper into Kandal. But no one asked me.

I remained at the home of Comrade Yem. I was told to wait for an assignment to a work team.

On April 30—I could sense my situation would not last.

Angkar was organizing. There would be a stricter routine. The forces of Angkar could not be resisted. As the month of May began, I could sense changes would come and they would not be good.

16

Collapse: Part 2

April 28–29 1975

I STOOD ON THE SMALL gray concrete balcony outside my second-floor room at the Caravelle and scanned the square below before turning in. "A peaceful transition, a controlled solution"; the talk of the night before seemed so far-fetched. Illusion minus reality had been so much a part of the thinking about Vietnam and Cambodia.

The National Assembly building in front of me was dark. I doubted it would ever again serve for government use. Across the square at the Continental Palace, the curfew had shuttered the Continental Shelf bar. The wild nights I witnessed there in 1972 were now firmly consigned to the past. To my left, the doors of the old military briefing building had closed. The South Vietnamese no longer provided daily news briefings—the language of kill ratios, body counts, protective reaction strikes, and advances by ARVN troops very much relegated to history. I closed the balcony door and went to sleep wondering what was next.

I did not have long to wait. In the early morning darkness of Tuesday, April 29, a barrage of rockets and 130 mm artillery fire slammed across the Tan Son Nhut Airbase runway. The attack dealt a crippling blow to all fixed-wing aircraft operations that were meant to carry out most of the Saigon evacuation. The American C-130 flights that had been shuttling in and out had finally been halted—permanently. The next American plane to Saigon would fly into a renamed Ho Chi Minh City Tan Son Nhut Airport in 1991—sixteen years later.

After a personal inspection of the runways by Ambassador Martin, all air operations shifted to helicopter. Washington ordered the start of Operation "Frequent Wind."

The plan made the Tan Son Nhut Defense Attaché Office compound the primary helicopter evacuation point. The US Embassy downtown would serve a secondary role in a plan that would soon have to be changed.

I learned later that a disc jockey at the American-run radio station was ordered to send out an evacuation signal to all remaining US personnel. He would read the words "The temperature in Saigon is 105 degrees and rising" and play several times the Bing Crosby favorite "I'm Dreaming of a White Christmas." The DJ would then put on a long-playing tape and leave.

I never heard the music. I don't know anyone who did. Frequent Wind was underway before the music played. NBC and other news agencies sent their personnel to assembly points where US Marine buses would transport evacuees to Tan Son Nhut.

The nearest pickup point to most news bureaus stood just across from the gates of the French Grall Hospital at the corner of Hai Ba Trung and Ly Tu Trong.

As journalists and many others raced to the evacuation point, I rolled out the old Citroën DaLat parked near the Caravelle. I picked up Neil and headed up Hai Ba Trung. We would follow the evacuation.

When we approached the old hospital, which the French had named Hôpital Grall in 1925 to honor a French colonial military doctor, I saw French gendarmes manning the gate engaged in a shoving match with young Vietnamese trying to enter the grounds. Hospitals in war zones have often become places for the fearful to seek refuge—if only temporarily.

Saigonese feared the worst.

By mid-morning, panic overcame many Saigon residents as they began to accept that the war was lost and that anybody who wanted out better get out now. Unlike in Phnom Penh, I found few Vietnamese who clung to the possibility of a peace without pain and a regime change without reprisal.

Across from the hospital, dozens of our colleagues mingled, chatted, waited, wondered. Neil joined them, encouraging them to believe that everyone from NBC was leaving too.

Dark olive-green buses began to pull up to the evacuation site. US Marines guarding the doors urged evacuees aboard. Each struggled with their overstuffed backpacks.

"Only one bag per person!" shouted the marines—orders which were soon disobeyed.

One by one the buses pulled out, beginning a meandering and chaotic route through Saigon streets. North on Hai Ba Trung, left on Phan Thanh Gian, right on to Cong Ly, with short stops to board more passengers along the way. Gaining speed on Cong Ly, the buses headed straight for Tan Son Nhut.

Neil, CP-16 camera at the ready, jumped in beside me. I gunned the little DaLat to keep up with what became a long caravan of buses.

Quickly the evacuation gained attention. Streets became flooded with motorcyclists, weaving in and out, waving, screaming, heckling, beseeching. It seemed all of Saigon's three million people wanted to board those buses for a massive escape.

Before the melee and not far from the hospital, the buses slowed nearly to a stop. Neil and I spotted two young Vietnamese girls standing on the sidewalk. They simply stared at the buses. Tears streamed down their faces. They carried small bags.

Neil shouted, "Stop!" I did.

"What's happened?" Neil asked the tearful girls.

In a stumbling mix of English, French, and Vietnamese they told us that their parents had left for Europe with instructions they should follow.

They appeared to be from a well-to-do Saigon family. They were barely out of their teens. They explained their exit papers had not yet come through. They heard Tan Son Nhut airport had been closed. What should they do?

Seeing that the buses were again on the move and without another thought, I shouted, "Get in the back!" They did.

We raced after the buses. One bus stopped just before turning on to Cong Ly. Neil grabbed the girls' arms and dragged them to the bus. He shouted and banged on the front door. A US Marine opened it and Neil pushed the girls roughly on board.

The buses surged forward. Off the girls went. Off we went in our little DaLat.

At Tan Son Nhut, we saw the buses disappear through the entrance to the defense attaché's compound. Neil captured some shots of the gates and transport helicopters in the distance. He waved goodbye and got back in the car. Escaping the pandemonium, I nudged the DaLat through the traffic back to the center of Saigon. We looked at each other. We felt even more confident in our decision not to join the evacuation.

More than a year later, Neil got a note. Somehow he had managed to slip his business card into one of the girl's bags. The note came from a young woman in Belgium. "Thank you," she wrote, "for pushing us on the bus on April 29, 1975. We reunited with our family. We now live in Brussels."

■ ■ ■

Back in Saigon, Neil raced off to capture more of the chaos enveloping the US Embassy especially. I ran up the steps to the NBC bureau at the Passage Eden. Anh was the only one there.

I got on the telex machine, reporting to New York that most of the Saigon press corps had left for helicopters or would be leaving soon. Anh was able to get a radio circuit up through the Saigon PTT to New York. I filed a radio report on the evacuation and the growing panic among Vietnamese suddenly desperate to leave.

Late in the afternoon, Neil and I learned that most helicopter evacuations had shifted from the defense attaché's compound to the embassy.

A few days later, when I visited the attaché compound, which I knew as MACV headquarters back in 1972, nothing was left but rubble. The Americans had blown it up. The roof of what once housed the command of one of the largest military operations in the world buckled inward after repeated detonations. Just down the road from the compound a large billboard remained standing. It read "The Noble Sacrifice of Allied Soldiers Will Never Be Forgotten."

■ ■ ■

Word of the stepped-up embassy evacuation spread quickly. At 5 p.m., after filing some updated radio news reports, I decided to get closer to the action. The NBC bureau seemed too far away. I gathered my camera, typewriter, and tape recorder and moved. I ran up Tu Do toward the Saigon Cathedral, taking a left on Han Thuyen Street to the Reuters office. There I met Nayan Chanda of the *Far Eastern Economic Review*. The *Review* had use of Reuters' facilities. I could send messages to NBC and help Nayan with whatever extra detail I could provide for that week's edition of the *Review*.

Reuters offered me a better position. It was a short run to the embassy and back. If I stood at the door off to the left, I could see through the trees the Presidential Palace, now occupied by retired general Duong Van Minh.

What I could not see was what was happening inside. Amid the gathering chaos, Minh was still trying to negotiate a ceasefire. He sent a "neutralist" delegation out to Camp Davis to meet the NLF's Colonel Vo Dong Giang. Giang was in regular contact with commanding general Van Tien Dung.

General Dung told me in 2000, "Our orders from Hanoi were clear; we were to achieve reunification." No negotiation. Dung also confirmed he had orders not to interrupt the American evacuation, but admitted he was growing impatient.

■ ■ ■

Outside the embassy gates I watched a scene of continuing chaos.

Thousands of Vietnamese tried to force their way through the gates or climb over the walls to join the evacuation. An extra contingent of US Marines flew in from aircraft carriers 30 miles off the coast to hold them back.

The embassy pressed into use two helicopter LZs. CH-46 "Sea Knights" came and went from the embassy roof. Larger CH-53s, which could carry up to fifty people each, used a new landing zone in the parking lot behind the embassy building, where a large tree had been felled to make room.

The constant roar of chopper engines reverberated across central Saigon. They flew about 45 minutes from the embassy out to ships, 45 minutes back. The relay stopped for a while, then resumed.

An extraordinary armada waited 12 miles or so from the Port of Vung Tau. "Task Force 76" comprised more than twenty naval vessels including nine destroyers, two large aircraft carriers, and smaller helicopters carriers. Among them sailed the Okinawa, on which I had spent a night after my evacuation from Cambodia just a few weeks earlier.

In addition to the helicopter evacuation, a flotilla of ships was making its way down the Saigon River to the sea. The ships would eventually carry more than 50,000 Vietnamese to the Philippines, Guam, and the United States.

At 6:30 p.m., April 29, New York time, John Chancellor led the NBC *Nightly News* with a radio report on the evacuation by my friend Brian Barron of the BBC (another reporter who also elected to stay). Chancellor read some of my telex reports describing the scene at the embassy.

> NBC reporter Jim Laurie, who remains in the capital, says South Vietnamese civilians by the thousands have tried to scale the walls of the embassy. He says he saw people claw their way to the top of wall only to have fingers mashed by United States rifle and pistol butts held by United States Marines.

Darkness set in just before 7. The helicopter evacuation, more dangerous at night, continued. At the Reuters office I managed to get the embassy on the phone. I reached the ambassador's office. A woman answered. The ambassador's long-serving secretary Eva Kim still answered the phone!

"How long would the evacuation continue?" I asked.

"As long as we can," she answered before she hung up.

As it turned out, the helicopter shuttle continued all night.

Ambassador Graham Martin stalled as long as he could. He finally boarded a helicopter a little after 5:00 on the morning of April 30.

Including the helicopter that carried the ambassador, the two-day helo lift rescued 1,373 Americans and more than 6,000 South Vietnamese and other nationalities. More than 2,100 were taken off the embassy grounds alone.

CIA analyst Frank Snepp, in the embassy until 3:00 that morning, later wrote of his anger about the conduct of the evacuation. Ambassador Martin's delays and the inevitable chaos, in Snepp's view, resulted in "squandered lives, blown secrets and the betrayal of United States friends and agents." "Our handling of the evacuation was an institutional disgrace," wrote Snepp. Many people left behind were most in danger because of collaboration with the Americans. Many who got out had little or nothing to fear.

■ ■ ■

After dark on April 29, it was too late for Neil to shoot his daylight Kodak film. Using lights in the Saigon melee was out of the question. Radio circuits went down for the night. I telexed all I could from Reuters. I returned to the NBC bureau and then to the Caravelle. A small group of us watched the drama at the embassy from the Caravelle roof.

As I looked out, I thought of Sinan and of Cambodia and about the contrast with what I had seen a few short weeks before.

At the American evacuation from that schoolyard in Phnom Penh, no one frantically clambered to escape. Available seats on helicopters testified to that. Many people surely felt misled and betrayed, yet many took a fatalistic view. We are all Khmer, I would hear more than once, as if that were a recipe for peace and a better life.

On the other hand, the South Vietnamese greeted defeat with anger, greater panic, and a much deeper sense of foreboding.

As it turned out, Vietnamese with close ties to the Americans had much to be afraid of, but Khmer—no matter who they were—had much, much more to fear.

■ ■ ■

Close to 10:00, at the NBC bureau, I found Neil counting 16 mm film stock for his durable camera. Anh assisted while polishing up an older, heavier Auricon camera we would use for backup. Neil wanted to know how long the film we had would last. "We could be here a long time shooting 'the liberation,'" he joked.

With Anh's help we practiced some new Vietnamese words that might come in handy. "Giai phong" (liberation), "giai phong bo doi" (liberation foot soldier), and Neil's suggestion: "Chao mung dong chi" (Welcome, Comrade).

17

"Prison Without Walls"

May 6, 1975—Saang District, Democratic Kampuchea

IN THE EARLY DAYS of May, Soc Sinan's emotions fluctuated widely. She felt a mixture of isolation, exhaustion, anxiousness, and a strange sense of exhilaration.

The exhilaration stemmed from being thrown back in her mind to an earlier time. The village on the Bassac River reminded her of her childhood home in Thlok Chhreu on the Mekong, where she had been supremely happy living with her grandparents. Sinan somehow also had a sense that her mother was with her, her spirit here in Saang.

> I simply looked backward to my childhood. The fresh air and nature around us in this remote area made my thoughts dwell on indefinite memories.

The anxiety that Sinan felt, however, never left her. Fears rose and then subsided. Fear of exposure. Fear of being taken away.

A new vocabulary came into use. She was a "new" person, a city person, sometimes called a "parasite." Those who had been "liberated" in earlier years were "base" people: part of the reliable, indoctrinated, rural base.

Sensing danger, Sinan took some precautions before Angkar could consolidate control. She repacked her possessions once more. She had never been subjected to a thorough inspection. She rearranged the contents in her remaining suitcases. Her most valuable items she kept with her at all times, sewing some of them in secret pockets.

There was a small pagoda at Prek Touch, not far away from the house to which she had been assigned. She thought it might be a good hiding place. Sinan had a lifelong talent for hiding. She had always squirreled things away. But this time her talent failed her.

The wat was abandoned. Angkar did not permit worship of Buddha. The monks had been taken away. So I hid my possessions here. It turned out that was a mistake. Within a few days my suitcases were stolen. I never found out who did it. A Buddhist wat provided no protection.

Still she retained her most precious items and the most potentially dangerous—key documents, jewelry, a small amount of medicine, other items that might be traded with the base people for food or better treatment.

In early May—I can no longer remember the exact day—Comrade Eng said he had orders from Angkar. We were to be moved.

Life in Yem's little house would have to end. Comrade Eng told Sinan that Kunthea and her grandson would have to go elsewhere. People would be separated into work units depending on whether they were old, young, men, women, healthy, unhealthy, married, or not.

One morning, soldiers led Kunthea and her grandson away.

Sinan could see fear in Kunthea's eyes. Tears trickled down her cheeks. The boy's eyes had that same wide, unknowing expression Sinan had seen back in that clinic where they first met.

"A shiver of fear overcame me," said Sinan. Her friends left. She never saw them again.

• • •

Angkar ordered Sinan to pack and move.

Her short stay in Prek Touch was fortuitous. Although she lost two friends and many possessions, she established herself in a category of people that would serve her well in the years ahead: "orphaned girl."

The nameless Khmer Rouge soldier who shared some food and the "base woman" named Yem who housed Sinan for a week spared her some hardship.

• • •

More than forty years later, Mrs. Nhem Yem still lived in the hamlet of Prek Touch.

With the help of Dany Long, a man who has been tracking down people affiliated with the Khmer Rouge for more than ten years, I found Yem.

She sat sorting scallions in a small thatched-roof house not much different from the one that sheltered Sinan. Yem, 74, had traded her Khmer Rouge black "pajamas" for a blue checkered blouse and boldly colored plaid trousers. Her eyes, however, narrowed as she talked. She turned evasive as she spoke. Among the old people from the families of old revolutionaries, memory is often selective.

"Several families and city people came to my house in April–May 1975. I was ordered by the local party chief to take them in.

I don't really know who they were or where they went. I treated them well. I was not responsible for anything that happened to them."

Yem went back to sorting scallions.

■ ■ ■

It was a short boat ride from the abandoned Prek Touch pagoda where Sinan tried to hide her possessions to the west bank of the Bassac River. From there Sinan walked another hour to reach the next destination assigned to her by Angkar: the Troy Sla zone in the Saang district of Po Kandal.

I learned that in the old days the Troy Sla zone was one of the richest along the river. The people were better off than elsewhere. Rice, corn, and other crops were plentiful.

Angkar leaders chose this area on which to build a new people's commune. They sought to develop the perfect communal lifestyle that was at the heart of the radical revolution.

Angkar would break up the family unit, arrange marriages, and assign children to communal day care centers. They forced people to work, eat, and live together in work brigades to create the perfect egalitarian society.

From Troy Sla, Sinan would be pressed into forced labor. Rice fields needed planting and harvesting. Dikes must be built. Canals must be dug. She would join a woman's mobile work brigade. She would experience both exhaustion and tedium. One day's work would merge into the next.

She soon came to detest the guardians of her prison.

The chief of the Angkar commune was Comrade Eng—a "pure" Khmer who had worked in the region under a wealthy landlord.

He stood about 5 foot 6 with a stocky build. Maybe 45 years of age, he had large eyes, which for some reason were bloodshot much of the time.

Known for his loud voice and his daily recitations of patriotic slogans, he warned loyalty to Angkar was paramount. He decided who would work and who would live. His judgment of the "new people" seemed to be final. Judge, jury, executioner.

He traveled around Saang District on his shiny new "Dera" bicycle —made in France.

In all the four years I lived in Troy Sla, I never saw him do any work. His main talent lay in his ability to talk, to speak hours on end. His patriotic speeches were required listening. His gruff and commanding personality made people fear approaching him.

Comrade Eng's best friends were the chhlop (the secret police) and other officials of Angkar.

Comrade Eng's boss, Comrade Bo, was chief of the Saang District. I thought it unusual, for Comrade Bo was a woman. I would see her occasionally arrive in a Chinese jeep to preside over big meetings.

She was about 5 foot 2 but rather heavy by Khmer standards. Behind her back, some joked: "The comrade leader does not work enough to burn off any fat."

She was tough, unsmiling, and also a good speaker. She received and enforced the production quotas from officials on high.

"Three tons of rice per hectare," she commanded.

Above Comrade Bo was Comrade Sean.

Sean had been apparently promoted several times since early 1975. He commanded the whole southern zone including Kandal Province and Takeo. Takeo, I learned, was one of the most "revolutionary" areas, known for its record for the highest number of deaths. Had the truck that brought me here not had a flat tire, I might have ended up there.

Many considered Comrade Sean handsome. At 5 foot 8, considered tall, he displayed some education. He may have been a killer but in public he always showed a pleasant face.

■ ■ ■

Soon after her arrival at Troy Sla, Sinan discovered that not all the base people were hardened Khmer Rouge who saw new people only as enemies.

On arrival, a woman named Aung Eaang and her family took Sinan in. Eaang's daughter Cheng was about Sinan's age. Khmer Rouge cadre placed trust in Eaang's husband Ngorn, a farmer who had been working in the liberated zone since 1971.

Sizing the family up carefully, Sinan decided she could trust them—to a degree. As she had done before, Sinan used her "orphan" strategy.

She had been married, she told the family, but her husband deserted her and her parents were dead. She was all alone. Might old Aung Eaang adopt her as another "daughter"?

Aung Eaang agreed.

I found Mrs. Eaang to be a base person who had a good heart. I was alone. She treated me as her daughter. She sought to protect me.

I told her little about myself. When I trusted her enough, I gave her a few of my valuables. Outside her house one night I buried in the ground my papers and my most precious items. I had no idea if I would ever need them.

■ ■ ■

The leaders of Angkar had been honing their philosophy since the early 1960s. Sinan knew only one name among the Khmer Rouge, Khieu Samphan.

Khieu had two brothers who worked for SONATRAC. Sinan also knew of Khieu's reputation as a leftist in the early 1960s who sought to be a deputy for the district in which she now lived.

More powerful members of the communist politburo would reveal themselves later in 1976.

Five revolutionaries formed a tight-knit, secretive group. Pol Pot, Ieng Sary, their wives (who were "revolutionary sisters"), and Nuon Chea forged their politics in Paris. They acted in remote areas of Cambodia, becoming, as one scholar put it, "full-time revolutionaries" in 1962.

Pol Pot, a name unknown to most people at first, emerged as the most infamous of the killers who ruled Cambodia.

Born Saloth Sar in Kampong Thom Province in the center of the country in 1925, Pol Pot managed to land a scholarship to travel to France in 1949 to study electrical engineering. After achieving poor exam results in radio electronics, he joined a small group of Khmer friends who studied Marxist Leninism. He also read of Stalin and Mao and liked what he read.

Some years after he returned to Cambodia, Saloth Sar changed his name to Pol Pot and began to build a revolution at home. Multiple visits to Hanoi and Beijing from 1965 onward had the greatest impact on the communist leader.

He came away from Hanoi fearing Vietnamese domination. They would want to control the Khmer Communist Party.

In Beijing, Pol Pot embraced the more radical and totalitarian features of the perpetual revolution that Mao Zedong preached. What became known as "The Great Proletarian Cultural Revolution" (1965–76) was underway when Pol Pot visited. Purges of "bourgeois capitalists" and "shang shan xia fang" (the Chinese down to the countryside movement) appealed to the Cambodian.

In China, hundreds of millions suffered persecution in the 1960s and early '70s. An estimated twenty million people died, including those who perished in famine after gross economic mismanagement.

On a per capita percentage basis, Pol Pot could do better.

In late June 1975, after the cities were emptied, with the commune system implemented and tens of thousands of people already executed, Pol Pot received the highest blessing.

Mao, in one meeting, told the Khmer, "You have achieved in one stroke what we failed to do with our Chinese masses." Later a Beijing delegation to the renamed Democratic Kampuchea proclaimed that Cambodia was now "a radiant democratic nation emerging in the east like a glowing red sun rising."

Pol Pot must have been proud. He was proclaimed "Brother Number One."

■ ■ ■

As 1976 began, Sinan's assignment to a women's mobile work brigade took her on a grueling three-month mission.

Far from my commune, I worked on a dike system which Angkar leaders said was very important to increase production.

The women's brigade worked, ate, and slept communally. My sleeping shelter was better than others I had seen. My biggest challenge was to keep mosquitos away. With mosquitos I worried about disease.

When the dike was done, we were given an afternoon off and one good meal. For the first time desserts: sweet rice with coconut milk, sugar palm, and black sesame mixed together.

I lay down for a while and looked out. Wild birds flew across the blue sky. Nearby monkeys jumped back and forth on the branches of the Kadol tree. I marveled at how much freedom the monkeys and the birds had.

There was an old saying: "where there is beauty and paradise, there is also hell."

This was my hell. My prison without walls. I kicked myself for being so ignorant. There was no sense looking back. The next morning, we gathered a few things from the communal shelter and began the long walk back to Troy Sla.

As soon as I was back I went to see Mrs. Aung Eaang and her daughter Cheng. Living near the communal cafeteria, Mrs. Eaang now worked at the communal kindergarten taking care of children while their parents worked in the fields. In some cases their parents had simply disappeared altogether. No one talked about them.

It was good to see Mrs. Eaang and Cheng again. They had become my adopted family.

I went to the Bassac River to bathe. I stayed there a long time. It was fresh even though recent rains had rendered it slightly muddy. It was far better than bathing in the B-52 craters where I had tried to stay clean for the past three months while with the work brigade.

By 4 a.m. the sound of the roosters. I was awake. No time to linger.

Comrade Tieng, our stern brigade leader, ordered the team to assemble at the old Wat Por, used as a staging area for the women's mobile work team.

In the past, monks cared for the trees here—bananas, papaya, and orange. Now the monks were gone. The trees were dead.

There were eighty-five women in our work brigade. Comrade Tieng always counted them before we started off for the morning assignment.

Most were "new people." Clearly many of the "native" or "base" people did not like us.

Some of the men among the "base" commented that the "new" women were prettier than the old. That only made their wives jealous and made our lives more difficult.

Most of the women were considered "wives of traitors." Nearly all the women in my team were now single, as their husbands had been taken away and never seen again.

I stayed with the women's work brigade for more than three years. Our tasks varied little from day to day. As a mobile group, we traveled away from the village to carry out three tasks, over and over again. We dug small canals around the fields, cleaned brush, and chopped trees to make way for more land for planting. And we worked on the bigger projects like building those dikes which Angkar said were so important.

I tried as often as possible to stay at the commune village, to be near Aung Eaang's family.

Being near the village enabled me to try to keep an eye on my few hidden possessions, to keep track of the political situation, to hear if there were any changes, to hear when danger seemed greater, or seemed less.

My biggest worry was becoming sick or injured. Some "new people" not used to walking in the mud fell, broke or sprained ankles. I stumbled and sprained my ankle once, fortunately only a minor injury.

If you got sick or injured, there was little that could be done. The Khmer Rouge clinic was run by people who knew nothing about medicine. We used to call the medicine they had "monkey turd medicine." I kept some of what I had taken from the Phnom Penh pharmacy. I used it to barter and kept some for myself. But of course, it soon ran out.

During the rainy season, work was lighter. We were assigned to the warehouse next to the kitchen for three or four hours straight, separating husks for the kitchen or shelling peanuts.

The work also showed me how cowardly and two-faced the Khmer Rouge were. The chief comrades would come by and fill their pockets with shelled peanuts so they had something extra to eat the following day. If *we* did that, and we were caught, we'd be punished severely. A new person could face death for breaking even those rules.

■ ■ ■

In late 1977, conditions around Sinan became worse. The number of disappearances increased. However, Sinan's strategy, playing the orphan girl, seemed to be working. Occasionally she would show her old surgical scar to get out of the hardest work. One of her saddest days came when she witnessed the attempt to destroy the culture of the Cham people and their devotion to Islam.

The Cham were an ancient people. Many settled in Cambodia as fishermen. I remember happy times watching them when I was a little girl on the Mekong.

One day Angkar brought two Cham families to live with us—the new people. I watched as the communal kitchen prepared rice and pork. The Cham were prohibited from cooking their own meals. I watched sadness and anger welling up in their faces. At times I could hear their murmured prayers to Allah.

Several months later, the Cham were gone. The rumor was that they refused to stop praying and refused the pork diet. They were then killed.

We heard an Angkar slogan over and over. It's hard to translate.

"The wheel of history is moving fast. If anyone tries to put their arms or feet into the wheel to cause it to stop, those arms and feet will be broken!"

As Sinan watched in horror and fear, more people disappeared. She was shocked by the reaction of some of those around her.

Some in the commune welcomed the disappearance of both the Cham and the new people. They were open about it. As categories of people disappeared, the food, the rations for the rest of us improved. Survival in a prison camp is like that. Survivors come to think only about themselves.

■ ■ ■

Painstaking research by Chanthou Boua (who had helped me visit Sinan's home village of Thlok Chhreu) provides context for Sinan's situation.

From 1975, Angkar divided Kampuchea into five zones and 106 regions, some more faithful to Pol Pot and the central leadership than others. Conditions varied. Sinan found herself in the most prosperous part of Southwest Zone, Region 25. Saang was advantaged owing to its position between two rivers—the Bassac and the Mekong. The rich basin produced a variety of crops, and even in the worst times, starvation was not known. Region 25 had a population of about 1.5 million.

About 400 "new" people from Phnom Penh were allowed to live in Sinan's district—at first. Sinan estimated the overall population on her communal work farm at a little over 1,000.

Later, comparatively flexible policies tightened. The number of people who disappeared sharply increased. Chanthou Boua, in her work with Ben Kiernan, found that many of those removed were sent on long, often deadly treks to Battambang in the northwest. Others were simply executed.

■ ■ ■

My prison without walls offered some learning opportunities. The raising of pigs and cattle.

While raising pigs was fairly easy, the commune cattle were more difficult to raise and keep healthy.

If cattle became ill, someone was blamed and often punished. At political meetings, "the cow," said Angkar cadre, "were second only to humans in importance." It seemed to me the cows were far more important.

Self-sufficiency in rice and corn were commune priorities. Angkar said we were always short on rice. When we ate, the rice was usually mixed with corn, sweet potatoes, banana, or "Kadouch."

Later it became clear. Angkar removed rice from the commune and shipped it out. We would see river steamboats pick up rice. We did not know where it was going or how the rice was being used. We lived in a world where we knew nothing and where no questions could be asked.

■ ■ ■

China became the principal beneficiary of the revolution, the true, steadfast friend of Angkar.

In late 1975, China shipped rice to the new Democratic Kampuchea. In 1976 and after, rice went in the other direction.

The state sent to China rubber from a limited reopening of plantations. China bought a range of animal parts for Chinese medicine.

Even the lowly lizard became a prized catch. Khmer Rouge communes gathered tons of geckos and shipped them to China. With their distinctive nighttime "geh-ko" sound, the only chattering member of the species was silenced for a while.

■ ■ ■

Every household was required to raise chickens.

Angkar officials came by to register the chickens in each household. Laying hens were registered. The number of eggs produced recorded.

Sometimes people would cheat and take eggs, boil them, and eat them without permission. They were always careful to bury the eggshells or throw them in the Bassac.

Every person received black uniforms two times a year. We never had clean clothes, as we were often working in the mud or dust. When the clothes were clean, we spent time sewing them and patching them up.

Angkar did not provide shoes. If we had sandals, as I did, we could wear them. Two-thirds of the people on my commune walked barefoot.

The top Angkar cadre wore rubber shoes. When we saw the comrades and their shoes, we smiled bitterly and remembered the Angkar slogan: "Everybody is equal. No rich. No poor. It is a just society."

■ ■ ■

In 1977, the southern region enjoyed a bumper rice crop. Comrade Sean ordered brigade leader Comrade Tieng to take Sinan and her work brigade on another important assignment. Tieng ordered the brigade out on one day's notice.

They were to walk 20 miles west and take a boat across Boeng Cheung Loung lake to Tonle Bati and on to the neighboring province of Takeo.

I went back to Aung Eaang's house to prepare for the trip.

In the old days Takeo was known as the place where "the water is sweet." The sugar palms produced an abundance of sugar.

I told Mrs. Eaang and Cheng about the news.

They devised a plan to get some personal benefit out of the Takeo visit. I was surprised that an old "base" person like Mrs. Eaang was willing to break the rules. She told me Takeo had a surplus of sugar, which we needed. We had some extra tobacco.

So Mrs. Eaang gave me tobacco. I promised to return with brown sugar. Bartering was strictly against Angkar rules. It was quite a risk. But that old stubbornness in me gave me the resolve to take a chance.

We started off early. In the old days, the road we walked along would have been busy. Now apart from a few chhlop patrolling by motorbike, it was empty.

Comrade Tieng urged us to walk faster.

At around 11 we arrived at Phnom Saang. One of the "new people" in my group knew the area.

"In the old days there was a lovely pagoda here," she said. "My family came here for the Khmer New Year celebration." The mention of Khmer New Year sent a shiver down my spine.

As we got closer, I could see the pagoda was destroyed. As we walked by, we prayed silently to Buddha in the hopes that the spirits at the old temple were at least safe.

■ ■ ■

The reason for Sinan's new "mission" soon became apparent. While Takeo produced abundant rice, there were not enough people to harvest it.

As the work brigade ventured further into the area, Sinan discovered why.

The rice fields had been cleared nearly two years ago by new people.

We heard that by now most of those people had died of starvation or malaria.

As we walked through villages, we noticed 70 percent of the people were women. Rumors spread quickly. Most of the men in this part of the country were dead.

As we walked, we passed other work camps, which made us realize how lucky we were. Takeo was a vast killing field. Far worse than Kandal, much, much worse than Saang.

We saw from a distance a large group of teenage boys building a giant dike in an area more rugged than where I had helped build dikes. The terrain made digging difficult. The boys had only hand tools.

The young boys were supervised by hardened chhlop agents. Twice I heard gunshots—into the air to warn the boys to keep working.

We learned later the boys were all children of "new people." We assumed the parents had been executed.

Arriving at the commune of Kandung in Takeo, we looked out. As far as my eyes could see were fields of uncut rice.

The trek totally exhausted us. We could smell soup being prepared for our first meal. We rushed to the communal kitchen, not even stopping to wash. Rice, soup, green banana, and fish was our first meal at Kandung.

We then built our own shelters fashioned from palm leaves and bamboo poles. Shelters ready, no sleep was permitted—at least not yet.

First a political meeting.

"We must uphold the reputation of our commune," shouted Comrade Tieng. "We will make good on Angkar's plan."

"We promise," we replied in unison. We raised our right fist in allegiance. Everyone repeated the promise again.

Although it was turning dark, all were forced into the fields to begin the harvest. The comrades set up lanterns to work by.

Again I was fortunate. I was assigned lighter work. Threshing: I would separate the grain from the husks and straw, removing the chaff.

Some women were so exhausted that they slumped to the ground.

Comrade Tieng called a halt to work for the night at 10.

We were rewarded with a dessert: sweet rice with palm sugar and a bit of shredded coconut on top. To me it was very good. I even saved a small bit for breakfast.

Finally we bathed. We were permitted only to bathe with a small tin of water. We were sound asleep this night by 11.

The bell rang at 5 a.m. "Get up, comrades! It's time to go to work!" I was ordered to start cutting rice.

The harshness of the work was made bearable only by the beauty of the location.

A soft mist across the paddy, rugged hills in the distance, and around us hundreds of palm trees—the source of the brown sugar the region was known for.

This area was less fertile than Saang. Shortages were common. In the old days it did not matter. A vibrant trade moved goods all over the country. In Sihanouk's time you could get anything. Under Angkar, there was no trade, no commerce between regions.

"Whoever sows will harvest." They forced each commune to exist on its own. The only trade was that in human beings: the supply of slave labor we provided.

Takeo formed the center of a strict revolutionary zone, a dangerous place for us new people. We went about our work quietly, worked hard, kept on our best behavior.

I told my friends in the work brigade, "Open your mouths only to eat."

Comrade Tieng constantly watched the brigade, with a special eye on me.

She ordered me at one point to stop cutting rice. I was too slow. She ordered me to tie the dry paddy in bundles instead.

On the fourth day of the harvest, I took a tremendous gamble. Perhaps I thought I would do it to spite Comrade Tieng.

An old lady told me that a short distance to the west was a warehouse where palm sugar was stored. I decided to investigate whether I could trade my tobacco for sugar.

The risk was great. First, traveling away from the work team even for a few hours was prohibited. Second, trading was strictly prohibited by Angkar law.

Still I set off with a small can of dried tobacco under my sarong, telling my two friends in the work brigade to cover for me as best they could.

I chose my timing carefully.

Comrade Tieng had become more relaxed. The harvest was going well. It was nearly complete. Angkar would be pleased by her success.

I got to the sugar stash. Made a quick tobacco-for-sugar deal and went back to the work team unnoticed.

It wasn't much. Only a half a kilo of sugar. Still it was valuable. I felt for the first time in a long time—victorious!

■ ■ ■

During the long, arduous trek back to Troy Sla, Sinan gained strength from the thought she had defied Angkar, succeeded, and survived.

As a "new person" I had done well. I always showed obedience, kept my secrets, and was deferential to my prison keepers.

I was always alert, protecting myself.

There's an old Khmer saying: "Whenever a cow has a wound on its back, it must open its tail to protect it from the flight of the corbeaux [the vulture]."

Back in Troy Sla, after Takeo, work settled quickly into its monotonous routine.

■ ■ ■

Early in 1977 something happened which frightened many of us in the women's work brigade.

We had just completed another large dike. When completed, the leaders staged a big ceremony. A large crowd stood in the middle of a field near the completed dike.

Comrade Sean, who was now district chief, arrived on his Yamaha 90. He rode with his escort holding an AK-47 rifle high in the air so all could see.

A dozen men all in black on motorcycles accompanied him.

We stood at attention and listened.

"Congratulations on the dike's completion. Thanks to Angkar, water can be stored and released from behind the new dikes. We will increase our production. We'll produce 3 tons of rice per hectare. We'll have good water through all the dry season. We will achieve self-sufficiency!"

It was hot in the fields. Comrade Sean's speech was long. We had to take off our hats to listen. We pulled our krama over our heads. The sun beat down. I was getting sleepy. I suddenly stirred when Comrade Sean's voice turned more stern. He changed the subject.

"I now must address a serious concern of Angkar. There are enemies here who hide in our district. They want to destroy our revolution. But their plans have been discovered by Angkar.

"Dear Comrades, if you know of anyone causing trouble, report to the chief of your work brigade.

"If you know something and keep it secret and Angkar finds out later, you will be punished as a traitor. You should watch everyone's behavior. Listen for treasonous speech. Angkar is counting on you to continue the work of the revolution."

I was struck by the remarks. It was clear Angkar was about to come after more new people. One mistake, one wrong word by me or other city people, could result in our deaths.

I resolved to remain quiet. Renew my patience. Comment on nothing. No longer would I take chances—even for a half kilo of delicious brown sugar.

I was certain Comrade Sean was right. Angkar would eventually find out everything. Death was only a matter of time. A matter of time before my luck would run out.

There was a Khmer saying: "Angkar has eyes like a pineapple. It can see everything."

The meeting was over.

18

Giai Phong

Wednesday morning, April 30, 1975

I WAS RUNNING LATE. The sun rose shortly before 6. Saigoners always get out at dawn to catch the fresh air before the heat becomes oppressive. On this morning, Wednesday, April 30, I wanted to pick up where I had left off the day before—in front of the US Embassy.

I ran downstairs to retrieve the Citroën DaLat and pick up Neil Davis. Outside the front door, I looked to the right, next to the old South Vietnamese Assembly building, and cursed. The vehicle was not where I parked it. Someone had hot-wired and stolen it during the night.

Back inside the Caravelle, I found Neil relaxed and casually sipping his ca phe den (rich black Central Highlands coffee). He spread more pineapple jam on his morning croissants.

"No worries, mate, about the Citroën. Relax. Embassy's not far. Maybe we'll steal another car." He laughed. We knew that Anh, the de facto NBC bureau "Mister Fixit," kept safe NBC's blue Ford crew car.

As we walked the half mile to the embassy, I noticed that Saigon had taken on a slightly different feel from the night before. Whatever limited law and order prevailed in the city had disappeared.

We heard a few scattered rounds of rifle fire. Somebody tried to keep order. It did not sound like combat.

The gates secured by US Marines the night before stood wide open. As far as I could see, the embassy was abandoned. Thousands of Vietnamese streamed in and out of the compound, looting anything they could find, anything that was not fastened down. They carted off air conditioners, light fixtures, chairs and desks, files, and file cabinets. A young woman rode on the back of a Honda motorbike clutching yellow sofa cushions in one hand and an electric fan in the other.

There were some angry faces but most simply displayed the determination of opportunism. Perhaps, I thought, they were just trying to get back at the Americans, who had been here so long and now were cutting and running, deserting them.

Across the embassy grounds, papers strewn everywhere blew in a hot morning breeze. We learned later that despite a determined last-minute effort to shred or burn all sensitive documents, embassy staff failed to destroy important ones.

I looked to the rooftop helipad. Not everyone had left the embassy. I could just barely make out the silhouettes in the early morning light of what looked like uniformed US Marines, M-16s at the ready.

From the east a giant helicopter flew in at low altitude and set down on the roof. Neil raised his camera to the sky.

He captured the final helicopter removing the last marines from the embassy roof. The chopper quickly gained altitude, heading east to the carriers in the South China Sea.

I looked at my watch: 8:00. We had witnessed the end of the American embassy evacuation.

With the last Americans gone, Neil scrambled up the stairs through a cloud of teargas fired by the retreating marines. On the rooftop, he found hundreds of Vietnamese sitting on the helipad waiting for rescue. They hoped for more helicopters that we knew would never come.

Down below, in front of the building, I was besieged by desperate Vietnamese.

Some showed me identification cards proving they had been employed by United States government agencies.

A woman in a floppy white hat with concern embedded on her face pleaded with me. "I worked for USAID. My family and I need to get out. Can you help us?"

I explained I could not do anything as the last helicopters had gone and I was remaining in Saigon. She looked at me in desperate disbelief.

A young student spoke to me in halting English. "We think the Americans must have some methods, must have many ways to save us from the communists. We don't want to stay here."

A short distance away, a fire erupted at the American consulate facility, where only a week or so ago consular officials had been busy stamping visas into South Vietnamese passports.

More Vietnamese approached me, expressing anger, disappointment, a sense of betrayal. Yet every one of them did so in almost a polite way. No one tried to take their anger and frustrations out on me.

I turned to Neil's camera and recited a piece:
> This is what is left of the American involvement in Vietnam. The US Embassy behind me has been completely looted. The South Vietnamese are obviously angry at the American withdrawal. Many of them said they worked for the Americans and were left out of the evacuation. They will now have to stay. They will have to stay and cope with communism in South Vietnam.

I spotted Brian Barron and his cameraman Eric Thirer from the BBC.

Barron was talking to an animated, panic-stricken American named Gerald Posner. Posner had arrived in Vietnam two days before, on April 28, on a mission to rescue his wife and her Vietnamese family and friends. He missed the last choppers.

Posner, a 25-year-old postal worker from Brooklyn, New York, served in the army in Vietnam from 1970 to 1972. He met and married a girl from the Mekong Delta. His wife returned to Vietnam to attend to family matters, and now Posner was desperately trying to reunite the family.

"I was staying at this Vietnamese family's house on the edge of Saigon. There was curfew. I couldn't get here. I've got air tickets for the two kids and papers for these people. I'm married to a Vietnamese. What can I do?"

There was nothing Barron or I or anyone could do.

Barron told Posner we were all staying at the Caravelle. Later Posner showed up there trying to figure out his future.

I empathized. I realized I was not alone in wanting to rescue a loved one from the mess that was Indochina.

Neil and I completed our shooting around the embassy and parted ways. I wanted to see if I could pull up a radio circuit to report to NBC what we had seen. Neil headed on foot to the Presidential Palace.

Anh anticipated my needs. He had already secured an audio circuit through the PTT to New York.

A little after 9:30, I began filing accounts for radio of the last American helicopter, the looting of the embassy, the city now waiting for the arrival of the Vietnamese communists.

NBC television in New York had booked a primetime network news special.

Anh monitored Saigon radio. He ran back and forth across the room to the radio booth to provide me updates.

We kept the circuit up. A little after 10, Anh translated the words of the retired general and the last president of the Republic of Vietnam, Duong Van Minh.

I got back on the circuit at once. They patched me through to the television side. A short time later NBC's John Chancellor went on the air.

> NBC News correspondent Jim Laurie is one of the few Americans left in Saigon. In the city President Duong Van Minh went on the radio and told the Viet Cong that his country would surrender unconditionally and that he had told its army to lay down its arms. Here from Saigon by radio hookup is Laurie's report on the surrender.
>
> "In the words of General Minh, we are here to hand over the power of government to you in order to avoid bloodshed. It is a unilateral ceasefire and an unconditional surrender … The 30-year war in South Vietnam is at last over."

The radio circuit remained up for another hour.

I ran outside and snapped a photo of a North Vietnamese tank rounding the corner near the Caravelle. I watched two tanks heading southeast toward the river. Another tank crew checked their maps on unfamiliar roads and moved toward the Presidential Palace, the headquarters of the "Saigon puppet regime."

It was astounding. The war was over. My thoughts flashed back to 1970, riding those US tanks and helicopters in Cambodia, and to 1972 and that near-miss B-40 round in Quang Tri. Battles, deaths, misery over so many years. What was it all for? This was it. This is how it ends.

Only a few people stood on the streets. The chaos earlier in the morning and the night before had dissipated. Not knowing what to expect, most people went home, took cover. The few on the corner of Tu Do at Lam Son seemed stunned. They stood silently watching the tanks roar by.

South Vietnamese troops waged the final defense of the city on a bridge across the Saigon River. The 12th Airborne Battalion stood at Cau Tan Cang, what we called "Newport Bridge," in the port area.

Just after dawn, a sharp exchange of fire was followed by the destruction of one of Hanoi's lead T-54 tanks by the bridge defenders. At 10:25, the Airborne were about to blow the bridge when General Minh called from the palace and ordered the unit to lay down its arms.

. . .

The voice circuit to New York went down at about 11:20 a.m. I continued to file written updates, typing furiously on the NBC bureau telex machine.

"CALLING NBC NEWS NEW YORK 232346A OVER"

At about noon a message all in caps typed by an unknown operator at the Saigon Post and Telegraph building clattered across the telex. The keys stuck as the notice went out.

SGN TLX 18

VERY SORRY

AS PER SENTEL SAIGON

WE HV TO STOP THE TRANSMITTEEEEE TRANSMISSION NOW AND WE ARE STANDING BY THE NEW ORDER+ TKS BIBI +.

I simply typed in response, "UNDERSTAND MERCI ET BONCHANCE."

The operator on the other side at the PTT replied, "WE WILL INFORM YOU WHEN POSSIBLE TKS BI."

Communications were cut immediately. They were not restored for one week. The new order was in charge.

■ ■ ■

Leaving the embassy area, Neil Davis positioned himself at the Presidential Palace.

He found General Minh in the hallway on the first floor. Minh had just returned from delivering his address at the Saigon radio station. He awaited the formal surrender.

Looking somber but composed, he said simply, "The other side will be here shortly."

Neil left the building and decided to remain in the open, on the grass in between the front of the palace and its imposing three front gates.

Nayan Chanda stood just inside the door at the ground-floor Reuters office where I had been the night before.

"Suddenly I saw crossing the frame of the door a large tank and at the back of the tank flew a red, blue, and gold flag," Nayan told me. "I looked out and said, 'Wow, they're here.'"

The flag was that of the NLF, the communist movement or Viet Cong of southern Vietnam. The yellow flag with red-stripes of the old Republic of Vietnam disappeared within hours.

In a few days another flag appeared, with a solid red banner and gold star in the center: the flag of North Vietnam. It was a reminder of reality. Hanoi was in charge. The North had won.

■ ■ ■

Camera ready, Neil held his ground. His viewfinder caught one of the wrought-iron gates of the palace. As Neil later reported,

> Tank Number 843 smashed through the gate. It didn't quite make it the first time. One gate fell off its hinges. It backed off and smashed through again. A soldier on the front of the tank holding a huge Viet Cong flag jumped off and ran towards the palace. I followed him with my sound camera rolling.

A North Vietnamese soldier raced forward, his AK-47 at the ready. The soldier stopped long enough for Neil to utter the well-practiced Vietnamese that Anh had taught us.

"Welcome to Saigon, comrade," Neil stammered.

"You are an American?" the soldier demanded.

"Non, Uc dai loi," shouted Neil over the noise of the tank engines. "Australian."

The soldier lowered his rifle, nodded, and ran toward hundreds of South Vietnamese soldiers who had stripped off their uniforms down to their underwear. They huddled on the palace grass in surrender.

Neil continued filming.

The gates were breached at noon. The entire area erupted in gunfire as several North Vietnamese soldiers waved the Viet Cong flag from the top-floor palace balcony. The gunfire aimed into the air served as the sound of celebration.

At an underground bunker about 20 miles north of Saigon, General Van Tien Dung got a radio message that the palace had been captured. He radioed Hanoi. General Dung told me years later, "A cheer went up in the bunker. We were crying with joy and hugging each other. Our great spring victory was at last ours."

At the palace, a tired and stooped Duong Van Minh officially surrendered. He was led away in the early afternoon. Hanoi authorities finally permitted "Big Minh," held under house arrest, to depart for exile in Paris in 1983.

Nguyen Van Thieu, South Vietnam's president from 1967 to April 21, 1975, took up residence in England and only later moved quietly to America. Bitter to the end, Thieu blamed Henry Kissinger and the Americans for his defeat.

■ ■ ■

I rejoined Neil late in the afternoon for a final combat operation, certainly one of the more unusual for either of us in all our years covering the war. This time we accompanied communist forces, the young men we came to call "giai phong bo doi" or "liberation foot soldiers."

The giai phong bo doi began a mopping-up operation. They crept slowly forward, knowing they had all the time in the world. They didn't seem to mind if we tagged along. "Just keep your head down," Neil reminded me as I followed behind.

About forty or so armed South Vietnamese troops defying Big Minh's surrender orders hid out near Ho Con Rua (Turtle Monument), not far from the palace.

Ho Con Rua had a history of somewhat uncertain origin. The turtle complex with its lotus-shaped tower sits in the middle of a roundabout just one kilometer from the northernmost point of the Presidential Palace. The palace, a Vietnamese fortune teller said, housed the head of a dragon. The giant turtle lay at the tail of the dragon. So long as the two remained aligned and the dragon slept, the reign of the occupant of the palace would be ensured. If the dragon awakened and swished his tail at the Turtle

Monument, the ruler in the palace was doomed. The tail was clearly flailing now.

Neil and I followed a few feet behind the Hanoi soldiers. We heard scattered rifle fire from just behind a thick growth of trees. I ducked. Neil kept filming. The liberation troops held their fire. They moved forward, surrounding the South Vietnamese holdouts. They shouted out the equivalent of that old Wild West command: "Surrender or else! Come out with your hands up!"

About an hour later, as darkness approached, our mission with the giai phong bo doi ended. The "Saigon puppet" troops surrendered.

∎ ∎ ∎

The early days of May seemed almost sleepy. Small groups of bo doi gathered around the city center. Clusters of Vietnamese civilians—led by young students—came out to talk to the boys from Hanoi. These hardened young soldiers seemed naive, rather shy country boys from the north, awed by Saigon and not sure what to make of it all.

The giai phong (liberation) of the Cach Mang (Revolution) seemed remarkable in its absence of violence or reprisals. As far as I could tell, in the first days, no one had been arrested by the new rulers. "Hoa binh" (peace) seemed to be on everyone's lips.

There had been some suicides. I found the body of a Saigon army officer a few blocks from the post office. His service revolver lay on the street.

I walked up and down Tu Do Street chatting with people. They greeted giai phong with some apprehension but mostly with smiles of relief. Relief, because the city had been spared heavy fighting.

On May 2, Anh drove Neil and me in NBC's blue Ford van to Cholon, the Chinese sector of the city and always a center of new enterprise. We discovered a small factory churning out flags. Local merchants were painting signs for the new rulers' propaganda campaign.

The signs read "Vi dan, cho dan, boi dan." Government—"For the people, of the people, by the people." The words were credited to Ho Chi Minh as borrowed from Abraham Lincoln's Gettysburg Address.

■ ■ ■

On May 4, I woke up at the Caravelle at 3 a.m. in a cold sweat. I jotted the outlines of my dream in the diary.

In a recurring nightmare, I dreamt of Sinan forced to work in the Cambodian paddy. I dreamt of leeches as she planted rice, knee-deep in water. Giant, impossible to shed, slimy leeches from the soggy wet fields clinging to her skin. I felt the leeches on my legs from my knees to my toes.

■ ■ ■

Neil and I may have been trapped in communist Saigon, but unlike our colleagues in Phnom Penh, we lived in comfort. We ate well. Givral's Café on the corner of Passage Eden opposite the Continental reopened. It again served "Foremost" American-style ice cream: strawberry, chocolate, and vanilla. I still ordered my hearty morning bowl of Chinese soup, and just because it was there, some ice cream!

The black market off of Ham Nghia Street reopened. I saw bo doi wearing their almost colonial-style green pith helmets wandering around photographing each other. I stopped and helped a Hanoi soldier take a picture. The soldiers marveled at the array of goods on offer in the black market. They examined carefully and laughed at toy AK-47 rifles. One soldier got a good deal on a South Vietnamese–made knock-off watch. Or maybe the bo doi had been ripped off, as I saw the merchant smiling.

Communications with the outside world remained cut.

With some amusement, Neil and I sat in Givral's Café listening to BBC news on my shortwave radio. "As all communications have been severed, the fate of as many as eighty foreign journalists remaining behind in Saigon is not known at this time," the BBC World Service newsreader pronounced in somber tones.

■ ■ ■

On May 1, 1975, a story appeared in the Worcester, Massachusetts, *Telegram* under the headline, "Area Newsmen Still in Indochina: In Saigon and Phnom Penh."

The article described how Syd Schanberg, the *New York Times* man in Phnom Penh whose family lived in Clinton, Massachusetts, and I, whose family was in Worcester, remained behind after the communist takeovers. We were described in a slight exaggeration as "among the last Americans in Southeast Asia." The article quoted my mother as saying she hadn't heard anything from me but saw "her son when she flipped on her television set at 11 p.m." a few nights earlier.

Months later back in America, I discovered how my mother and father really felt. Dad had bought a tape recorder to document everything on radio and television that he could find about me or by me. And Mother simply said, "I wasn't worried. You'd been gone in faraway places for so long, I just figured you knew how to take care of yourself."

■ ■ ■

On Monday, May 5, Neil and I were getting restless. We wanted something different. A drive outside the capital might give us a better sense of how Hanoi forces were consolidating their new rule.

I suggested we drive west—along Route 1 toward Cu Chi. I had Cambodia on my mind.

On Sunday I had had lunch with Khoeun Rigaud and Amy David.

"There are reports," said Khoeun, "that a number of Cambodian refugees have made it across the border near Bavet near Route 1 on the border."

"It seems unlikely that Sinan would be among them," I replied. "How would she get all the way from Phnom Penh across the Mekong to the border?"

"But *peut-être*, maybe she did!" Amy added.

The next day, I asked Neil if we might drive west to the Cambodian border. Neil, with slight impatience in his voice, noted that "looking for your lover, mate, is like looking for a needle in a haystack. I'd rather drive south into the Mekong Delta. It's more of what Vietnam is about. We need to see if Vietnam is returning to normal."

In the NBC office, Anh listened to us both and said we had gasoline enough for only one day's travel out of town. Gasoline in Saigon was scarce. Black-market petrol prices skyrocketed.

The giai phong bo doi settled the issue.

For the most part North Vietnamese soldiers left us alone. We couldn't file stories, but we were free to travel locally and gather news.

Driving northwest toward the Cambodian border on Route 1, however, we encountered a roadblock. Only a few soldiers manned the outpost. They had erected a small barrier which they could raise or lower. A small wooden guard shack sheltered them from the sun. There was no questioning their orders; the bo doi were polite but firm: You cannot drive westward. We have no more information. Please turn around.

My Cambodia plan ended there.

Retracing our route, we headed about two hours south into the Mekong Delta as Neil had wanted. As we headed toward the port town of My Tho we came across a sea of discarded army hats, boots, clothing, and weapons. The South Vietnamese army had clearly fled rather than put up a fight. Villages we entered showed no sign of major battles.

In rice fields, a few days after Hanoi's victory, South Vietnamese women were doing what only the war had prevented, planting rice.

Then Neil had an idea that I thought most peculiar. He wanted to visit the island of the Coconut Monk!

The man Neil wanted to see was a French-educated engineer turned monk named Nguyen Thanh Nam. Known as the Coconut Monk because it was said he lived for three years on nothing but the white flesh and juice of coconuts, Nam had become a symbol of a peace movement in the Delta. He lived on Phoenix Island, "a sanctuary from war."

We reached the island. Ong Dao Dua, the Coconut Monk, greeted us warmly. He remembered Neil from a previous visit.

As I wandered around the complex, I marveled at this strange man. He wore Buddhist robes but a crucifix around his neck. He practiced a religion which seemed to embrace everything, much like the Cao Dai sect in Tay Ninh Province near Cambodia. Ong Dao Dua's utopian dreams of peace included dragons and gargoyles and columns with mythical creatures wrapped around them.

At one time perhaps 5,000 devotees followed Nam. He preached peace and he preached reunification between the North and South.

Now the monk's unification had been achieved by force.

"I saw liberation soldiers nearby in the river town of My Tho," the monk told us. "They seemed well behaved."

We agreed that My Tho's markets were thriving and Hanoi was quickly rebuilding infrastructure. The Coconut Monk voiced optimism about the future.

We departed the Coconut Monk and wished him well. I came away wishing we could have made it to the Cambodian border.

And the Coconut Monk's optimism turned out to be misplaced. In 1976, the communists declared Ong Dao Dua's religion a "cult." The wizened monk was put under house arrest; his few remaining followers dispersed. Nguyen Thanh Nam died mostly forgotten in 1990 in Vietnam at age 81.

■ ■ ■

On May 8, the first face of the new rulers appeared.

We were invited to the Presidential Palace, now Doc Lap (Independence Palace), to a news conference chaired by General Tran Van Tra, head of the Saigon Military Region Management Committee. General Tra was a deputy to General Dung, the architect of Hanoi's victory.

Tra had a reputation as a frank, outspoken communist. Unlike many in leadership, he was a southerner. Later in life, Tra would come into conflict with northern members of the politburo. In a memoir he published in 1983, he complained that southerners had been sidelined in the new Vietnam and that Hanoi had made serious mistakes in the famous Tet Offensive of 1968. For his candor, General Tra was thrown off the politburo and ended his days in seclusion.

In May 1975, however, General Tra was there to assure us that conditions in "reunified" Vietnam were returning to "normal."

"The road to reconstruction," Tra admitted, "will be long and difficult." He urged the cooperation of all.

He stressed an issue very much on the minds of many who feared the communist takeover—"bloodbath."

For years, Americans had spread fear in South Vietnam of widespread executions if the communists came to power. Uncertainty fed frightening rumors. I met young girls who feared their painted artificial fingernails would be ripped out by police. Or they feared they'd be forced to marry war-wounded, disabled North Vietnamese soldiers. It didn't help as word spread of what was happening to the urban elite in next-door Cambodia.

General Tra denounced reports of "bloodbath" as "despicable slander." He called on Vietnamese who had fled the country to return and help rebuild a unified Vietnam. "With the exception of a small number of ringleaders or reactionaries," Tra told us, "most had nothing to fear from the Provisional Revolutionary Government."

After the general's first meeting with the media, communications that had been cut for the past week were suddenly restored.

I raced back to the NBC office from Doc Lap Palace only to be disappointed. While telex and cable traffic returned, radio circuits remained blocked, making voice reports impossible. We also still had no way to get our television film out.

I cabled New York that Davis, Anh, and I were in good shape, restaurants and shops had opened, and the city was returning to conditions similar to those before the fall. I noted that "American ice cream was being dished out at Givral's."

I learned later that Bill "thanks for filling a hole" Corrigan thought that with the "ice cream" comment, I was trying to send some coded message. NBC News New York just couldn't figure out the secret code.

Soon John Chancellor began quoting me in brief "readers" on *Nightly News*. As intended by the new authorities, General Tra got a mention.

My stories began to appear again in the *Far Eastern Economic Review*. Nayan Chanda also pounded away on his stories at the Reuters office. On May 16, my piece on "Big Minh's Last Hours in Office" appeared. On May 23 the headline on my story about General Tra read "A Sense of Relief after the Bullets." It pretty much summed up the atmosphere during those early days of May.

During the week of May 10, several ominous developments in Saigon gave us reason to worry about the future in communist Vietnam.

The ruling Saigon military committee began the week by issuing an order that all Vietnamese report to street-side army posts to "register" with the new regime. Registrants were required to provide detailed information about their backgrounds, their work, their connections.

Several of my Vietnamese friends got nervous. One friend took to hiding in her home day after day. She feared coming out. She had worked for a foreign agency as a journalist. That alone would be enough, she argued, to condemn her. In the end, with the assistance of her former employer, she was allowed to emigrate to France.

Others were not so lucky. I saw registration as a first step. Hanoi authorities singled out former Saigon officials, army officers, and those with American connections. Later, upon institution of a new policy of Hoc tap cai tao, or "reeducation camps," more than 300,000 southerners were sent to primitive prisons and "reform through labor" facilities. Some remained in the camps a few months, many more for up to seventeen years. Many died in the camps.

Other signs in mid-May emerged that the tolerance of the new rulers would be limited.

One Sunday, Neil and I were filming at Saigon's Ben Thanh Central Market. Shoppers stocked up for the week ahead. Everyone was out and about but worried about higher prices and dwindling cash supplies. Banks still had not reopened.

As we explored the area, we saw a group of giai phong bo doi tearing down street stalls and clearing books from shelves. They appeared to be preparing a bonfire for a book burning.

Neil began to film. An officer saw us. He sent two of his men to greet us. The liberation soldiers marched us with AK-47s trained on our backs the three-quarters of a mile up Le Loi Boulevard back to the Caravelle.

I did not have enough time to jot down exactly which books were being earmarked for the bonfire. In a place where everything from the latest *Playboy* magazine to Orwell's *1984* could be had at a fraction of its cost in the West, I could only imagine.

As Vietnamese were ordered to register, the Foreign Affairs Section of the Military Management Committee asked me to report as well.

I presented my passport. I met Phuong Nam, the PRG officer who had lived at Camp Davis for more than two years. The "man of the south" looked at me curiously. "There aren't many of you Americans here, you know. I will assume you are a progressive one." I assured Phuong Nam of my progressive ideology.

I was duly registered and received certificate number 131.

Generally, I experienced little trouble as an American in communist Saigon. Attaching myself to Neil helped. If I were challenged by a hostile cadre, I would say, "I'm with him—*Uc dai loi!* Australian." Neil joked that I must learn to say "G'day" the proper way: "Ga-die!"

It was fortunate I registered with the communist authorities when I did, for two days later I would meet some "Saigon cowboys."

■ ■ ■

For years thieves on motorcycles proved a constant menace in the cities of South Vietnam. They would come out of nowhere to swoop down on unsuspecting pedestrians. In the early '70s we dubbed them "Saigon cowboys."

I was in a hurry to meet a friend at Brodard's café. I wore my satchel bag carelessly over my left shoulder as I hurried down the sidewalk. Roaring down Tu Do Street came two men on motorbikes. Suddenly my bag disappeared into a plume of exhaust fumes as the cowboys gunned it in the direction of the port. In the bag—my passport, gone in a flash, nearly two weeks after the US Embassy had fled.

A day after I reported my loss to the military committee, Saigon radio announced a war on street crime.

Warning against "reactionary elements" in Saigon, the radio reported that "liberation security forces" responding swiftly to an attack by thieves on an American television correspondent "apprehended the thief and shot him dead on the spot." The broadcast sent a clear message. But as far as I knew, no one had been shot and I never got my passport back.

In the end, the French Embassy came to my rescue. Consul Jean Grosboillet could not have been more accommodating. On

May 16, he presented me new travel documents. I would travel on French "laissez-passer No. 318/75."

• • •

The month of May marked a series of important celebrations for "unified" Vietnam's new rulers. On May 7 Hanoi marked the anniversary of the French defeat at Dien Bien Phu. On May 19 the Vietnamese observed Ho Chi Minh's birthday and decided to rename Saigon after him. The name change became official in early 1976.

On May 15 the communists organized a massive victory parade. French, Russian, and Chinese journalists arrived from Hanoi. A large group of Vietnamese Communist Party leaders flew in, northern and southern cadre.

My diary contains a long list of the names. Most are now long-forgotten leaders, many of whom were replaced in several years by more hard-line members of the Hanoi politburo. The man who really ran the show at that time as head of the "collective" leadership, Le Duan, was nowhere to be seen. Behind the Vietnamese on a large platform in front of Doc Lap Palace stood their Soviet backers from Moscow and their Chinese allies from Beijing. They waved and smiled as truckloads of young soldiers from Hanoi saluted them while standing at attention in the back of army vehicles.

A large banner read in Vietnamese Ho Chi Minh's words: "Nothing is more precious than freedom and independence."

I thought, as I watched from the sidelines, they had fought long and hard for this day. I guess they deserved their day in the Saigon sun.

• • •

A few days after the big celebration, Phuong Nam of the Military Management Committee called me in to give me a choice. Leave Saigon for Vientiane, Laos, in the next week or so with more than 20 days' worth of unexposed newsfilm to process and air on NBC, or stay a bit longer and not get the film out. There was no real choice.

Neil Davis would remain as long as he could. I would board a special plane to Laos carrying three giant onionskin sacks containing his film. The Military Management Committee made all the arrangements.

On Saturday, May 24, I packed my bags and said goodbye to Khoeun Rigaud and Amy David, with hopes that we could still somehow find Sinan.

I bid farewell to Saigon. The next twenty-four hours kept me in constant motion with a rather convoluted travel itinerary.

The Russian-made Ilyushin to Vientiane was packed: Peter Arnett of the Associated Press, Barron and Thirer of the BBC, and several dozen other journalists. We were joined by diplomats and foreign civilians who needed to get out. This was the first opportunity since the early morning hours of April 30 to leave Saigon. A few hours' delay. The plane's air conditioning failed as we waited on the baking Tan Son Nhut runway. Finally, we were off.

In Vientiane, my colleague George Lewis greeted me and handed me a new passport—quite an achievement. The NBC bureau chief in Hong Kong had persuaded the US vice consul there to issue me a new passport using a three-year-old photo.

"No time to waste," cautioned Lewis. "NBC has booked a special live broadcast out of Hong Kong for Monday. You have to be there tonight to start processing film. You've got a month of film to review. I'm not sure you're going to make it!"

"What's the route, George?" I asked. I knew there were no direct flights to Hong Kong from Laos.

"From a few miles down the road, you'll cross the Mekong by boat to Nong Kai, Thailand. A driver will take you an hour to Udon Thani airport. NBC has a single-engine charter plane standing by. It will take you to Bangkok in time for the last flight of the day to Hong Kong at 1730. Off you go!"

As it turned out, the Mekong boat crossing slowed me down and I was late meeting the charter at Udon Thani. I reached Bangkok too late to catch the last flight to Hong Kong.

NBC, however, was prepared to spare no expense.

The network scrambled. They placed a chartered Cathay Pacific Boeing 707 Jetliner with seats for 180 passengers on standby.

Nayan Chanda and I wrote up the extravagant story in "Travellers' Tales" in the *Far Eastern Economic Review*:

> Networks with newsfilm were particularly anxious to get their stories out, but the new Saigon authorities did not seem to have the immediate means …
>
> The BBC contacted an Asian airline in an attempt to arrange a charter to go into Saigon and bring the story out …
>
> In the end, the Provisional Liberation Government (PRG) handled affairs their own way. An Ilyushin from Hanoi of Hang Khoan Dan Dung (People's Airways) ferried foreigners to Vientiane for US$120 a ticket (about double the previously normal Saigon to Vientiane fare).
>
> The chartered aircraft story did not end there. NBC News, with exclusive film of the communist takeover, hired an aircraft to fly the film from Bangkok to Hong Kong for a special broadcast. For the

first time in the history of Cathay Pacific Airways, a Boeing 707, with a crew of nine including four flight hostesses and 37 hot meals, carried a passenger load of one ragged reporter and three film bags.

This ragged reporter finally got Neil Davis's film into the "soup" (the Kodak processing lab in Kowloon, Hong Kong) and edited it down to twenty-five minutes of somewhat organized vision.

With no time for a shave or a haircut, and wearing a borrowed, oversized green jacket, surrounded by veteran NBC network anchors and veteran Vietnam reporter Peter Arnett as guest, I sat glumly in front of the camera helping narrate my twenty-five days in communist Vietnam.

The Monday, May 26 program opened: "We delay the start of the *Tonight Show* starring Johnny Carson to bring you the following NBC News Special Report—Communist Saigon."

∎ ∎ ∎

Looking back at my time in April and May 1975 in Indochina, the stark contrasts between Vietnam and Cambodia stand out.

Along with the loss of Sinan, I struggled with the news of the horrific evacuation of the Cambodian urban centers and the brutality of the Khmer communists. Yet in Vietnam, I observed an orderly takeover with fewer deaths than most expected.

Given the long war, shouldn't South Vietnam's communist takeover have been bloodier?

I pondered the naivete of the Khmer and the cynicism (or realism) of the Vietnamese. I questioned why Khmer soldiers outside Phnom Penh fought on for five days after the American left them on their own.

However, in Vietnam, young soldiers pushed women and children out of the way to escape on planes and helicopters. Only a few South Vietnamese units put up a determined defense of their homeland. Within hours of the American departure, the war ended.

I was struck by a meeting Neil had with a young communist cadre who arrived in Saigon in mid-May from Hanoi.

"What I don't understand," he said, "is why the South didn't fight harder for all their riches." He pointed to a TV, a radio, and some furniture in his new Saigon apartment. "Don't you understand how destitute we were in North Vietnam?"

■ ■ ■

For one young American who nearly lost everything on April 30, escape from giai phong took fifteen months. On August 1, 1976, the young US postal worker Gerald Posner from Brooklyn, New York, put his arm around his wife, Tu Thi Nhan, as they landed safely in Bangkok. Gerald, the desperate 25-year-old we had met in front of the US Embassy, had a broad smile on his face. For fifteen months he remained trapped in Saigon. Reduced to poverty like most Vietnamese were, he lived on about $30 a month. Working with the International Red Cross, he found his wife in the Mekong Delta. Vietnamese authorities allowed the couple to leave together.

It was an accomplishment that a certain young journalist—roughly the same age as Posner—could not claim. Soc Sinan was still nowhere to be found.

19

"Change Will Come Soon"

THE LONGER SOC SINAN REMAINED on the commune in Saang, the more Angkar stepped up political indoctrination. The longer she stayed, the more careful she became, as one by one people she knew disappeared and the number of "new" people dwindled.

The political rallies with their endless harangues about the virtues of Democratic Kampuchea became a regular if monotonous feature of Sinan's life. Behind the rhetoric, she discovered some new meanings.

As 1977 ended, intense political struggles were underway, struggles accompanied by harsh new rhetoric. Sinan watched and listened.

Comrade Eng or Comrade Bo in her Chinese jeep would visit to speak two or three times, then half a dozen times during a year.

We were forced to stand for hours and listen.

We had no idea of the leadership of "Democratic Kampuchea" except from these meetings. Everything was a secret. Sometimes leaders would turn on a communal radio on loudspeakers to hear news from the top leadership. In the closed world in which we lived, it remained a mystery. They were simply the Angkar Loeu: "The High Organization."

The cadre spoke endlessly of the good Angkar was doing. The importance of self-reliance. Independence. Hard work. No rich. No poor. Equality for all.

Over and over, they reminded us that the Americans and their puppets were to blame for destroying Cambodia. "You have seen for yourselves the destruction they did by their bombing for so many years."

Sometimes nearly a thousand people would sit for hours under the shade of mango trees as they "washed our brains."

Then in early 1978 the political meetings revealed a new enemy: the Vietnamese.

The Vietnamese? I thought the Vietnamese communists helped build the Khmer Rouge and made their success possible. The past. Now Angkar must triumph OVER them.

I befriended one of the "base" people with a kindly twinkle in his eyes. He was perhaps 50, but looked older. Hard work clearly took a lot out of him. Comrade Hok was his name.

After one long meeting, Hok turned to me. He could see I was tired. His wrinkled face brightened with a slight smile. He whispered, "Be patient. A change is coming. Change will come soon."

As I walked slowly back to the commune women's work brigade barracks, I shook my head. Change? I could not believe Comrade Hok.

While Sinan doubted that she would ever see change, remarkable events were transforming Asia: developments no one in the work camps of Kampuchea could possibly know about. These events would intersect to decide Sinan's fate.

■ ■ ■

Not many weeks after their victory, Khmer Rouge extremists began to pursue what they saw as their manifest destiny. Based on territorial claims hundreds of years old, the new Khmer rulers saw parts of Vietnam as theirs. During the chaos of May 1975, Pol Pot ordered Khmer Rouge troops to seize the island of Phu Quoc at the very tip of the Mekong Delta. The Vietnamese easily turned back the attack, but it did not stop Khmer Rouge raids on Vietnam's territory.

By June 1977, Kampuchean forces attacked along a 60-mile front. Hanoi seemed to have been caught off-guard by the offensive. Hundreds of Vietnamese were killed.

At first Hanoi tried negotiation. The Khmer Rouge stalled, then boldly accused Vietnam of aggression.

Phnom Penh severed diplomatic relations with Hanoi, and by October 1978 the situation reached a critical stage. As the border war intensified, *Time* magazine reported, "The regime of Pol Pot was staggering under the weight of its own excesses."

Denis Gray of the Associated Press wrote, "The terror in Cambodia is gaining in viciousness, defying the macabre optimism of some Western diplomats who thought the government would run out of people to kill."

Nayan Chanda, in his 1986 book *Brother Enemy*, summed up the change that swept across Indochina and drew in China and the Soviet Union.

The French and the Americans "by their long intervention had interrupted the natural order of things, had brought competing nations, divergent cultures, conflicting ancient histories together."

"Now," wrote Chanda, "nationalism would trump ideology."

It would not be long before this rush of violent events and political re-alignments would impact the life of Soc Sinan and millions of other suffering Cambodians.

In America, people had lost interest. They had turned away from the never-ending wars of Indochina. After the collapse of

South Vietnam, the new battles that embroiled the region drew little media attention. It did not help that from late 1975 through 1978 access to Vietnam and Cambodia by Western reporters was nearly impossible.

■ ■ ■

After my month in communist Vietnam in 1975, NBC threw me into a long list of assignments. I welcomed the work if for no other reason than to keep my mind off personal pain. I accepted a long assignment in India. Then off to Beirut to cover the Lebanese civil war. Once a war reporter, always a war reporter.

I tried to maintain, as best I could, my Cambodia connections. France possessed a large, vibrant, educated Khmer exile community. If anybody had news of Sinan or other Cambodians now trapped as rural prison laborers, they might be there. But I could find nothing. A horrible blanket of silence descended over the nation whose rulers had the audacity to name it "Democratic Kampuchea." I rather naively applied for visas for Kampuchea, through the Democratic Kampuchea Embassy in Paris. I received no reply.

Saorun and Eric Ellul reached Paris safely in 1975. Now divorced, Saorun lived in an apartment in the 11th Arrondissement on la rue de Charonne.

I went to Paris to see her in June. I learned the heartbreaking story of her last meeting with Sinan on April 12. She recounted the harrowing story of her own escape from Cambodia through the French Embassy.

"What do you think?" I asked Saorun. "You've seen conditions. Is there any hope? Can Sinan survive?"

Saorun shook her head with a mixture of sadness, distress, and just a glimmer of hope.

"Je ne sais pas," replied Saorun, "but if anyone can escape death, it would be Sinan. She is very resourceful."

■ ■ ■

I also decided to reach out to Sinan's "Le Commandant," Major Walt. From Paris, I flew to Washington.

I felt the two men who failed her should meet. Walter had tried so hard. What kind of man was he? Would he blame me for Sinan's fate? I was certainly ready to accept that blame.

We set up a lunch meeting at the Shoreham Hotel.

He arrived at the restaurant—tall, thin, with that military bearing of authority. He was quiet and gracious. No accusations.

I told Walter of my meeting with Saorun in Paris.

"I'm not sure I know Saorun," Walter replied.

Still, he was grateful for the story of Saorun's last encounter with Sinan in Phnom Penh.

"I still can't understand why she wouldn't leave." There was a question in his statement.

I began a long reply on the importance of friends and family and the Khmer New Year. I refused to examine the possibility that Sinan had remained because of me. These were thoughts I would not explore with Walter.

"Does the Pentagon or the US government have any intelligence of what is going on inside Cambodia?" I asked, trying to bring the conversation back to a professional level.

"Not much," Walter replied somberly, "but what little there is is not good."

"Do you think Sinan can survive under those conditions?"

"I have grave doubts," Walter said after a long pause. "I think people of her background are put to death."

A long silence. Then two men—a 40-year-old former MEDTC officer and a 28-year-old reporter who had by now witnessed three wars—choked up. Tears for lunch at the Shoreham.

"Le Commandant" came across as neither the tough military careerist that Sinan depicted nor a man who would place blame on me for Sinan's fate. Perhaps she was projecting her father's traits onto the man in front of me.

We came out of the meeting, two men who had been in love with the same woman, concluding that there was very little hope. We agreed Sinan was just the kind of Khmer who in the ongoing carnage would be doomed, certainly if anyone found out she was connected to us. We both pledged to do what we could to find and rescue Sinan.

As years went by though, Walter gave up hope.

Walter turned to Denny Lane, now the Southeast Asia Intelligence desk officer at the Pentagon. He asked Lane to explore the possibility that Sinan was still alive. Lane prepared a short report concluding that the best information available suggested that Sinan "could not have survived."

Walter had to move on. He wanted a family. He retained an obsession with Cambodia. By 1978, he had met another Khmer woman, an early refugee from the war. Davi too was beautiful. She and her family had made an early escape to Vietnam from the horrors of Cambodia. Walter described Davi as the "light of my life." They married and settled down in Virginia.

Change was best for everyone concerned.

· · ·

In the District of Saang, the woman who had in effect been declared dead at the Pentagon watched and waited.

As Sinan listened, the speeches of the Angkar cadre became more strident. They spoke of great victories over the new enemies of Democratic Kampuchea.

We could hear in the distance the sounds of rockets or artillery, certainly some big guns. It seemed to be coming from an area east of Saang.
I was happy when I heard it.
Before April 17, 1975, in Phnom Penh—rockets were a source of fear for me, total terror. Now sounds of rockets were a source of hope.
Maybe Comrade Hok was right. It must signal some kind of change. I was eager for war again.

Sinan quickly recognized that not all the communist leaders in Kampuchea agreed a war with Vietnam was necessary.

There was something different about the harvest of 1978. It was a good harvest. We now worked on two shifts. I looked around me. There were fewer people in the work brigades than in the past.
More disappearances. Now it was not only the "new" people who became victims. Angkar began weeding out unreliable revolutionaries. "Base" people disappeared.
In Saang there were signs of new ethnic turmoil. Angkar began to separate people according to blood. People who were 75% Chinese or 75% Vietnamese were forced out of the region. Those who were pure Khmer or those who were 80% Khmer like me remained and in some ways received better treatment.
Angkar also changed the leaders of districts, cantons, communes, and villages.
I did not know what happened to the old leaders, or the Vietnamese and Chinese, but I heard later that at least some of them were put to death.

■ ■ ■

Inside Democratic Kampuchea, an internal war among its leaders was underway. Communist turned on communist. The records of the destructive purges were later revealed at the Tuol Sleng Prison in Phnom Penh.

The Communist Party of Kampuchea (CPK) was breaking down along the lines that Sinan noticed in her apartment on April 20, 1975.

With an AK-47 pointed threateningly at her head, Sinan had the presence of mind to notice the young Khmer in black uniform and the older Khmer in green. Green—cadre from the eastern zone nearer to Vietnam. Black—the more extreme Khmer who took orders directly from Pol Pot, the then-unknown figure at the center. Pol Pot ordered anyone not in lockstep with him on Vietnam killed.

■ ■ ■

In Saang, faced with the challenge of staying alive, Sinan discovered she had some knowledge that might help her. She could perform a service that the cadre and their most dedicated followers wanted. Sinan figured out something else. Support for the regime was waning among the "revolutionary" farmers who had lived under the Khmer Rouge for years. The radical communists had destroyed three traditional values that made life worth living: land (no matter how small the plot), family, and religion.

On the commune, Sinan resolved to be as useful as she could.

I had perfected a treatment: rubbing coins on the backs of the weary. Coin rubbing and cupping were traditional medical treatments in

Cambodia. I practiced in my family. I found the technique was not known by these base people and the Khmer Rouge cadre who led them here.

They seemed grateful for my service. While I massaged and used the coins, I could learn from the comrades.

They would whisper their unhappiness and speak of their long years of revolutionary struggle.

Their enthusiasm for Angkar seemed strong during the war. People were far more worried then by American bombing than about Khmer Rouge cruelty. The Americans really helped the Khmer Rouge. Now things were different. The unity of Angkar was falling apart.

As 1978 dragged on, we heard the sound of artillery more often. More political meetings now warned of the treacherous Vietnamese.

This was a time to listen, to think. This was not a time to talk but a time to be extra careful and be as useful as I could to the "base" and the older members of the commune.

My new friend Ala seemed to know something. I don't know how. She was a native "base person." She had become an unlikely friend.

She had her political sources. "Don't worry too much, be patient and work hard. Our glorious day is approaching. Something will happen soon."

I admired her. A native person of maybe 35, she was old enough to remember the Sihanouk era. She harbored resentment against the Khmer Rouge and yet, as a farmer all her life, she had been living in the liberated zones for more than eight years.

Ala got along with all of the chiefs as well as the ordinary people, both from the countryside and the city. To me she seemed to be the perfect spy, the perfect double agent.

I listened to her without comment.

As I rubbed the coin on Ala's back, we heard the rumble of artillery.

No one expressed enthusiasm for the sounds of war as I quietly did. But I could tell. The people, the base, would not oppose change when it came, as it seemed it would soon—out of the east.

■ ■ ■

The harvest continued. The sounds from the east grew louder.

Most of us stopped working. We looked up in the direction of explosions. Having heard the sounds in Phnom Penh, I was sure I knew what it was.

Comrade Tieng would get angry when everyone stopped for work.

She shouted through a loud hailer: "Comrades, don't be startled. Our cadres are blowing up rocks in the Saang Hills to build some new roads. Pay no attention. Back to work!"

I didn't believe her. Few did. We kept our mouths shut, did as we were told.

To me the explosions were melodious. I wanted to hear more.

20

Letters of '79

April 10, 1979—Route 1, Kampuchea

HEADING WEST, OUR BEAT-UP Ford van from the Ho Chi Minh City Tourist Bureau bumped along Route 1 toward Phnom Penh. The old French-built route posed different challenges from those when I last traveled this road nine years before.

This time I did not fear for Khmer Rouge ambush. At least, I thought we were safe.

Responding to repeated Khmer Rouge provocations, the Vietnamese had invaded Cambodia in December. They took the capital on January 7. Now, three months later, Hanoi was in charge. Yet Ong Viet, my guide from the Ho Chi Minh City Foreign Affairs office packed his Russian Makarov semiautomatic pistol. He placed it conveniently under the front right seat of the van—just in case.

We were the only passenger vehicle on the road. Occasionally we had to make way for an armored personnel carrier or other military vehicle driving west.

After we crossed the Mekong on the Neak Leung ferry, the highway was packed not with military trucks but with people. A steady stream of people—ragged, sad, sacks of meager possessions on their backs, with desperate looks on their faces—trudged wearily westward. They were leaving communes. Freed from the labor camps, they were trying to go home, the homes they were forced to leave in April 1975. Many of them were bound for Phnom Penh.

I looked out the window. I examined every woman's face I could see. Might I see someone I knew? Might Sinan be among these survivors?

■ ■ ■

My return to Cambodia occurred nearly four years to the day after I had fled Phnom Penh by helicopter.

In 1978, at the end if my NBC contract, I joined ABC News with the new assignment to increase coverage of Southeast Asia and to open a bureau in China. I set to work on regaining access to Vietnam and Cambodia as soon as I could. I badgered Vietnamese authorities for visas. I approached anyone with contacts in Hanoi. It finally paid off.

My colleague, producer John Lower, our Vietnamese guide, and I drove across the border with a Japanese film crew from Nippon Denpa News, an agency which had maintained close relations with the government in Hanoi for almost twenty years.

■ ■ ■

The artillery exchange Sinan heard on her commune in late summer 1978 developed into a full-scale Vietnamese invasion of Cambodia.

Hanoi had prepared well. In addition to assembling a large invasion force of more than 200,000 men, the Vietnamese as early as 1977 began to train a new core of Khmer leaders. They drew them from disenchanted Khmer Rouge and Cambodians who lived in Vietnam. Hanoi cultivated Khmer like Heng Samrin, who had commanded a unit that entered Phnom Penh in 1975, and promoted a young man named Hun Sen who lost an eye in combat and then fled to Vietnam.

Hanoi moved decisively on December 22, 1978. In less than three weeks, Vietnam's massive force sent Pol Pot and the Khmer Rouge fleeing toward Thailand. Declaring victory in Phnom Penh on January 7, Vietnam renamed "Democratic Kampuchea" the "People's Republic of Kampuchea."

■ ■ ■

The last 20 miles of our drive into Phnom Penh was slow going.

My film team and I stopped about 2 miles outside Phnom Penh. The remains of an old government dormitory served as a makeshift shelter for perhaps a thousand people seeking to return to what remained of their homes in Phnom Penh after nearly four years.

Vietnamese troops prevented the Cambodians from going further. Entry to the city was being carefully controlled. The Vietnamese army feared Khmer Rouge saboteurs might reenter the capital and attack the Vietnamese encamped there.

They needn't have worried about the people who sat before us this day.

These were the dispossessed. These city people, Phnom Penh residents, mostly professionals or merchants, were educated people who, like Sinan, had been forced from their homes into harsh rural commune life.

A large group gathered on the side of the road when they saw us stop. They approached us hesitantly at first and then seemingly all at once.

Dozens of men, women, and children stepped forward with tears in their eyes. They looked at us beseechingly. Many spoke French or English.

John Lower engaged them in his fluent French. I alternated between my rusty French and English. I was overcome with that choking feeling you have when trying to suppress your emotions.

Was it too much to hope that Sinan might be among this group of returnees?

With unfailing politeness, each person asked us for help.

We met the former Khmer manager of the Phnom Penh office of Air France. He tearfully told me of his imprisonment under the Khmer Rouge and the fate of his family. "When we left our home in 1975, we were separated from our family, our parents, until now. I met my sister three days ago. They killed them all."

"The Khmer Rouge communists killed your parents?" I repeated.

"Yes—as well as my brother and my other sister too. Dead. All dead!"

As we talked, dozens more approached us with letters, some written on meager scraps of paper. I started giving out pages of my notebook so that others could write messages.

Please, a young woman asked me, send this to France:

To Mms Vanna Volent, 7 Route de Bazement 78, Aubergenville France.

Dear Chin, Our parents were died. I name Eng and my five children are alive in P. Penh. But very sad living.

With love your second sister Ly Yok Eng.

We accepted their letters, one by one.

Cheng Sokum sought his cousin Chin Saream in New York.

Kim Bopha Darany wanted me to send a letter to her sister in Morocco.

Marie Clementine Meng wanted her relations in Paris to know she was alive.

Cheng Heng asked me to tell his daughter Narinnee in Knoxville, Tennessee, that he survived.

Sometimes, I would simply take names and addresses of loved ones. I promised to write on their behalf. We gathered as many names and letters as we could.

I turned to address the camera for a piece which Peter Jennings introduced on ABC's *World News Tonight* a week later.

> In the last few hours here we have been given dozens of letters from people wishing their relatives and friends in the outside world to know they are still alive. They have survived the four years of the Pol Pot regime. For all of them, this is the first opportunity they have had to communicate with the outside world.

I spoke emotionally, waving scraps of papers around as if they were evidence in the prosecution's case against genocide.

> Our impression was of a people emerging from a holocaust. We talked with more than fifty people here on the outskirts of Phnom Penh. All had similar horror stories. Doctors, bankers, technicians, teachers put to dawn-to-dusk work on communes with little food. Most said they survived by pretending to be someone else.

In this short time, we collected twenty-three letters with addresses of relatives in Europe, Africa, and the United States. I relayed all the details to the International Committee of the Red Cross in Geneva.

The number of people we helped reunite was tiny compared to the millions who sought to find loved ones.

For the rest of the year I received notes from all over the world hoping I could help relatives the next time I went to Cambodia.

On May 17, I got a telegram in the ABC News office in Hong Kong:

To M. Jim Laurie

Acknowledge receipt of your letter concerning my sister Kim Bopha Darany. Sincere thanks for your kind help.

Kim Pong Reaksmey, Rabat Morocco.

Still, the extraordinary visit to Vietnamese-occupied Cambodia was a disappointment. I received no letter from the one person I hoped to hear from. No trace of Soc Sinan.

On Saturday, April 14, I boarded the Ho Chi Minh tourist van once again and retraced the route back to Ho Chi Minh City. I felt rotten. I assumed the worst, but I vowed to return.

∎ ∎ ∎

In Saigon all the familiar names had been changed. The city had been officially renamed Ho Chi Minh City.

The colonial Majestic Hotel built in 1925 on the Saigon River waterfront was now the Cuu Long. Hotels, restaurants, and even coffee shops had been nationalized. The Ho Chi Minh City Revolutionary Committee in many cases replaced old Western names with simple numbers. One of my old hangouts—Brodard's in French and Bo Da in Vietnamese—was now simply Nha Hang 131, Restaurant #131.

The younger brother of Le Duc Tho (the tough negotiator who hammered out the fatally flawed 1973 Paris Peace Accord with Kissinger) had been rewarded. The hard-line Mai Chi Tho served as mayor and Communist Party boss.

Tho imposed short-sighted policies which stifled economic recovery.

He ordered the construction of "economic zones" outside the city to soak up unemployment and try to kickstart a stagnant economy. I visited one in Tay Ninh, a province near the Cambodian border. The barren location, littered with land mines and absent of cultivatable land, proved unfit for settlement. The government sent thousands to Tay Ninh. People drifted back to the city to eke out a living on the streets or in new urban black markets.

Vietnam was a mess. Rigid policies held it back. The nation was also now burdened with a massive military occupation in Cambodia. Vietnam would not begin to recover for another ten years.

■ ■ ■

From my base living in Hong Kong, I threw myself into work.

I tried to focus on three major events: emerging China, famine-stricken Cambodia, and struggling Vietnam. I bounced from China to Southeast Asia and back again.

I met China's leader, Deng Xiaoping, in Beijing, then accompanied him on a four-city tour of America.

In Hanoi, I interviewed Vietnamese leader Pham Van Dong. The prime minister vigorously defended Vietnam's invasion of Cambodia. "In the future more nations will see clearly the justice of our actions."

Much to my surprise, Dong inquired about my days in Saigon in 1975.

"Do you know Mr. Frank Snepp?" he asked. "I have read that CIA man's book *Decent Interval*. It provides good reading to understand Vietnam's refugee situation."

From Hanoi, I drove to China's border with Vietnam, reporting on the impact of a 27-day Chinese invasion of northern Vietnam. The Chinese, it was said, wanted to "teach Vietnam a lesson" for Hanoi's invasion of China's ally, Cambodia.

An outpouring of refugees from both Vietnam and Cambodia reached a peak in 1979. I visited dozens of refugee camps: from those housing Cambodians in Thailand to those housing Vietnamese in Malaysia.

After weeks of extensive traveling, I arrived back in Hong Kong on Sunday, October 7.

The next day, back in my office in Wanchai, I began to sift through a stack of mail on my desk.

One handwritten letter stood out.

The small blue hotel envelope had apparently been taken from Saigon's Cuu Long. Yet it was postmarked Singapore and addressed to my old NBC News office in the same building, forwarded upstairs to ABC.

I opened it at once.

Dated August 17, 1979, it had taken nearly two months to reach me. I recognized the neat handwriting instantly.

Dear Jim

It is 4 years 4 months since April 17, 1975, that I didn't hear any news from you.

Where have you been? In Hong Kong or U.S.A.

I have received your last visiting card which you put by the door of my house before you leave P.Penh in the morning of Saturday April 12, 1975. I keep it until now.

Since April 27, 1975, I leave the city by the Khmer Rouge truck. They took me to the district of Saang in the province of Kandal. I live there from that date.

I have so many strong deceptions on life since the K.R. came to P.Penh. I left P.Penh alone without a family. No sisters or brothers. I didn't have any happiness for one minute. I know how big mistakes I have made at that time.

I came one time to my house at P. Penh on July 1979. I was very sad and I burst into tears. I had all of my early memories. I couldn't find my father and all of my sisters and brothers. I do not know if they have life or not.

I get very tired of this situation and I don't want to go to P Penh or stay there anymore.

I would like to get out of this country but I couldn't find the best way to go. I would need some help from you. Could you please find the good way to take me out from this situation?

I still have a ticket from Sabena from Bangkok to New York.

My life doesn't have the sense for me to live.

I hope you are very well and very happy in life and business and that you travel all over the world.

I suppose that I will meet you in the far off days:

My address: Mrs. S. Sinan

Phum Por Kandal

Khum Troysla

District of SAANG

Province of Kandal

CAMBODIA

I live on the east side of the Bassac River about 40 km in the South from the city.

Thank you in advance. My best thoughts to you.

Your remote friend

SSinan

N.B. I send this letter by someone who goes to Saigon. The K Government does not yet open a P.O. in P.Penh."

"Your remote friend, SSinan."

My eyes welled up. I was dumbstruck. How was it possible?

The letter seemed so matter of fact and yet awe-inspiring and profoundly sad. What could I do? I resolved at once to do what I should have done in 1975. Sinan must leave Cambodia! I must get her out!

I quickly drafted a ream of letters.

To the International Red Cross. To the United Nations High Commission for Refugees (UNHCR). To my Vietnamese Foreign Ministry contacts in Hanoi. To the US Embassy in Bangkok. To everyone I could think of.

The two most important notes went to Chum Bun Rong in Phnom Penh and Bui Huu Nhan in Ho Chi Minh City.

Nhan was the Vietnamese NLF official I had met in Paris so many years ago after the Peace Accord was signed. I had seen him again in Vietnam in May. I knew Vietnamese officials controlled all visas to Cambodia. I would have to win them over. Nhan possessed an intelligence and sophistication I had rarely seen in government officials. He spoke five languages, including some Russian and Khmer. He also served as special adviser to the Vietnamese ambassador in Phnom Penh. I felt Nhan could be trusted with the delicate mission of extracting Sinan from her prison.

And Chum Bun Rong in Phnom Penh. He served as my guide in Cambodia in April. I had told him Sinan's story when we first met. He seemed sympathetic. I asked him to get a message to Sinan. I was determined to return to find her as soon as I could.

In October, I flew to Thailand again to report on the growing refugee crisis and something more. A devastating famine had begun to take hold of Cambodia. The war, the massive dislocation of people, and the mismanagement of resources by the Khmer Rouge merged to create a major catastrophe.

I wrote a story on singer Joan Baez. She had flown to Thailand to show support for efforts to assist starving refugees. The last time she had been in the region was in 1973 when she traveled to Hanoi just after Nixon's 1972 "Christmas bombings."

The celebrity of Baez brought attention to the story. On October 12, the plight of Cambodia placed high again on the evening network news.

I phoned Dick Richter at the ABC News New York *Close-Up* documentary unit suggesting we develop a new project—a major film on Cambodia.

I knew that John Pilger, a well-known British writer, had already completed work on what would be a powerful telling of the Cambodia story. Pilger released *Year Zero: The Silent Death of Cambodia* in late October.

On October 15, a man with a long association with Vietnam, who had the trust of Hanoi officials, approached ABC News with a proposal, which I urged New York to accept.

Don Luce worked and lived in South Vietnam from 1958 until 1971; he was another Vietnam specialist nurtured by the organization IVS—International Voluntary Services.

Most media organizations reported the Cambodia story from Thailand. Luce was willing to use his connections to get me and a three-person team back inside Vietnamese-occupied Cambodia for an extensive look. In a few days, we had a deal.

Veteran ABC cameraman Yasutsune "Tony" Hirashiki and I would join Luce and photojournalist Ed Rasen to film a one-hour ABC documentary.

We would travel extensively across Vietnamese-occupied Kampuchea. From New York, producer Phil Lewis and a second team would be assigned to the Thai border. While one team roamed Cambodia, the second captured the horrors of Thai refugee camps. Lewis and his team also landed a rare interview on the Thai border with the ousted radical communist leader, "Brother Number One," Pol Pot.

Pol Pot told Lewis that all the reports of bloodbath in Cambodia were lies. "All theater created by the Vietnamese aggressors." He pledged, with Chinese help, to take Cambodia back.

We prepared to enter Cambodia via Vietnam on November 12.

I struggled with an internal emotional battle. As a reporter, I believed in keeping work and personal matters separate. And yet, the intensity of my desire to make this documentary was driven by my pledge to rescue Sinan.

I decided to tell Luce and Hirashiki of Sinan's story. Until then I had not confided in many colleagues.

Hirashiki suggested that if we could find Sinan and film the reunion; we would have a better documentary than the one ABC News *Close-Up* envisioned.

What better? A youthful story, complete with love, loss, recovery, and maybe rescue. I told him I would think about it.

A film featuring my personal drama? In those days I subscribed to an old-fashioned view of television news. Tell good stories about people, but remain, as much as possible, dispassionate and uninvolved. The reporter was not the story. This 1979 notion seems almost quaint today.

. . .

Upon arrival in Hanoi, the four of us were met by Tran Ngoc Thach from the Foreign Ministry. "Little Thach" we called him, to not confuse him with his boss—Vietnam's Foreign Minister Nguyen Co Thach. Little Thach and I seemed to develop an instant bond. He was a good man who would skillfully broker most of our arrangements for the next six weeks in Cambodia.

On November 22, from Ho Chi Minh City, I once again headed down Route 1 to Cambodia.

Bui Huu Nhan accompanied us. The sympathetic Nhan had received my letter. I provided him more details of Sinan and her situation.

■ ■ ■

By the time of our November arrival, Hanoi controlled 85 percent of Cambodia and had stationed at least 50,000 troops across the country. Khmer Rouge resistance under Pol Pot appeared to be confined to small pockets in the far northwest and sanctuaries in Thailand.

What made our situation especially complicated was that the United States refused to deal with Vietnam. Washington now supported a coalition of Cambodian factions including the Khmer Rouge, once again headed at least in name by Norodom Sihanouk. Washington forbade aiding Cambodia through Phnom Penh. Any US-backed assistance to the starving Khmer people must go through refugee camps in Thailand.

Again Cambodians became victims of cruel politics. It struck me as inhumane. Food was scarce inside Cambodia. But in effect the Americans were saying that if Cambodians wanted to eat, they should flee to Thailand, where American relief would be waiting. Of course, to get to Thailand meant walking hundreds of miles, crossing Khmer Rouge front lines, and risking land mines, which were planted along the border. The United States once again, in my view, was playing politics with people's lives.

Back in Phnom Penh, I met with Chum Bun Rong. He had been invaluable on my visit in April. He offered at once to ride his motorcycle down to Saang District on the Bassac and see if he could find Sinan.

Meanwhile, the documentary shoot began.

The next day Hirashiki, Luce, Rasen, and I embarked on twelve remarkable days of travel by road across Cambodia.

Our able interpreter Kim An worked out all the arrangements. We headed northwest first: Sisophon, Battambang, Poipet, Siem Reap, the Angkor temples. We drove southeast to Kampong Cham and finally further south to Cambodia's seaport and Kampong Som better known as Sihanoukville.

Four images of those extensive travels stay with me all these years later.

The killing fields. As we traveled to the northwest, we stopped at multiple mass graves where hundreds, perhaps thousands, of skeletal remains provided shocking testimony to Khmer Rouge genocide.

Hunger, especially among children. Everywhere we went, food was being delivered to the needy, but not enough and not quickly enough.

And death, often by cerebral malaria.

One afternoon, on the road heading north from Kampong Som, we came across a small hospital: a hospital really in name only.

On the steps of the facility a man lay dying. I watched in shock as the man's body twitched in agony. A stream of what looked like white foam spewed from his mouth. In a minute or so, he was still. Dead. I had seen a lot of death covering wars and disasters over the years, but this was the first time I had seen a civilian, afflicted with malaria and no medicine, no doctors, no help, die right in front of my eyes.

My fourth lasting impression was bitter-sweet. A pleasant excursion walking through the abandoned temples of Angkor in a small way lifted my spirits. As I walked around the complex, with Vietnamese troops providing security, my mind wandered back to 1970 when Sinan and I planned our visit to Angkor before war intervened. It would have been so much better if Sinan and I had been there together.

■ ■ ■

Back in Phnom Penh, Chum Bun Rong came to me with news I had been waiting for.

He had returned from a motorbike trip to Saang District. He had located in the little village of Khum Troysla a young woman who now taught school to children deprived of education for four years. He had found Sinan.

Sinan could stay at his house in Phnom Penh. I would be reunited with my "distant friend" Sunday morning.

21

Reunion

Sunday, December 9, 1979

A SMALL ABANDONED SHOP stood across the street from the Monorom Hotel on Monivong Boulevard, less than a half dozen blocks from the deserted fourth-floor apartment which Sinan called home for six years.

Kim An whispered that Sinan would be there waiting for me. He and Bun Rong had arranged her transport. He suggested a quiet meeting that would not attract a lot of attention.

The ever-enthusiastic Tony Hirashiki had other ideas. He raised again the idea that I said I would consider. "Jim, this is a great opportunity. A great human story. We really must capture it on tape."

I hesitated. Then agreed.

Tony grabbed his camera and ran after me across the street.

The door of the shop opened. My eyes needed time to adjust after the bright morning light.

There in the darkness stood Soc Sinan.

I couldn't believe it. She had really survived. First she, then I, dissolved into tears.

Tony moved in with his camera and turned on the camera lights, and I'm afraid I lost it.

"No, this is not right," I muttered. "No filming, Tony. I think we need to keep this private."

Tony years later remembered it this way: "Jim shouted at me 'not now Tony,' and waved me out of the room. I think he forgot he agreed to record what I thought was a beautiful love story. But I retreated as he wished."

Sinan later thanked me for not making our reunion a public spectacle. When the one-hour ABC News *Close-Up* "This Shattered Land" aired in March 1980, the Soc Sinan story did not become part of the television documentary.

■ ■ ■

At first there was silence. Just tears and a long embrace.

Neither of us was certain of the politics of what we were doing. What should we say? The Khmer Rouge may have been gone, but Sinan's survival tactics, which lay in well-kept secrets, remained.

We whispered caution. We did not know who might be listening.

Still, in that moment on a December Sunday, in an abandoned shop on Monivong Boulevard in Phnom Penh, in hushed voices, we developed a plan to get Sinan out of Cambodia.

We must have a case to present to authorities. We knew the Vietnamese had to be won over first, and then the Kampuchean Foreign Ministry. The Vietnamese had installed the Khmer Rouge defector Hun Sen as foreign minister. I knew little about him. I would consult with Bui Huu Nhan.

I jotted down in my diary our plan.

> Arguments to present to Vietnamese regarding Sinan's rescue:
>
> Sinan was supposed to leave with me on April 12, 1975. True.

She had no family in Cambodia. All had been killed. As far as Sinan and I knew, that was also true.

She was not a security risk. She would not damage the reconstruction of Kampuchea. True.

One issue must be kept secret. There could be no mention of Major Walt, no mention of her relationship with the American military. Hanoi still referred to American actions in Vietnam and Cambodia as "war crimes." President Jimmy Carter had condemned Vietnam's Cambodia invasion. Normalization of relations remained fifteen years away.

Because I was a reporter with a large media organization, the publicity for the People's Republic of Kampuchea, I reasoned, might provide another argument in our favor. The ousted Democratic Kampuchea would not be capable of this kind of humanitarian gesture. Sinan too would tell her story of imprisonment under Angkar.

In that darkened room that Sunday, we put together, I thought, a pretty good plan to extract Sinan from Cambodia.

■ ■ ■

At 3:00 p.m. on Tuesday, December 11, I sat down to interview the foreign minister.

Hun Sen was little known then. Later he came to dominate Cambodian politics, as only Sihanouk had before him.

His history was both colorful and unique—a come-up-from-nothing, rice-to-riches story.

Hun Sen underwhelmed me as a leader. The casually dressed 27-year-old possessed a slightly stooped, beaten-down bearing not unlike some of the Khmer refugees I had interviewed. Remarkably thin, skinny really, he had served as a battalion commander fighting on the side of the Khmer Rouge in eastern Cambodia in 1975. As border tensions rose, he defected to the Vietnamese in 1977. He wore a poorly fitted artificial eye, which gave his face a slightly misshapen look.

Hun Sen spoke quietly. He seemed almost shy. He stuck to a script, written, I assumed, by his Vietnamese mentors. He reflected on the new government and how it was trying to rebuild a devastated nation, overcome by famine, destroyed by the Pol Pot regime. His voice rose slightly. Kim An provided the translation: "It is beyond understanding that Western governments including the United States still recognize the Pol Pot regime and not our new government, which has liberated millions of Cambodians from murderers."

At the end of our talk, I raised the Soc Sinan question and expressed the hope that with the foreign minister's help, I might be permitted to leave Kampuchea with her. Hun Sen promised to look into the matter. I came away encouraged.

I thought I had a few advantages in obtaining Sinan's exit. Behind the scenes with his close Vietnamese connections, Don Luce was hard at work. And I had Bui Huu Nhan on my side. He had the ear of Vietnam's Ambassador Ngo Dien. In 1979, nothing in Cambodia happened without Ngo Dien's green light. Mentor to Hun Sen, he was in effect Hanoi's governor in country.

The efforts to obtain Sinan's exit continued through December. I saw Sinan briefly at New Year's. We had to be careful until we were guaranteed paperwork for her departure.

■ ■ ■

On January 2, 1980, a second meeting with Hun Sen included Sinan. We shook hands. I excused myself. Hun Sen wanted to speak to Sinan alone.

The foreign minister told her he was making an exception to normal procedures. He then lectured Sinan on life in the West, where Hun Sen had never been. Be careful of "temptations" that may "corrupt" your life in America, he warned.

With that Hun Sen ordered Sinan's exit papers. The documents, prepared in French by the "Ministere Des Affaires Etrangeres of the Republique Populaire du Kampuchea," granted Soc Sinan a laissez-passer: one-way permission to leave Cambodia for the United States. "Une fois, pour se render a U.S.A."

Sinan was naturally delighted. She had more confidence in me pulling this off than I had in myself.

When Chum Bun Rong brought her to Phnom Penh at my request, she had already said goodbye to Saang District, to her new position as a teacher in Troy Sla, and to her old Khmer Rouge protectors, Mrs. Aung Eaang and her daughter Cheng. Sinan was ready to go.

There was one catch. The exit pass was valid for only two days. It expired on January 4.

I must get Sinan out quickly. It was up to me to find a way. I had less than 48 hours to arrange something. I could not fail Sinan again.

In January 1980, there were no commercial flights to cities where transit on to the United States could be arranged. The American embargo against both Vietnam and Cambodia and the absence of any diplomatic relations severely limited my options.

We needed to get straight to Bangkok or Singapore, where the United Nations High Commission for Refugees and the United States Embassy could be pressed into service. We needed a direct route out.

I scrambled to seek help from the global relief agencies which had reestablished themselves the year before.

OXFAM proved to be my savior. Founded as the Oxford Committee for Famine Relief in Britain in 1942, OXFAM in 1980 was one of the most effective relief organizations around. OXFAM scheduled weekly humanitarian supply flights to Singapore.

"It will be coming in tomorrow," the OXFAM representative told me. "We can get you and your friend out on it."

The flight scheduler then asked me if Sinan had all the papers she needed. I told a half truth. I said yes and showed her the exit papers: the laissez-passer. I neglected to mention that I knew she had no visa for Singapore.

Sinan met me at the Monorom Hotel. She had packed all her belongings and had just returned from a newly opened Phnom Penh market, where she bought some clothes, simple but perfect for travel.

She then suddenly produced for me what she managed to hide from the Khmer Rouge for nearly four years:

My business card left under her door on April 12, 1975.

An expired Sabena Airways ticket to the United States via Europe.

Her immigrant visa and alien registration documents signed on March 31, 1975, by John Francis McCarthy III at the US Embassy.

450 French francs and 1,555 US dollars.

The next morning Sinan and I and several new friends from the Foreign Ministry gathered at Pochentong Airport to await the OXFAM charter.

Dressed simply in a stunning combination of Khmer and Western attire, Sinan appeared as beautiful as ever to me. Looking at her, I found it hard to comprehend the pain and hardship she had been through during her years of internment.

In late morning, we boarded the OXFAM plane. The pilot invited us to the cockpit. A smiling Sinan posed for pictures. In a few minutes, the plane lifted off for Singapore.

On Thursday, January 3, 1980, Sinan was finally free.

Well, not quite.

Upon arrival at Changi Airport, we were promptly detained. Immigration refused to recognize her travel documents. She had no visa for Singapore. The Singapore government did not acknowledge the Vietnamese-backed People's Republic of Kampuchea. They still recognized the government of Khmer Rouge, Democratic Kampuchea.

We were in trouble.

Airport officials hustled us into a waiting room while they figured out what to do.

"Please call both the United States Embassy and the UNHCR," I demanded.

"Just wait!" the Singapore immigration officer ordered.

I was a bundle of nerves. Tears were welling up in Sinan's eyes. "I cannot go back," she whispered.

After an hour, a senior Singapore immigration official came to see us.

He did not have good news.

"You have violated Singapore law. The lady will have to return to Phnom Penh on the first available flight. You, Mr. Laurie, and the OXFAM pilot will be charged with attempting to assist an illegal entry. OXFAM will be held responsible for the return to Phnom Penh and any costs incurred."

My passport was seized. Sinan's laissez-passer became a useless piece of paper.

"Please," I pleaded. "Call the United States Embassy and the United Nations High Commission for Refugees. We have no desire to stay in Singapore. We simply want to proceed to the United States."

I raised my voice, no doubt with a bit too much outrage and arrogance in it. "I am an American journalist. My friend is a victim of the genocidal Khmer Rouge communist regime. She has been held in captivity for four years."

I worried I might have gone too far. Would the official see in my words a threat that I would write that Singapore was siding with killers over an innocent Khmer survivor?

He did not respond. Clearly upset that he had to tackle this mess, he left the room.

We settled down to spend the night at a holding room at Changi Airport. Sinan was a prisoner again. This time I shared her cell.

A few hours later, I was permitted to plead our case.

The cavalry arrived. A representative of both the UNHCR and the American Embassy joined Singapore officials in the holding room. This time I pulled out all the documents Sinan had so carefully and daringly kept. Though expired, the papers showed clearly that Sinan possessed a visa to enter the United States. There were plenty of grounds to allow us to leave.

I made one more move that I thought might influence Singapore authorities in our favor. "Sinan's release," I argued would be good publicity for Singapore. Before I left Phnom Penh, I had sent a telegram to Eddie Chan, the Singapore stringer for ABC News. He knew we were coming and expected trouble. He alerted some of the Singapore media in the hopes that the right kind of publicity might ease our entry. Reporters had already been phoning Singapore's Foreign Ministry and immigration authorities inquiring about our unique case.

After nearly five hours in detention, Singapore authorities made their final decision. They released Sinan to my responsibility.

The broad smiles as we posed for a picture together in front of the duty-free store at Changi Airport were those of exhaustion and relief.

In the taxi into the city we sat in silence. Sinan simply looked out the window. I felt I knew her thoughts. I could see tears in her eyes. She likely reflected on what had just happened, on the pain of the past four years, on a new sense of relief. After my months and her years in the shattered land that was Cambodia, we both marveled at the lights of the modern city we glimpsed from the speeding car.

It was nearly midnight when I checked the two of us into the Singapore Peninsula Hotel. With a close embrace and whispered thank-yous, we said good night.

On Friday morning the Singapore representative of the UNHCR visited Sinan. In a rare exception to policy, Singapore officials provided her a special pass to remain in the city-state.

Sinan now had permission to move around Singapore. She had money. I arranged for accommodations. We awaited news on when she could depart for America.

Our time together in the Lion City proved short-lived.

A phone call came in from ABC News. I was needed in New York on Monday to start work on writing and editing the Cambodia documentary film.

I wanted more time in Singapore. Perhaps we could get to know each other again. Perhaps we could turn the clock back five years, or ten years. I thought for a moment about calling New York and asking the ABC documentary unit to start without me. Then Sinan spoke words I had heard before from her.

"You have your work. Your career must come first. Go. I will be fine."

Sunday morning, January 6, I again said my goodbyes to Sinan with promises to meet in America. I would leave her alone once more. This time at least I knew I had made all the proper arrangements for her to follow.

At Changi Airport, I waited to board the Pan American flight to New York.

As the plane lifted off, a heavy tropical rain doused Singapore.

Sinan looked out the window of the Peninsula Hotel and wrote me a short note with the touch of sadness that had always marked her letters.

C'est tellement triste de vois la pluie pur la premiere fois lors de ma sortie du Kampuchea, en plus, je reste seule a Sing'Pore.

"It's sad to see the first rains since I left Cambodia and that I remain alone in Singapore."

■ ■ ■

The next day, Sinan ventured out to Singapore's Cinema Lido to see her first film in six years.

The movie was *Big Wednesday*. Not a great film to be sure. Gary Busey, Jan-Michael Vincent, and William Katt become friends, do drugs, dodge the Vietnam War draft, lose a friend in the war, and enjoy surfing in California. A critic wrote of Sinan's first post-liberation American film, "The surprise is not that Director John Milius has made such a resoundingly awful film, but rather that he's made such a bland one."

Still, for someone just out of the killing fields, a coming-of-age film about young surfers in California provided a true escape.

■ ■ ■

On Wednesday, January 9, Sinan made the front page of the Singapore *Straits Times*. Eddie's media blitz, somewhat belatedly, kicked in.

> "How Khmer Woman escaped to Singapore …
> with TV newsman's help"
> By Evelyn Ng

A young Kampuchean woman, who managed to fly out of her country last week with the help of an American television journalist, is staying "with friends" in Singapore, informed sources said yesterday.

The woman, Soc Sonan, 27, flew into Selatar airfield in a Red Cross aid plane last Wednesday with American Broadcasting Corporation journalist James Laurie, 32.

The sources said she arrived with an exit permit but it is not known who had issued it or how she had obtained it.

Second Bid

It is believed that the United States has agreed to accept her as a refugee and it is under this condition that the Singapore authorities have allowed her to remain here. She is expected to leave for the US in the next few weeks.

Singapore's policy on refugees from Kampuchea allows a manageable number to stay if a third country has agreed to accept them within 90 days.

Mr Laurie, bureau chief of the ABC office in Hong Kong, is understood to have flown to New York—evidently to hasten procedures that would enable Soc Sonan to join him.

She is described as Mr Laurie's "close personal friend."

It was learnt that this was the second attempt by Mr Laurie to arrange for Soc Sonan's escape.

His first attempt was in 1975, in the last days before Phnom Penh fell to the Khmer Rouge.

Then owing to a slip-up, she missed his message telling her to meet him at his helicopter. The helicopter flew off—one seat still empty.

Just Made It

Mr Laurie did not hear from Soc Sonan in the intervening years, and he did not know if she was alive.

But she contacted him when he made a 26 day trip into Kampuchea recently to shoot a documentary film on the country. It was then that he made his second attempt to get her out.

Even then, they only narrowly made it. The exit permit for the girl was to expire January 2. They waited tensely for a Red Cross plane that would fly to Bangkok. When it was late, they decided not to take any more chances, and hopped on another plane heading for Singapore.

Close friends and associates of Mr Laurie had sworn not to tell the tale, afraid that somehow they might jeopardize Soc Sonan's attempt to get to safety.

The article went on to mention that Sinan had worked in a "commune" in Cambodia, that reporter Ng tried but could not find her in Singapore, and that neither the UNHCR nor the US Embassy would release any information about her.

Evelyn Ng's story may have been slightly off in some details—but it served its purpose.

The story reaffirmed Singapore's policy on refugees while casting the government in a benevolent light in allowing Sinan to stay. Through most of the 1980s Singapore would maintain a tough policy on refugees. The small city-state argued that, despite its wealth, it lacked resources to handle a rising influx from Indochina. The navy provided food, water, and fuel and towed most Vietnamese back out to sea. Singapore was not alone. Much of Southeast Asia in the 1980s suffered a sad case of compassion fatigue.

■ ■ ■

A week after Sinan arrived in Singapore, her paperwork was finally ready.

On Friday, January 11, 1980, Sinan boarded Pan Am 006 bound for San Francisco with a connection on TWA to Washington, DC.

The following day Sinan tried to put the trauma of Indochina behind her. She moved into her new temporary home: a room I had arranged for her at the Windsor Park Hotel on Connecticut Avenue.

The next few years would be particularly difficult. She would have to adapt to a new country while still recovering from the trauma of Khmer Rouge imprisonment. She would also be forced to confront the realities of two men in her life.

Her "Commander" remained at the Pentagon. Assuming the worst, he had moved on with his life. There could be no reunion or reconciliation there.

Sinan would also discover that the man who finally rescued her from Cambodia was too self-absorbed, too unreliable, to provide her the psychological and emotional support she really needed.

In 1980, Sinan would start building a new life with little support. Eventually she would find a man who she trusted and who provided her the stability she always sought.

She would also struggle with her memories and her desire, which came and then went, to tell her story for all the world to know.

22

Food for Thought

Washington, DC

THERE USED TO BE a place on Connecticut Avenue just north of Dupont Circle with some curious food (it was among the first to offer barbecue avocado burgers and tofu platters) and even curiouser clientele.

Food for Thought, it was called.

It closed its doors in 1999. And when Linton Weeks wrote its obituary for the *Washington Post*, he captured completely the place and its place in time.

> There was a time when everybody knew "Food for Thought"—the hippie-trippy, hummus-shoveling health-food hashery at the absolute bleeding heart of the Washington Left. Here nonprofit serfs in tie-dyed T-shirts and faded jeans met, played chess and read the New Age Journal. Here the sandalistas gathered to plot the revolution. Ah, the '70s and '80s. Those were the days, my friend. We thought they'd never end.

At Food for Thought one hot July day in 1981, Soc Sinan surveyed the bulletin board under housing. In the eighteen months she had been in Washington, Sinan had changed living arrangements twice. Finding a good place to live was a challenge. She needed a change.

Adjustment to American life proved difficult for Sinan, as it is for many refugees. Her oldest friends like Saorun now lived in Paris. She had few new friends. Saorun wrote her, suggesting a move to Paris might be better for Sinan. No one had as yet "adopted" Sinan in Washington as Mrs. Aung Eaang had in Khmer Rouge Cambodia.

Sinan remained very much alone.

At the bulletin board this day at Food for Thought, she was just looking.

And so was he.

A new man was about to enter Sinan's life.

Walter Teague could only see her from the back as he looked up from his coffee toward the popular bulletin board. He knew instantly that the woman in front of him was beautiful and someone he must know.

And so they met. He approached her almost at once, just as I had at that military briefing so long ago. Teague helped find her a new place to live. He fell in love. They moved in together. With every passing year, their bonds strengthened, their relationship grew.

The second Walter could not have been more different from the first. Teague too started his career in the military, stationed in Okinawa.

But Teague became a confirmed pro-peace, anti-war political activist. When he returned from Asia, the racial injustices he saw both in America and in Asia in the early '60s set him off. After a campaign dedicated to the US civil rights cause, 1963 saw him refocus his attention on the injustices of the American war in Vietnam.

"To me the assassination of South Vietnam's President Diem in 1963 provided another piece of evidence of the corruption and futility of American efforts," Teague told me years later.

"Johnson's escalation of bombing in March 1965 spurred me to think of how I could contribute more significantly to the effort against the American war. After the bombings, I joined others to form a committee which opposed the war by focusing on promoting the reasons for the Vietnamese resistance."

In 1967, Teague became one of the organizers of the march on the Pentagon, the biggest anti-war protest to that date.

What was it that John Guare said about six degrees of separation? "Everybody on this planet is six or fewer steps away from each other."

Teague and I might have met in October 1967—but didn't.

While in college, I began a part-time gig as a reporter at a local Washington radio station. On October 21, I reported live on the radio from the steps of the Pentagon.

Tens of thousands of people responding to the call of the National Mobilization Committee to End the War in Vietnam marched across the Memorial Bridge from the Lincoln Memorial and descended on the sprawling headquarters of the military establishment.

Novelist Norman Mailer immortalized the march in what he called a "non-fiction novel" titled *Armies of the Night*. The book won the 1968 Pulitzer Prize for non-fiction. Teague was not too pleased by his portrayal in the book.

Teague met Mailer in a jail cell after they were both arrested by federal marshals outside the steps of the Pentagon.

Teague recalls Mailer as arrogant and annoying, portraying that day's massive anti-war demonstration as mostly about Mailer.

Mailer saw Walter Teague less as a legitimate war protester and more as a "revolutionary."

"The other man's philosophy probably began with Lenin's remark the revolution needed people who would work, sleep, think, and eat revolution twenty-four hours a day," wrote Mailer.

His portrayal of their time in a cell together is told in Mailer's third-person style.

"Why were you arrested, Mr. Miller?" asks a helmeted US marshal. (The marshal perhaps on purpose calls Mailer "Miller," much to the author's irritation.)

"For transgressing a police line as a protest against the war in Vietnam," replies Mailer.

By contrast, the leftist activist Teague seems well practiced in protest and relaxed in arrest.

"And why were *you* arrested?" the marshal asks Teague.

"As an act of solidarity with oppressed forces fighting for liberty against this country in Southeast Asia," he recites.

"Walter Teague," Mailer wrote, "lay down immediately on the floor with his white motorcycle helmet for a pillow, and went to sleep."

The Walter that Sinan came to know was a passionate activist who was also now cautious and caring. After the war years were over, he turned his attention to counseling. Teague earned a degree at Washington's Howard University. He began practicing psychotherapy in 1980 and enlarged his practice in 1981. Walter, with his background in counseling, provided Sinan the understanding she so needed and deserved.

■ ■ ■

By 1987, Sinan finally found stability, a new life, and happiness.

She moved to Maryland and bought a house with Walter Teague.

In the 1990s, Sinan developed a new career. In her efforts as a paralegal, she displayed the same diligence and reliability she had shown at SONATRAC in Phnom Penh. She provided French and English translation services for the Khmer community. She worked with new immigrants, helping untangle their complex legal problems in a nation they struggled to understand. She pushed for immigration reform to allow a more open America which would welcome all.

Indochinese refugees encountered enormous difficulties adapting to life in the United States. As with all refugee groups, language and education posed the greatest impediments.

The American war, the subsequent hardships in communist Vietnam, and the genocide in Cambodia produced a massive outpouring of refugees. The refugee flow continued from the late 1970s until it finally tapered off in the late 1990s. New diaspora communities sprung up in France, Australia, Canada—nearly everywhere—and most significantly in the United States.

In a first wave from 1975 to 1980, more than 530,000 Vietnamese were able to adapt through tight-knit family and community structures in the United States.

Many of the 140,000 Lao and Hmong people who arrived before 1995 had limited education. Speaking only their native languages, they found adjustment particularly slow.

Among the 158,000 Cambodian refugees, only 5 percent found good white-collar jobs in America. These were usually educated Khmer who arrived before the Khmer Rouge atrocities. About 40 percent of the Cambodian newcomers, in waves after the Khmer Rouge were overthrown, managed to find blue-collar jobs. Most of the rest—more than half the total—relied on welfare and other public assistance. Many of the new Khmer settling in California had been born in Thai refugee camps in the 1980s and had received minimal education. Because the Khmer Rouge killed men at such a high rate, women became the principal breadwinners in many of the refugee households.

Support for women, refugee education and job training, confronting post-traumatic stress disorders, from which many suffered—all proved an enormous challenge. Sinan worked for more than twenty years to help struggling women get ahead.

Sinan also assisted Walter Teague in building his counseling practice. She was known in the small community where she lived as selfless and generous with her time.

She bridled at what she saw happening in the Khmer community. Scrupulously honest, she accused the Buddhist monks in the Maryland community of ripping off poor people in demands for large donations. She cut her ties to the Buddhist clergy.

She watched from afar developments in Cambodia. While she was grateful to Prime Minister Hun Sen for his help in her 1980 departure, his increasing dictatorial tendencies and his accumulation of extraordinary wealth for family and friends disturbed her.

In 1998, the prime minister's office invited Sinan to meet Hun Sen on the sidelines of a United Nations General Assembly meeting. Reluctant at first, disapproving of his politics, she nonetheless owed him at least a visit. She traveled to New York for a short courtesy call.

Our mutual friend Chum Bun Rong, however, was not spared Sinan's disappointment. Although he was in New York at the same time, Sinan refused to see him. Bun Rong, who later became Cambodia's ambassador to Washington, told me he was hurt by the snub.

"Why didn't she ever call me?" he asked.

The answer was complicated.

It may have been unfair, but Sinan saw Bun Rong and his rise within the Cambodian government as personification of the corruption within the system.

Like Sinan, Bun Rong was also a survivor. Unlike Sinan, Bun Rong seemed keen to make up for lost time, to gain material wealth and rise within the regime.

But there was more to it. In 1987, after she became more settled with Walter in Maryland, Sinan began to cut herself off from old friends.

Gradually, as Sinan built a new life, she wanted less to do with the old.

Sinan wrote less frequently to her friends Khoeun and Saorun in France.

Vann, who had separated from Jimmy the aircraft mechanic, settled in Nevada. She told me years later that Sinan emerged from the killing fields a changed person.

They met once in Reno, where Vann had become a blackjack dealer at a casino.

The changes in Sinan seemed understandable given what she had been through.

"She was now a very serious girl," recalled Vann. "That carefree nature, that easy laugh was gone. She cried easily. She quickly changed the subject if I mentioned good times in Cambodia."

Not all the changes were bad, Vann admitted. "I was always the party girl. Sinan not so much, but she joined in. Now she no longer thought about frivolous or material things like gold or silver jewelry. She stopped dressing with any fashion. There was a new selflessness in her. She was always someone who would befriend people easily. She did it now but with purpose. She just wanted to help people."

Youk Chhang later shed some light on Sinan's changes. Youk, whom I met in 1997, runs an organization in Phnom Penh dedicated to investigating the crimes of the Khmer Rouge and documenting the stories of survivors.

His observations about other survivors rang true for Sinan.

Sinan began to bury her past, both the good times of the early '70s and the horrors of the final years of the decade.

"Some survivors seek to totally disassociate themselves from their past," Youk told me. "They sometimes even change their names, to make a break, to start a new life."

"Another characteristic is to compartmentalize thoughts and actions, to shut out pain," Youk continued. "To survive you had to keep secrets. After the killing fields, it becomes natural to maintain those habits and remain secretive."

Thursday, January 10, 1980

As Sinan began her difficult adjustment, I was not there to help her. Instead, a representative of the International Rescue Committee was. I messaged its Washington office. The refugee assistance agency IRC America, which had its roots in 1933 when it began to assist Germans escaping Hitler's persecution, now aided Cambodians fleeing Khmer Rouge genocide.

While Sinan adjusted, I remained in New York, totally immersed, writing my Cambodia documentary, *This Shattered Land*, which after some delay aired in March.

Capitalizing on our scoop as one of the few American networks to visit Vietnam and Cambodia in 1979, ABC News public relations arranged for dozens of interviews for me. When I wasn't helping write, edit, and narrate the film, I was talking to or writing articles for any magazine or newspaper that would publish

Cambodia's story. I found myself in my element: telling anyone who would listen of a country I loved.

My emotions were torn. How much did I want to re-involve myself with Sinan? How much now did Sinan need me?

I did accomplish what I promised to do in 1975—rescue a woman I loved. Oh, it wasn't the swashbuckling, sweep-her-off-her-feet, sprint to freedom in a dramatic helicopter airlift that I wanted. Rather, five years later, it was a negotiated bit of subterfuge, persuading diplomats that this small gesture would be in their interest.

At the same time, hidden guilt remained behind a stream of questions, which I could not easily answer. Why had I allowed her to remain in Phnom Penh in the first place? Did I encourage her to stay? Was it my fault that she suffered nearly four years under the Khmer Rouge? Why had I not married Sinan? Would that not have been right? The passion had certainly been there in 1970. Didn't Sinan now need a protector? Was providing protection a reason for marriage?

With my support, Sinan enrolled at the local Strayer College to improve her English-language and office management skills. She marked her 32nd birthday studying. She began to work part-time at a law office.

As my film was nearly complete, l took a short break. I invited Sinan to New York.

We dined together at Nanni's on East 46th Street. Its throwback classic Italian décor reminded us of La Venise, one of our favorites in Phnom Penh ten years before.

We talked about Sinan's adjustment to America, her school. As she described her new life in Washington, I thought the independence she had displayed so clearly in Cambodia should serve her well in America.

Then I broached the subject of writing a book.

"You—we—have a remarkable story, Sinan. We should share it."

"I have too much else to think about it now," she replied.

"But perhaps we could at least start. We can write down some things and record your memories?"

Wanting to please me, she agreed, flashing that engaging 1970 smile of hers.

Yet we avoided the question that I feared she really wanted to ask: What about us?

"I'll help you any way I can, Sinan," I said. "Just let me know."

"Don't worry, I know you have your career in Asia," she said. "I'll be OK."

Commitment averse, I breathed a sigh of relief that she had again let me off the hook.

In Washington, I introduced Sinan to a string of friends, people I knew from my college days. I thought, in my absence, they might provide a bridge to a new world.

A few were knowledgeable Asia experts who were sensitive to both Sinan's cultural roots and her Khmer Rouge experience. Others less so.

When one friend pressed her on her experience, she burst into tears. She soon excused herself and left the gathering.

Another friend, in apparent innocence and obvious ignorance, asked Sinan what she did for fun on weekends on the Khmer Rouge commune.

■ ■ ■

With the documentary complete, I flew back to Hong Kong and on to a dozen new assignments in Japan, South Korea, and China.

In June, I returned to Washington. I thought perhaps we might try once more to rekindle our romance of 1970. I asked Sinan if she might drive with me to Florida.

The road trip settled two issues. First, and I thought this a positive sign, Sinan opened up more about her captivity. We recorded some long interviews. But it also resolved a second issue: we would remain friends but not lovers. I could not bring myself to commit.

■ ■ ■

I continued to see Sinan when I could, usually on short visits to the United States when ABC News summoned me back for meetings.

We remained in touch through a stream of letters—mine short and hurried, hers long, handwritten descriptions of whom she met and where she went.

I saw Sinan for dinner for the last time on Friday, June 21, 1985. I had bought her an Amtrak ticket from Washington to New York. We ate at a small Japanese restaurant. I can't recall the name—it was around the corner from Carnegie Hall.

A diary entry on June 23 noted, "Good to see Sinan again, the first time in two years. Seeing her always takes me back. Fifteen years has passed since Cambodia and a time of discovery, happiness, and innocence."

There was no great finality to that last dinner in 1985. Just a drifting apart. My life moved on. Hers did as well.

■ ■ ■

More than twenty years later, I sat with San Arun over dinner in Phnom Penh. Arun, one of Sinan's quintet of "city girls" from Cambodia, explained to me what should have been obvious.

"You, of course, know that Sinan was very much in love with you," Arun said quietly. "She had a Cambodian man before you, but you were her first foreigner. The first Western man she made love to. That's a big thing for a Khmer woman."

I sat in silence.

Arun paused to consider how best to deliver what amounted to a list of grievances.

"In her view you betrayed her three times. First you left her in 1971. You went off with another woman.

"You came back in 1975. I know you didn't mean to hurt her. I know you wanted to rescue her. But you failed. The helicopters left without her. She suffered a lot under the Khmer Rouge. It affected her mind.

"And 1980. It wasn't surprising that Sinan reached out to you rather than Walter, the Major. She knew you were resourceful. You were. You got her out. But what did you do next? You left her alone in America. You failed to provide the one thing she wanted. You!"

Arun stopped, looked down, and asked another question. "Did you know that I also betrayed Sinan in 1987?"

"You? No, really, how?"

"Sinan moved to Maryland with a man who she could rely on. She made me promise not to give you her address. But I did. She was angry. She did not want to hear from you again. When you wrote her letters, she kept them—unopened. Walter saw them. Walter, as you know, intervened to bring you two back together at the end of her life."

Again silence. A very long silence.

23

Reflections on Genocide and Survival

TWO OLD SCRAPS OF PAPER were kept in a box in Maryland at the comfortable suburban home where Sinan lived for the last twenty-three years of her life. It is hard to make much out of them. Handwritten in the Sanskrit-like language of Khmer, the faded blue ink on one side of the thin paper bleeds through to the other.

I asked Youk Chhang at his Documentation Center of Cambodia in Phnom Penh to take a look. He and his researchers could only conclude that the writing was part of a longer document and the document seemed to be a forced confession.

I had seen similar confession documents in Phnom Penh at the Tuol Sleng prison and execution center. Khmer Rouge officials demanded those accused of class or political crimes write long detailed biographies before they were put to death. Often the accused would weave both fact and fiction into their narrative in hopes the executioners might somehow spare their life. It seldom worked.

At Tuol Sleng over three years, more than 20,000 people were imprisoned. Only twelve were known to survive, including five children.

Sinan revealed the scraps of the document only a few months before her death. She had never shown them to me. Perhaps she was trying to purge herself of painful memories, finding closure at the end of her life. But the scraps looked very much like the prelude to a Khmer Rouge sentence of death.

Sinan told Walter she found them in Angkar's Saang district office on January 7, 1979, the day the Vietnamese army swept through the area, forcing Khmer Rouge cadre and military to flee westward. She said she was scheduled for arrest three days later, on January 10. She believed the Vietnamese invasion saved her life.

The scraps of paper remain part of the mystery in the story of Soc Sinan's survival.

■ ■ ■

What was the secret of Sinan's survival? Was it a matter of character? Cleverness, willpower, faith? When faced with the most extreme conditions, why do some survive and others not? How does one walk that fine line between life and death?

Sinan's story pushed me to search for answers to such questions. On that long drive to Florida in 1980, I asked Sinan her explanation.

She had no clear answer. *"J'ai simplement eu de la chance?"* she told me.

Can it really be simply by chance?

If Sinan had been sentenced to death before the Vietnamese invasion, Angkar most likely would have taken her to a small island in the middle of the Bassac River, about 5 or 6 kilometers north of the Troy Sla village. Sinan spoke to me about the island. Years later I decided to go there.

■ ■ ■

On April 7, 2004, I sat in the back of a small motorboat as it tuk-tukked 10 minutes from the east bank of the Bassac to a tiny island in the middle.

The island comprises a bit of lush land, fruit trees, and palms spread across less than a mile at its widest point.

Villagers along the Bassac knew the island as Koh Kor. Others called it "death island" or the "island of widows."

The Khmer Rouge built a prison and interrogation center there in 1976, out of sight and almost out of sound of the work communes on the banks of the river.

Here the chhlop would determine who would live and who would die.

Sinan told me that she learned of the island from the hushed voices of fellow workers when the chhlop were asleep or away. She could never be sure, but she believed several of her commune friends who had suddenly disappeared died on Koh Kor.

On nights when the wind was right, when Sinan and some of the more daring women of the commune bathed in the waters of the Bassac, Sinan told me she thought she could hear from somewhere across the water the faint sounds of screams. Wretched sounds made after torture and confessions and just before death.

■ ■ ■

One of the most painful parts of her "prison without walls," Sinan told me, was meeting good people, getting to know them, and then suddenly finding they had disappeared.

For nearly a year, her best friend was Chantha, a simple girl, a little younger than Sinan, who had worked in Phnom Penh's Central Market. Chantha said little about her family but Sinan suspected she had a military background.

Chantha and Sinan looked out for each other. They covered for each other if one or the other was tired or sick. They bathed together in the Bassac. They lay on the embankment under the stars and dreamed—dreamed of escape.

In 1977, resentment seemed to be building against some on our work team. Chantha seemed at the center of it. Chantha prayed to Buddha too much. She talked too much of her husband. She loved him deeply and longed to be with him. I cautioned her. It was not good to talk much.

Chantha could not contain herself. Her disdain for the Khmer Rouge ran deep. Once she spotted a few cadres struggling to start a stolen motorbike. Although she whispered, I feared someone might hear.

"Look at that herd of vultures! They really look like poor monkeys who've never ridden a motorbike before. Such peasants."

I simply nodded. Dangerous talk.

Then one morning, Chantha was gone. No one dared ask where she went. People whispered "Koh Kor." Chantha never returned. Sinan was shaken.

I was in shock. My friend was gone. I went to the communal kitchen at 7. I could not eat. My hunger pangs disappeared as I thought about the murder of my friend. I missed Chantha. I felt miserable now much of the time.

■ ■ ■

Later Sinan befriended a quiet, hardworking family.

The head of the family, Heang Chhay, had worked in the Finance Ministry before he was expelled to the countryside.

He arrived at the commune after I did. I saw him. He smiled. We spoke. He introduced me to his family. They were fortunate among new people. Heang had kept his family together. His wife Lim Him was assigned to the women's brigade. She worked hard. She got along with everybody. The old "base" people liked her.

They had a daughter Sokhavy, 17, and a son Sopheak, 12. They were assigned to the girls' and boys' work brigades. They were quiet, timid, slight in stature, and had fair skin. It may have been their fair skin that determined their fate.

Heang worked hard, fulfilling every Angkar demand.

But Angkar, with all its eyes, discovered Heang Chhay worked for the Ministry of Finance. As soon as it did, they disappeared. Only the daughter Sokhavy was allowed to live. Like me, she became an orphan. I tried to look after her. It was hard for me to accept. Hard for me to maintain my spirits. I had lost my friend Chantha to Angkar and now most of the Heang Chhay family. Who next?

■ ■ ■

During my visit to Koh Kor, I walked clear across the island. I discovered a small temple surrounded by a garden plot and a few wooden pens for pigs and chickens. It was less a temple really, and more a small stable with an attached steeple pointed toward the heavens.

Encased in this makeshift memorial was a grotesque display of hundreds of human skulls dug up from the fields nearby.

No one knew who they were, but one villager told me the bones dated from 1976 or 1977. They were no doubt "new" people unable to keep their secrets from Angkar. Was Sokhavy's mother, father, brother here among them? Was Chantha?

Many of the dead were men. Sometimes widows were left alive, imprisoned on the island.

Craig Etcheson, who researched the killing fields in the 1990s, reported that execution of "class enemies" usually occurred immediately on arrival. If families were not killed with the men, they were interned. "The Khmer Rouge were greatly concerned about the possibility of survivors from an enemy's family taking revenge."

Skeletal shrines remained a feature of Cambodia's countryside for years. Across the country, Etcheson identified at least 196 sites like Koh Kor.

For some of the survivors at Koh Kor, the trauma did not end when the Khmer Rouge were ousted. Fifty or so women remained for awhile. Many had nowhere to go, no one to look after them. They had been forgotten. A few foreign NGOs, charitable groups, tried to help. Foreigners came and went. The legacy of "death island" remained.

■ ■ ■

On a frigid early December day in 1994, I met a man from Paris named Charles Baron.

I walked with Baron across the bleak and horrific landscape of a camp on the edge of the town Oświęcim in southern Poland.

The place is better known by its German name: Auschwitz.

I had asked ABC News to assign me to do a feature story here. I did so with Sinan very much in mind. I had become fascinated with the experiences of survivors. How did surviving the German Holocaust compare with surviving the Cambodian killing fields?

I spoke to Charles Baron about what it meant to be a survivor and about the importance of preserving memories.

On July 16, 1942, French police under Nazi instruction launched Opération Vent Printanier, rounding up 13,152 Jews in Paris. Baron, barely 16, was among them, one of about 4,000 children. He began a journey to a half dozen Nazi concentration camps, including Drancy, Dachau, and Auschwitz. Baron survived them all.

When he got to Poland, in late July 1944, he was chosen for a work detail at a concrete factory and thus was spared the gas chambers. Only one in ten people brought to Auschwitz or its neighboring camp Birkenau survived.

"Everyone should visit this place," Baron told me in hushed tones as a sharp wind swirled around us.

"And when you do, bring a piece of yourself with you," he continued, "to observe, to think, to place yourself back in time. Put yourself in the position of those who lived and died here. Think what you might have done, how you might have survived."

I asked him how he explained his survival.

"Youth and chance," he replied. "I was only 16 when I was first captured."

Daring and deception surely played their parts. With a fellow inmate, he escaped from a transport train once and hid out for awhile, only to be re-interned just before the war ended.

"I had a stubborn and rebellious state of mind," Baron recalled, "but I tempered it just enough to satisfy the guards."

． ． ．

I sometimes reflect on how much more attention is paid to the horrors of German persecution and murder nearly eighty years ago compared to that paid to the Cambodian genocide just forty years ago.

It may be a case of degree. More than six million were killed compared to about two million. It may be the contrast between an "advanced" European society and a poor rural Asian nation. It may be the outrageous religious persecution.

In Cambodia religion was not usually a factor, except for the Muslim Cham people. Ethnicity, class, and education formed the main criteria for execution. Vietnamese were driven out. Chinese fared little better. Purity of Khmer bloodline saved some. Darker skin was favored over lighter. Later in 1978, ideology proved deadly. An explosion of hatred pitted Khmer against Khmer, hard-core communist against communist. Survival often hinged on a cadre's closeness to Pol Pot and his most radical adherents.

Perhaps neglect of history comes simply from the cruelty of repetition, to paraphrase Milan Kundera's "struggle of memory against forgetting."

The bloody massacres in Cambodia were quickly overshadowed by the slaughter at Srebrenica, in turned drowned out by the horrors of Syria and the cries of Myanmar's Rohingya, "so on and so forth until ultimately everyone lets everything be forgotten."

■ ■ ■

Whether in the death camps of Europe or in the communal work camps of Cambodia, survival depended on luck, cunning, compromise, deceit, determination, and usefulness.

In Phnom Penh in 1995, I met a schoolteacher named Kassie Neou. The Khmer Rouge selected him for death. Kassie was also a marvelous storyteller. I met probably the only Khmer who specialized in the study of Aesop's fables. He brought the Greek oral tradition to Cambodia. Kassie knew them all—"The Ant and the Grasshopper," "The Boy Who Cried Wolf," "The Tortoise and the Hare."

As he put it, "the Khmer Rouge soldiers were but children. And they wanted to hear more stories. So—they refused to kill me. They kept alive the storyteller, so he could tell more stories!"

The Jews in World War II who were not immediately put to death sometimes survived too through talent, wit, or deception.

A Ukrainian Jew named Zhanna told a story like Kassie's. She was part of a musical troupe entertaining occupying Nazi forces in Poland. The SS kept her alive so they could hear more music.

■ ■ ■

In the short time we had together in 1994, I asked Charles Baron whether he had read of the killing fields of Cambodia.

He had. The tragedy, he said, was that man's inhumanity to man was a constant feature of global history. All he could do was promote education and continue to tell honest accounts of the barbarism he witnessed.

"The most important task for people like me," Charles told me, "is to keep telling my story, to encourage the living to remember the past; to preserve what I call 'the kingdom of memory.'"

Baron died in Paris at age 90, still telling his story of survival to anyone who would listen.

■ ■ ■

Youk Chhaang reminds me a little of Charles Baron. In Cambodia, for more than thirty years, Youk has been doing what Baron sought to do: preserving "the kingdom of memory."

Born in 1961, Youk also survived. Like Baron, Youk was a teenager when he descended into internment.

Youk's painful journey took him from Phnom Penh, where his mother worked as a gem merchant, to the west of Cambodia. He witnessed the horrific murder of his pregnant sister. He escaped to a refugee camp in Thailand and eventually got to the United States.

Youk paints a more candid picture than most do of what must be done to survive. "Survival often meant stealing, cheating, lying, and pointing fingers at others."

In 1990, Youk returned to Cambodia with a mission to chronicle the atrocities of the Khmer Rouge. He's still at it.

With a diligent research team, Youk runs his operation out of an office near Phnom Penh's Independence Monument. His work provided much of the evidence for the "Extraordinary Chambers in the Courts of Cambodia," the war crimes trials that began 2006. His work also produced the first school textbooks to ensure the Khmer Rouge period is examined by young people. "A society cannot know itself," says Youk, "if it does not have an accurate memory of its own history."

Youk introduced me to his able researcher Dany Long, who helped me pursue Sinan's story in greater depth. On my behalf he traveled to Saang District to find some of "base" people who might have known Sinan.

Saang District has of course changed in the years since Sinan survived her internment here, but not in fundamental ways.

Route 21 from Phnom Penh is now fully paved, making the 20-mile journey easier. The local government has tried to promote some tourism. They built a new pagoda on top of a hill they call Saang Mountain.

On the east side of the Bassac, fewer than a thousand people worked on Sinan's commune. Today the population has doubled and private farming has returned, but people still grow what they always have—rice, fruit, and vegetables. Simple thatched housing has been enhanced with cement, tin, and sturdier wood.

Dany quickly located a number of Sinan's Khmer Rouge benefactors near Troy Sla.

Ngorn Kim Cheng beamed broadly as she remembered Sinan.

Cheng is the daughter of Aung Eaang, the kindly "base person" who adopted the "orphan Sinan." Sinan had buried documents and valuables in a hole next to her tiny house.

Mrs. Eaang died a few years ago, but her daughter remembers Sinan well.

"Bbat noh chea karpit—yes, that's true," Cheng recalled. "I remember when she returned to us after weeks away with the women's brigade. Sinan would always return and greet us with a big smile.

"My mother took pity on her. You could say that we protected her. I was about Sinan's age. She said she was an orphan and she asked my parents to be her godparents.

"Nearly 400 new people came to our village from April to June 1975," Cheng confirmed. Two years later fewer than one hundred, including Sinan, remained.

> We were told more workers were needed in other provinces. They were sent away. We also knew of the investigations of new people. We knew people were taken away at night to Koh Kor.
>
> We learned very little about Sinan's background. She said she could read English, had a husband who left the country, whom she could not join because of surgery on her abdomen.
>
> After some time with us, Sinan gave to my mother a gold necklace, a bracelet, and some American dollars. We didn't know what dollars were, but Sinan told us to guard them as they'd be valuable one day.
>
> My mother sewed the valuables in a secret pocket in her clothing. Because she was old and had lived so long in a liberated area, Angkar never bothered her.

Cheng recalled that in June 1975, Comrade Eng and another Khmer Rouge leader named Chuon began investigations of the new people. The old revolutionaries were told they must turn in any valuables they had. In a remarkable act of defiance, Cheng's mother simply kept quiet.

"Comrades Eng and Chuon asked my parents about Sinan. We were among the oldest of the base people. My mother, who was trusted by Angkar, told the investigators, 'She's just a poor orphan girl from Phnom Penh. She works hard. Let her live, leave her alone. We will watch her.'"

Dany found another villager named Thong Vantha who remembered Sinan. Sinan had the ability, he said, "to make people like her, but also feel sorry for her."

He recalled the arrival of the Vietnamese in 1979. "Comrades Eng and Chuon fled. Comrades Tieng and Bo also disappeared. Most likely they went to Thailand."

Within days the Vietnamese began to reorganize.

Sinan returned to live with Aung Eaang and Cheng's family. She began to teach school at the local Wat Po Andet Primary School. She started to give both Cheng and Vantha English lessons.

More than thirty-five years after Sinan left the village, Vantha, writing in a notebook, proudly showed Dani how he could still write his full name in English letters: "T-H-O-N-G V-A-N-T-H-A."

"Sinan taught me that!"

Cheng remembered the day Sinan left the village.

"My mother returned to Sinan all her valuables, but Sinan gave me an 18-gram gold necklace as thanks for protecting her and her secrets."

Aung Eaang, Cheng, Vantha, and the "old" people of Saang District, Troy Sla, Po Kandal, said their goodbyes to a young women they remembered as a "kind orphan girl with a kind smile and sweet voice."

■ ■ ■

For Sinan, survival came down to instincts and patterns of behavior that extended back into childhood.

In Phnom Penh, she refused to believe the warnings of the Khmer Rouge that she must evacuate the city because "Americans are going to bomb." Procrastination helped. Thousands who undertook immediate evacuation were doomed.

After a Khmer Rouge soldier put a gun to her head, Sinan learned that there were different types of Khmer Rouge—some more ideological than others. Recognizing divisions within Angkar helped her identify who might be more lenient and who would not.

Her scar. Sinan counted on the limited education of the Khmer Rouge. She portrayed herself an orphan and used her old surgical scar when she could to gain sympathy.

She made friends easily but was always cautious. She shared little about herself, revealing some facts while keeping important secrets well. All her life Sinan proved exceptional at keeping secrets.

Her skills at hiding were honed early in life as she escaped to the trees near the Mekong to avoid her father's agents. Sinan's early childhood gave her some knowledge of "river" life. She knew the Mekong. She came to know the Bassac.

She won important defenders: the trusted "old" revolutionaries in the village.

Like the singer at Auschwitz or the teller of Aesop's fables, Sinan provided a service to her captors. Word of the benefits of her ancient cupping therapy spread among the hardest Khmer Rouge cadre.

As improbable as it may seem, another old person named Lorn had one more theory. Lorn, 18 when she met Sinan, spoke almost adoringly of the woman she encountered in a work camp so many years ago.

"Sinan survived, I think, because she was kind and gentle and had a sweet way of talking which made everyone like her. Perhaps," said Lorn, "she was too kind to kill."

24

Ashes to Ashes

Sunday, November 7, 2010

I DROVE TO ADELPHI, MARYLAND, to the house that Walter Teague and Sinan bought together in 1987.

I had not seen Sinan since 1985. Walter reached out to me to arrange the reunion. He said Sinan wanted to see me one last time. My "distant friend" was in a very bad way. She was painfully thin, as cancer that spread from her liver was now tearing her once-vibrant body apart.

The best we could determine is that she had contracted hepatitis C sometime either just before or during her imprisonment in Cambodia.

The hep C virus ate away at her liver undetected for more than thirty-five years.

Sinan and I sat on a well-worn sofa, blankets arranged to shelter her from the cold.

On the wall above, a portrait of her as she looked in 1969 gazed down at us. The painting by a friend was inspired by the first photograph Sinan had given me in June 1970.

A demure, slightly smiling, vibrant beauty, who even those close to the Khmer Rouge acknowledged displayed both extraordinary strength and exceptional kindness.

Sinan spoke almost inaudibly.

At first she displayed anger. It was not fair that this disease born of her hardships in Cambodia was stripping her of life so soon. Her fragile body shuddered. She dissolved into tears.

Then she stopped. Sinan whispered a thank-you for events thirty-two years in the past. She remembered a photo of the two of us at the duty-free shop in Singapore. That was her first taste of freedom once outside Cambodia.

I muttered apologies for things done or not done over forty years: for being callous, irresponsible, for failing her at so many points in her life.

Too weak to speak, Sinan simply nodded.

A long silence followed. Then a painful but quiet cough.

Sinan motioned to the stairs, which led to a basement study. The study belonged to Walter, anti-war activist turned therapist turned loving partner.

Sinan said Walter was the best thing that had happened to her in the last twenty-five years of her life.

"He was the only one who truly loved me," she said in that nearly inaudible whisper.

She looked up. She tried to smile. "You, of course, did not need me. You always had your work. I always wanted you to be successful in your career."

We talked for an hour. In fact, we sat lost in silence for much of that time. She tried to focus through a blur of pain and medication. I tried to hold on to memories of so long ago.

One month and three days later, at 11:00 in the morning, Soc Sinan was gone.

Walter, her partner for twenty-five years, phoned me with news of her death.

Two old men wept openly.

Just after New Year's Day 2011, a celebration of Sinan's life was held at a home in Maryland.

Nearly a hundred people gathered in the spacious living room of the house owned by one of Walter's friends. Walter placed four photographs of Sinan at various periods in her life on the mantelpiece. One by one, friends young and old came forward. They stood in front of the large flagstone fireplace.

In turn each person delivered eulogies. Many of the Khmer who spoke had also struggled to adapt to a strange land. They recalled how Sinan had helped them: helped them build new lives. They thanked her for her consistent kindness and generosity. Said how she had been too kind to die.

After the memorial, Walter asked me if I would like to fulfill one of Sinan's wishes. He said it was something he could not do himself. Might I take her remains back to the village where she was born, the place on the river where she was most happy, as a little girl? I readily agreed.

January 31, 2011

It is dry season in Cambodia again. Old battlefields are quiet.

About an hour out of Phnom Penh, we edge closer to the Mekong near the district capital of Kang Meas. The rutted road turns to dirt. Dust plumes envelop the car. The going is slow.

At 8:35 we enter a schoolyard in the village of Thlok Chhreu. San Arun, Saorun, and Eric Ellul are with me.

In the yard, a welcoming committee has assembled a group of about twenty people.

A woman named Khun greets us first, her hands cupped before her. Khun and a group of older women say they knew Sinan as a little girl.

"We knew her mother too. Her mother died so young," they recall sadly.

Arun translates.

When pressed, unsurprisingly, memories are vague. "She was such a good little girl."

We sit in front of a makeshift altar.

Within the hour, the assembly grows larger as local villagers bring ornaments made from banana leaves, flowers, food, and other offerings, including an array of common household items.

"These are called Pralong," Arun explains. They are items needed, the Buddhist believes, for life in the next world. For a poor village it is an extraordinary effort.

"When you brought the ashes back, I could feel Sinan's soul returning to Cambodia. As you know, ashes are like the soul," Saorun reflects. "The ceremony provides a way for Sinan's soul to be blessed, by making her present among us, with her friends and family in her native land. We Khmer think the 'earth' at the place of birth is very important."

The other importance of these Buddhist rites is to permit the soul to live peacefully in a new world.

"We call this 'Phob Thmey,'" says Arun. "We enter a new world with no regret, no fear, no pain, no blocked feelings."

"It is 'un rituel de passage,'" adds Eric. "Mother says it helps free the soul."

I place the small black lacquer box containing Sinan's remains at the center of the altar.

Soon the achar arrives. A man in his early 60s, he will serve as the master of ceremonies in the ritual that follows. Two young monks, "Tveu bon," have been asked to join. They face the group in prominent positions.

The ceremony, Saorun tells me, is called Pram pi thgnay.

Normally this ceremony is held exactly seven days after cremation. We of course must make an exception, as Sinan's journey from Maryland has taken more than forty days.

Khmer Buddhist believers continue to mark the departure of a soul for many years to come. There are prayer services—mouyroy thgnay—after one hundred days and Khuob mouy chnam each year or every three or more years thereafter.

Saorun and San Arun, continue to sit facing the altar arrangement. Saorun sobs silently. Eric watches from the side.

Arun suddenly feels faint. She nudges me and I hold her arm to steady her. "It's Sinan's spirit. I feel it," Arun whispers. I am all too willing to believe.

A series of recitatives led by the achar summons Sinan's soul, calls on her to return and be free. The young monks bless us all with a sprinkling of water.

With the ceremony complete, a small group makes its way about a half mile to the banks of the Mekong.

My plan is to take a small boat out to the middle of the Mekong to free Sinan's remains, but there is one final obstacle.

Local village boatsmen object. The spirits warn this may not be such a good idea. Eric talks to them. I offer to add an additional incentive. The obstacle is lifted.

The climb is steep down the muddy embankment to the water's edge, where the small boat awaits us.

As I stumble down the ridge, I try not to upset the small black box, now placed in a decorative tray surrounded by flower garlands.

The achar takes the lead, followed by the young monk. Eric is at my side. I clutch the lacquer box. We scramble into the small boat on the bank of the Mekong.

Saorun and Arun watch from the top of the embankment.

We are seated. The young monk sits at the bow, the achar and Eric next, Sinan and I at the center, and the boat owner guards his investment from the rear. An expert oarsman stands at the stern as we cast off. Not a long journey—it's just a few hundred meters to the center of the Mekong.

A brisk breeze stirs the humid air. The heat rises. The sun sends glimmers of light streaking across the Mekong.

The achar chants a final prayer. He nods to me.

I open the lacquer box. The fine gray ash is disturbed only slightly.

I pour tentatively at first—a handful of the remains over the left side of the boat. Eric, armed with a video camera, captures the ritual.

The achar and the young monk throw flowers into the water as I scatter the ashes.

Then a sudden breeze picks up. A light dusting of ash surges upward and gently strikes Eric on the cheek.

Arun—with her marvelous mix of spiritual seriousness and sweet humor—says later, "That was Sinan, Eric. She was sending you a gentle farewell kiss, just like the ones she gave you when you were a baby in Phnom Penh."

The achar nods to me again as if to say "Finish the job, old man."

Half a box of ash remains.

I scatter ash more quickly. This time the wind rises up more strongly. A backlash of ash strikes me sharply across the face, into my nose and mouth.

Again, later Arun has the answer.

"That was Sinan once more, cher Jim." She smiles. "This time she was *slapping you* across the face for your betrayals."

Neatly the oarsman sets our course back to the shore. Eric puts down the camera. The achar and young monk are silent. The Mekong River glistens.

■ ■ ■

After a short visit to the village and the distribution of tveu tien (donations in Sinan's name), we said goodbye to Thlok Chhreu and made our way back to Phnom Penh.

Saorun, Eric, Arun, and I were physically exhausted and emotionally spent.

I took Arun to the Calmette Hospital on Boulevard Monivong—a short distance south from the French Embassy. She was suffering fainting spells.

Given the deep spiritualism rooted in every Khmer, I could not know for sure whether Sinan's spirit had really possessed Arun, causing her to be overcome, or whether more simply it was the impact of heat, dust, and fatigue.

What I did know is that—in their spiritualism—my Khmer friends summed up my feelings and my hopes better than I could myself.

As Saorun told me later: "I know Sinan is looking at us from where she is. She still watches over us. I believe she will take care of us in the days to come, as we all grow old and we have only our pasts to consider."

Afterword

IN 2020, APART FROM MEMORIES, there is almost nothing left of the Cambodia and Vietnam I once knew. Not surprising perhaps after forty or fifty years.

I have revisited Indochina often.

My slow January 2011 ferry ride across the Mekong River at Neuk Leung would be my last. On road trips between Saigon and Phnom Penh in 2017, I sped across the river on a spanking new suspension bridge built with Japanese government assistance. The leisurely ferry service had been discontinued.

In late 2019, I slept at Hotel Le Royal, dined with San Arun, and lunched with Eric Ellul. His mother Saorun had gone to the Wat Botum Pagoda to mourn the death of her friend, the great Khmer Ballet Dancer, Princess Bopha Devi, one of the daughters of Norodom Sihanouk who died in 2012.

Cambodia today is a nation of more than 16 million people. Nearly 70 percent of them having no memory of the killing fields. Phnom Penh has grown into a sprawling city of new skyscrapers and shopping malls. The city reminds me more of Bangkok, Thailand than the Cambodian capital I once knew.

The Angkor temples now attract more than six million tourists during most years. The majority travel from other Asian nations. China leads the pack. Some fear the crush of modern-day tourism on the ancient site will do more harm than the war ever did. Yet, on more recent visits, I came away encouraged by the remarkable new restoration work carried out by archeologists from France, Japan, Germany, and 13 other nations. With improved oversight by Khmer experts from the Angkor Archaeological Park, APSARA, in coordination with UNESCO, a vibrant heritage park has replaced the scattered, enchanting but badly decaying and looted temples I saw on multiple visits in the 1970's and 80's.

The young, seemingly shy, one-eyed Foreign Minister, who signed the papers making Sinan's departure from Cambodia possible, has made a remarkable transformation. He became Prime Minister in 1985 and in 2020 remained as one of the longest serving leaders in the world. At age 68, he rules Cambodia with near dictatorial powers. While leaders in Hanoi trained him and brought him to power, leaders in Beijing are now his greatest benefactors. China dominates the economy of the nation.

In late July 2020, the Khmer Rouge leader Khieu Samphan marked his 89th birthday. Convicted in November 2018 of war crimes by a United Nations Tribunal, Khieu remained the last major figure from the deadly radical revolution alive.

Next door in Vietnam, the politburo in Hanoi in 1987 relaxed the stifling Communist orthodoxy which imprisoned tens of thousands in "re-education camps" and held back the nation's economic potential following the 1975 "Giai Phong."

The appallingly bad government of the 1970's and 80's was replaced by continued single party rule – yes – but with a reformist agenda and more power transferred to local government. As I travelled around the country in recent years, I found Vietnamese provinces had made progress in improving healthcare, curtailing rampant corruption, and even permitting more freedom of expression. Vietnam seemed to be developing along more moderate lines at least in contrast to its giant more totalitarian neighbor to the north.

With orthodoxy consigned to history, a young nation of nearly 100 million people grows and thrives. Apart from Singapore, Vietnam is arguably the most vibrant economy in Southeast Asia.

Before the start of positive change, I witnessed many Vietnamese suffer. During visits from 1979 to the early 1990's, new and old friends hesitated to talk to me openly. During that time, nearly two million Vietnamese fled the country, many in crowded and leaky boats. Many thousands died at sea.

Yet the exodus spawned large, dynamic refugee communities across the world. Their children and grandchildren have worked to become the most prosperous among the Indochinese diaspora. Thousands of Viet Khieu, or overseas Vietnamese, returned to play a role in building the nation's new prosperity and encouraging reform.

My life too underwent a good measure of reform. My career in American network television news continued for another twenty years after Sinan's arrival in America. I later moved on to other media work—beyond TV news reporting.

Four years after my last dinner with Sinan in New York, I met in Los Angeles and later married in London another woman of Indochina. We raised a family of two sons of whom we are enormously proud.

Xuan Xanh, the Vietnamese woman who eventually settled me down, had her own dramatic story of escape from Qui Nhon to Phu Quoc to Saigon and down the river to the South China Sea. She faced challenge, change, and growth in a new world.

She became the sturdy "anchor" for a dozen "boat people" in her family who continued to flee Vietnam for fifteen years after her own terror-filled departure.

Xuan Xanh's story too is a remarkable one of stubbornness, courage, and survival against tremendous adversity. But hers is a story for another time, in another place. As I used to say at age 16 sitting in front of the microphone at that little "CBS affiliated" radio station in Worcester Massachusetts—"Stay Tuned!"

Acknowledgments

MEMOIR, PARTICULARLY OF EVENTS FORTY or fifty years ago, is a tricky business. Memory is imperfect and selective. Diaries and recordings provide contemporaneous thoughts but are frequently incomplete. I have, as faithfully as I could, recreated Sinan's story using her own words while editing them for clarity.

The following people have made indispensable contributions in helping me muster recollections.

Walter Teague, Soc Sinan's partner for the last 25 years of her life, loved and sustained her throughout, and shared with me a wealth of observations, photographs, documents, and recordings. Walter has much more to write about Sinan's later years. It is a story I hope he will complete.

Jacquelyn Chagnon interviewed Sinan at length in 1984. Her recordings were essential to this story. Throughout much of my writing, Jacqui remained in Laos, assisting hundreds of Lao people who, 50 years after the war, continue to be war victims due to unexploded ordnance and the hidden impacts of Agent Orange.

Sinan's oldest friends Saorun Tchou Ellul, San Arun, and Lisa Vannery Doa (Vann) showed great generosity in sharing their memories and sometimes their most painful experiences.

Eric Ellul at the Lycee Descartes in Phnom Penh not only responded to my frequent inquiries but also shot some of the photographs in this book.

Youk Chhang and Dany Long of the Documentation Center of Cambodia offered guidance, context, and interviews with the former "old people" of the Khmer Rouge period that I could not have accomplished on my own.

The Vietnam component of my story was enriched by the recollections of such colleagues as Nayan Chanda, Fox Butterfield, and William Dowell. My mentor, Neil Davis, died in 1985 of shrapnel wounds sustained while covering a botched military coup d'etat in Thailand.

Insights or encouragement over the years also came from Chanthou Boua, Chhang Song, Chum Bun Rong, Yasutsune "Tony" Hirashiki, Tran Ngoc Thach, Irwin Chapman, Donald Critchfield, Alan Dawson, Henry and Toni Farrington, Denny Lane, George Lewis, Don Luce, Larry Matthews, Jim Russell, and Dan Southerland.

Editors Katherine Pickett, Barbie Halaby, and Amanda Werts helped me shape and clean up an old TV reporter's sloppy manuscript. Book designer Peggy Nehmen guided me through the digital and paperback process. Map credit goes to Filippo Vanzo.

The beauty and solitude of my rural home in Oxford County, Maine eased the burdens of writing.

Special thanks go to my son Christopher for his critical eye and to Xuan Xanh for her understanding, tolerance, and especially her creativity in the choice of the title and cover of this book.

Whatever help I have received, I take full responsibility for any mistakes, omissions, simplifications, opinions, or distortions contained herein.

Photo Gallery

A Buddhist ceremony for Soc Sinan. Thlok Chhreu Village, Kampong Cham, January 30, 2011. Seated to Jim's left is San Arun and to his right Saorun Tchou. They were among Sinan's oldest friends.

The childhood home of Soc Sinan, where she was most happy. Thlok Chhreu Village, Kampong Cham Province.

Soc Sinan in a 1970 photo given by Sinan to Jim Laurie when they first met.

Students of the Royal Ballet. Among the pleasures in Phnom Penh in June 1970 was visiting the Royal Palace to watch the graceful young dancers learning classical Khmer dance.

Photo Gallery • 343

The Phnom Penh apartment building where Sinan lived. On April 12, 1975, "Two steps at a time, I bounded up to the fourth floor. The apartment was shuttered… How could she not be there?"

Military press accreditation issued by the Joint United States Public Affairs Office of the Military Assistance Command Vietnam. Journalists during the war were given by the US Military the equivalent rank of major in the US Army.

Seated just behind a US Army helicopter pilot provided some sense of security. These fliers were good. "The sharp crack of AK-47 fire... the pilot quickly pulled the Huey into an upward spiral."

A US Helicopter over Cambodia. Door removed, gunners ready, the durable Huey was the warhorse of the American war in Vietnam.

Photo Gallery • 345

Australian cameraman and journalist Neil Davis (1934-1985). After leaving Phnom Penh on the American helicopter evacuation, Davis and Laurie travelled together to Vietnam and resolved to remain in Saigon to cover the communist take-over. Photo: Givral's Café, Saigon. May 6, 1975.

A North Vietnamese tank in central Saigon April 30, 1975. A column of tanks headed down Tu Do Street toward the waterfront shortly after Hanoi troops took the Presidential Palace in what they called Giai Phong or "Liberation."

Jim on the balcony of the Caravelle Hotel in Saigon with the flag of North Vietnam behind on May 5, 1975. All flags of the defeated South Vietnamese government had been quickly removed.

Jim Laurie interviews Prime Minister Pham Van Dong in Hanoi, April 24, 1979. The Vietnamese leader, a longtime revolutionary colleague of Ho Chi Minh, said the world "will one day see the justice" of Vietnam's invasion of Cambodia to oust the Khmer Rouge.

Norodom Sihanouk and Jim Laurie exchange toasts in Pyongyang North Korea on July 28, 1985. The glasses were filled with orange juice. Sihanouk, the first ruler of independent Cambodia after French colonial rule, also offered the visitor American cookies and presented an audio tape of his music.

Jim on the ferry across the Mekong River at Neak Leung, April 9, 1979. Elements of the Vietnamese army on the ferry were heading west to reinforce units that invaded Cambodia in late December 1978.

Jim records a piece to camera in front of the abandoned United States Embassy in Phnom Penh on April 12, 1979, four years to the day after the American evacuation from Cambodia.

The Killing Fields. Driving northwest from Phnom Penh in November 1979, Jim comes across several exposed burial grounds with the remains of hundreds of victims of Khmer Rouge killings.

Vietnamese occupying troops with Khmer civilians in Siem Reap Province Cambodia, November 1979. The troops provided security for Jim as he and his camera team toured the Angkor Temples.

Photo Gallery • 349

The ouster of the Khmer Rouge by the Vietnamese in 1979 pushed an already starving nation into famine. As Jim travelled across Cambodia, suffering children like these were a common site.

At Angkor, November 29, 1979. Jim had hoped to travel to the famed 12th Century temples in 1971. War made that visit with Soc Sinan impossible.

Angkor 1979. Returning to Cambodia in 1979, apart from Vietnamese troops and a few Khmer civilians trying to recover from the impact of the Khmer Rouge regime, the Angkor Temples were abandoned. Large parts of the complex were inaccessible due to landmines.

Jim Laurie and Foreign Minister Hun Sen on January 2, 1980. Hun Sen, then 27 years old, had been installed by the Vietnamese. He went on to become Prime Minister of Cambodia in 1985, a position he still held 35 years later.

Rescue at last. Soc Sinan in the cockpit of an Oxfam Relief plane to Singapore January 3, 1980. Sinan had survived Khmer Rouge atrocities in what she called "my prison without walls."

Jim and Soc Sinan at Singapore Airport Duty Free after they had been released with the help of the United States Embassy and the United Nations High Commission for Refugees from hours of interrogation by Singapore authorities.

August 17th, 1979

Dear Jim,

    It is 4 years 4 months since April 17th, 1975 that I didn't have any news from you.

    Where have you been? at Hong-Kong or U.S.A.

    I have received your last visiting-card wich you put by the door of my house before you leave P.Penh in the morning of Saturday April 12th, 1975, I keep it until now.

    Since April 27th, 1975 I leave the city by the Khmer Rouge's truck. They took me to the District of SAANG province of Kandal, I live there from that date.

    I have so many strong deceptions on life since the K.R. came in to P.Penh. I left P.Penh alone without family, (nor sisters or brothers), I didn't have any happiness for one minute, I know how big mistakes I have maked on that time. I came one time to my house on July 1979 at P.Penh, I was very sad and I burst into tears, because I had all of my earliest memories. I couldn't find my father and all of my sisters and brothers, I don't know if they have the life or not. I get very tired from this situation and I don't want to go to P.Penh or stay there anymore. I would like to get out from this country but I couldn't find the best way to go. I would need some help from you, "could you please find the good way to take me out from this situation?"

I still have the ticket from "SABENA" from Bangkok to New York. "My life doesn't have the sense for me to live"

    I hope you are very well and very happy on life and business, you travel all over the world.

August 17, 1979 letter from Soc Sinan asking for help in escaping Cambodia. The letter was written about seven months after Vietnamese troops expelled the Khmer Rouge from her village. After receiving the letter on September 5th, Jim began his efforts to extract Sinan from Cambodia.

I suppose that I will meet you in the far-off days —

My address:

    Mrs S. Sinân
    Phum Por kandal
    Khum TROYSLA
    District of SAANG
    Province of KANDAL
    CAMBODIA

I live on the East side of Bassac River about 40 km. in the South from the city.

Thank you in advance.

My best thoughts to you.
Your remote friend
Sinan

N.B. Do you meet my good friend Mrs. Khoun Rigaud sometimes? Do you know where she lives now? Could you please tell her that I'm well but do not happy, I miss her and want to see her very much, I have never forgotten her even one time, maybe Goodbye for ever.

Thanks you very much.
I send this letter by someone who goes to Saigon to be stamped. K. Government does not yet open the P.O. at P.Penh.

How Khmer woman escaped to Singapore

...with TV newsman's help

Straits Times 1/9/80

By EVELYN NG

A YOUNG Kampuchean woman, who managed to fly out of her country last week with the help of an American television journalist, is staying "with friends" in Singapore, informed sources said yesterday.

The woman, Soc Sonan, 27, flew into Seletar airfield in a Red Cross aid plane last Wednesday with American Broadcasting Corporation journalist James Laurie, 32.

The sources said she arrived with an exit permit but it is not known who had issued it or how she had obtained it.

Second bid

It is believed that the United States has agreed refugees from Kampuchea allows a manageable number to stay if a third country has agreed to accept them within 90 days.

Mr Laurie, bureau chief of the ABC office in Hongkong, is understood to have flown to New York on Saturday — evidently to hasten procedures that would enable Soc Sonan to join him.

She is described as Mr Laurie's "close personal friend."

It was learnt that this was the second attempt by Mr Laurie to arrange for Soc Sonan's escape. His first attempt was in 1975, in the last days before Phnom ever, that Soc Sonan had previously worked in a commune.

The couple had apparently stayed at the Peninsula Hotel in Coleman Street while Mr Laurie was here.

Both checked out of the hotel on Saturday after 6 p.m., destined, as Mr Laurie told a staff member, for Jakarta. Other sources confirmed later than he is now in New York.

Hotel staff also overheard a "Chinese gentleman" assuring Mr Laurie that he would take good care of Soc Sonan.

The part-time ABC photographer who had gone with Mr Laurie to Kampuchea refused to disclose any info

Front page story in the Singapore *Straits Times* on Sinan's "escape." The story was controversial at the time as the Singapore government had a policy of discouraging refugees from Indochina. Singapore in 1980 also had no diplomatic relations with Vietnamese occupied Cambodia.

Photo Gallery • 355

Friends at the Hotel Le Royal, 2011. Eric Ellul, Jim Laurie, San Arun and Saorun Thlok meet in Phnom Penh to bid farewell to Soc Sinan.

Ashes to Ashes. January 30, 2011. Scattering remains on the Mekong River near the birthplace of Soc Sinan in Kampong Cham Province.

References

ON LANGUAGE: For the English language writer, the Khmer (Cambodian) and Vietnamese languages present challenges. There are at least four transliteration systems for romanizing Khmer script. Vietnamese, as romanized in the eighteenth century, requires diacritical markings for the language to be read and understood properly. The author therefore apologizes for inconsistencies in Khmer renderings and the absence of diacritical marks in the Vietnamese quotations.

Citations according to chapter that may be of interest for further reading or watching are listed below:

Chapter 2
Ben Kiernan, *The Pol Pot Regime: Race, Power, and Genocide in Cambodia under the Khmer Rouge, 1975-1979* (Yale University Press, 1996).

Chapter 3
Milton Osborne, *Sihanouk, Prince of Light, Prince of Darkness.* (Allen & Unwin Ltd. 1994), Chapter 13.

Chapter 5
Richard Nixon Foundation – "President Nixon's Cambodia Incursion TV Address, YouTube, July 21, 2020, https://www.youtube.com/watch?v=3cAAnoqmksg: "April 30, 1970: President Nixon announces his plan to eradicate communist sanctuaries along the Cambodia-South Vietnam border."

CIA, Intelligence Memorandum: The Central Office for South Vietnam (COSVN), November 1965 (declassified August 2003), https://www.cia.gov/library/readingroom/docs/CIA-RDP79T00472A000600040017-4.pdf.

Chapter 6
Meeting between Alexander Haig and General Lon Nol in Phnom Penh, May 23, 1970, verbatim text sent via cable to Henry Kissinger (declassified May 2010), https://www.cia.gov/library/readingroom/docs/LOC-HAK-503-2-13-6.pdf.

Emory C. Swank, US Ambassador to Cambodia September 1970 to September 1973, *The Association of Diplomatic Studies and Training Foreign Affairs.* Oral History Project (1988) pp. 20-38, https://www.adst.org/OH%20TOCs/Swank,%20Emory%20C%20.toc.pdf .

Chapter 7
John R.D. Cleland, Major General U.S. Army, *End of Tour Report MEDTC* 1972-1974 (declassified December 31, 1982).

Chapter 8
Secretary Melvin Laird as quoted by Dale Andrade, *America's Last Vietnam Battle: Halting Hanoi's 1972 Easter Offensive.* (University Press of Kansas, 2001), p. 11.

Col. G.H. Turley USMCR (Ret.) *The Easter Offensive: Vietnam 1972* (Naval Institute Press, 1985), pp. 207ff.

Chapter 16
Frank Snepp, *Decent Interval: The American Debacle in Vietnam and the Fall of Saigon*. (Allen Lane, 1980), pp. 469ff.

Chapter 17
Mao Zedong as cited by Kenneth Quinn, "The Pattern and Scope of Violence," Page 177ff in Karl Jackson, *Cambodia 1975-1978 Rendezvous with Death*. (Princeton University Press, 1989).

See also Nayan Chanda, *Brother Enemy: The War After the War*. (Collier, 1986).

Chapter 20
This Shattered Land – an ABC News Close Up Documentary 1980 available through Amazon as an "ABC News Classic DVD" https://amzn.to/3glIORg.

Chapter 22
Linton Weeks, "The Hippies' Last Stand," *Washington Post*, February 2, 1999.

Norman Mailer, *The Armies of the Night: History as a Novel, the Novel as History*. (Penguin-Plume, 1968), pp. 160ff (excerpts used with permission of author's estate).

Chapter 23
Milan Kundera, *The Book of Laughter and Forgetting*. (Harper, 1994), p. 7.

About the Author

JIM LAURIE IS AN INTERNATIONAL writer, broadcaster, and media consultant who has witnessed many defining moments in Asia's history over the last 50 years.

A recipient of multiple Emmy, Peabody, and Overseas Press Club Awards, Jim roamed the world first for NBC News (1972-1978) and then ABC News (1978-2000). He has produced or written documentary films on Cambodia, Japan, China, and Vietnam and interviewed noted world leaders over the years including China's Deng Xiaoping, India's Indira Gandhi, Cambodia's Norodom Sihanouk, the Soviet Union's Mikhail Gorbachev, Russia's Vladimir Putin, and the Dalai Lama of Tibet.

Dear Reader,

THANK YOU FOR READING *The Last Helicopter: Two Lives in Indochina.*

I very much appreciate your sharing my personal journey back in time to meet remarkable people in a dramatic period of history that should not be forgotten.

Your feedback is especially important to me. Please email me at focusasia1@gmail.com

If you found what you have read here worthwhile, do take a few minutes to write a short online review.

Post to Amazon, Goodreads, or at your favorite bookstore website.

You may also be interested in a Video Companion to this book. Check out my YouTube page, www.youtube/jimlaurie1.

I have put together a series of my videos from the 1970's which capture on film some of the historic episodes in this book.

Again, sincere thanks.

—*Jim Laurie*

Made in the USA
Las Vegas, NV
20 August 2021